THE
EVERYTHING
FREEZER MEALS COOKBOOK

Dear Reader,

I am so excited you are joining me in cooking freezer meals! It is especially thrilling because freezer cooking has the potential to change both the way you cook and the way you think about cooking. No matter what season of life you are in, there is something in this cookbook that will appeal to you. You can dip your big toe into the water and try out a few simple ideas, or you can put your scuba gear on and dive in! It's really up to you, and I am here to support you all the way.

I've enjoyed freezer cooking and teaching others about freezer cooking for many years, and what a joy to know that this knowledge makes a difference in the lives of others. With the busy lives we lead, we need all the help we can get. Sometimes just finding one recipe your whole family enjoys can make your whole week. And if next time you make two meals and freeze one of them? Even better! It's all about simplifying, learning, and improving the quality of our lives. We all need to eat, so let's have some fun in the process.

As Julia Child said, "This is my invariable advice to people: learn how to cook—try new recipes, learn from your mistakes, be fearless, and above all have fun!"

Your partner in cooking,

Candace Anderson

Welcome to the EVERYTHING Series!

These handy, accessible books give you all you need to tackle a difficult project, gain a new hobby, comprehend a fascinating topic, prepare for an exam, or even brush up on something you learned back in school but have since forgotten.

You can choose to read an *Everything®* book from cover to cover or just pick out the information you want from our four useful boxes: e-questions, e-facts, e-alerts, and e-ssentials. We give you everything you need to know on the subject, but throw in a lot of fun stuff along the way, too.

We now have more than 400 *Everything®* books in print, spanning such wide-ranging categories as weddings, pregnancy, cooking, music instruction, foreign language, crafts, pets, New Age, and so much more. When you're done reading them all, you can finally say you know *Everything®*!

QUESTION

Answers to
common questions

FACT

Important snippets
of information

ALERT

Urgent
warnings

ESSENTIAL

Quick
handy tips

PUBLISHER Karen Cooper

DIRECTOR OF ACQUISITIONS AND INNOVATION Paula Munier

MANAGING EDITOR, EVERYTHING® SERIES Lisa Laing

COPY CHIEF Casey Ebert

ACQUISITIONS EDITOR Katrina Schroeder

SENIOR DEVELOPMENT EDITOR Brett Palana-Shanahan

EDITORIAL ASSISTANT Ross Weisman

EVERYTHING® SERIES COVER DESIGNER Erin Alexander

LAYOUT DESIGNERS Colleen Cunningham, Elisabeth Lariviere, Ashley Vierra, Denise Wallace

Visit the entire Everything® series at *www.everything.com*

THE
EVERYTHING®
FREEZER MEALS
COOKBOOK

Candace Anderson
with Nicole Cormier, RD

Avon, Massachusetts

*This book is dedicated to my husband Steve,
the most loving and supportive guy a girl could
ask for, and our boys Zach, John, Jason, Chris
and Matt who are just amazing. I rawr you!*

An Everything® Series Book.
Everything® and everything.com® are registered trademarks of F+W Media, Inc.

Published by Adams Media, a division of F+W Media, Inc.
57 Littlefield Street, Avon, MA 02322 U.S.A.
www.adamsmedia.com

ISBN 10: 1-4405-0612-4
ISBN 13: 978-1-4405-0612-3
eISBN 10: 1-4405-0613-2
eISBN 13: 978-1-4405-0613-0

Printed in the United States of America.

10 9 8 7 6 5 4 3 2 1

Library of Congress Cataloging-in-Publication Data
is available from the publisher.

This publication is designed to provide accurate and authoritative information with regard
to the subject matter covered. It is sold with the understanding that the publisher is not
engaged in rendering legal, accounting, or other professional advice. If legal advice or other
expert assistance is required, the services of a competent professional person should be
sought.

     —From a *Declaration of Principles* jointly adopted by a Committee of the
American Bar Association and a Committee of Publishers and Associations

Many of the designations used by manufacturers and sellers to distinguish their products
are claimed as trademarks. Where those designations appear in this book and Adams
Media was aware of a trademark claim, the designations have been printed with initial capi-
tal letters.

*This book is available at quantity discounts for bulk purchases.
For information, please call 1-800-289-0963.*

Contents

Acknowledgments

I shall take the King's advice as given to the White Rabbit and, "Begin at the beginning and go on till you come to the end: then stop."

First and foremost, credit goes where credit is due. I could never have completed this project on my own. I quite literally prayed my way through it, so thank you Lord for Your sustaining hand.

A giant thank you to Neil Salkind, my literary agent, for making this all happen.

I have the most loving friends and family who graciously shared their favorite recipes, and cheered me on through this project. Thank you Mom, Dad, Monica, Mom Anderson, Marti, Sherry, Debra, Laura, Lisa, Becca, Judy, Denise, Lydia, Greg, and Carmela.

Thanks to my five boys who reminded me to take it one recipe at a time, were really good at telling me to get back to work, and were the best guinea pigs a cook could ever need.

Last and far from least, thank you Steve, my knight in shining armor. Thank you for supporting me from day one of this cookbook, for the hours of time you put into developing recipes with me, and most importantly for sharing your closely guarded multiple-blue-ribbon-winning chili recipe. The secret's out now, babe.

And really, next time we say "Let's go to Belize!" Let's go to Belize.

Introduction

WHY SPEND ANOTHER MOMENT staring into the freezer at frozen hamburger meat or chicken, trying desperately to decide what to cook for dinner? *The Everything® Freezer Meals Cookbook* solves the ever-so-stressful "What's for dinner?" dilemma by giving you all the tools you need to prepare and freeze delicious home cooked meals. Family dinners, once trending toward obsolete, are now becoming popular as the economy forces more families to eat at home. Here, you'll learn a variety of methods for filling your freezers with delicious meals like:

- Apricot Walnut Stuffed Chicken
- Salmon Patties with Dill Sauce
- Lemon Tarragon Sauce
- Cheese and Rice Enchiladas with Salsa Verde
- Garlic Parmesan Rolls
- Chocolate Banana Popsicles

In addition to saving time, you will be armed with money-saving tips such as how to take advantage of loss leaders at the grocery store; how to shop sales combined with coupons to maximize savings; and how to cook, portion, and freeze meat and other foods on sale that can be purchased in bulk. With everything you need to succeed, you can dive into the world of freezer cooking and enjoy the tremendous time- and money-saving benefits it will bring to your life!

If you have children, in all likelihood you feel like a taxi service, driving your children to school, games, sports practice, rehearsals, and other after-school activities. And if you are a working parent trying to balance the kids with a full- or part-time job, odds are you are stretched to your limit. Regardless of your situation, most days there never seems to be enough time to do all the things you need to do, and much less time for the things you want to do. After a full day of work or caring for the children, dinner is just one more thing on the to-do list that needs to be checked off. Dinnertime can be one of the busiest times in a household, and freezer cooking is a trouble-free solution that saves time when you need it most.

Just like with all good things, it takes practice to develop a habit and freezer cooking is no exception. Dedicate yourself to utilizing your freezer to its fullest potential. After all, you already own a freezer; why not get the most use out of it as possible, especially if that use will greatly benefit your life? Learn all you can about freezer cooking. Learn how to freeze a casserole, learn how to defrost and prepare meals, and find freezable recipes your family loves. Start small or start big, but start nonetheless. You'll never change your life without taking that first step in the right direction.

Once you do start freezer cooking and train yourself to think of cooking through the "eyes" of your freezer, you'll be amazed at the endless ideas and opportunities you'll encounter. Because you have a recipe for seasoning, cooking, and freezing ground beef in bulk, you can take advantage of sales and buy meat in large quantities. Putting together a chicken meal for the freezer can be as simple as putting chicken breasts in the bottom of a freezer bag, whipping up a marinade to pour over the chicken, and freezing it. With freezer cooking you can be as simple or elaborate as you want to be, but one thing is for certain: You will start to think differently, shop differently, and live differently.

CHAPTER 1

Introduction to Freezer Cooking

Freezer cooking is about making life easier by filling your freezer with prepared meals, side dishes, and ingredients you can mix and match into meals. It's about saving money at the grocery store, and saving time in the kitchen. Best of all, it's about reducing stress in your life and giving you more time to spend with the people you love. Imagine opening your freezer door and seeing it filled with prepared meals. The hard part has been done; all you do is choose a meal, defrost it, and heat it. Doesn't that sound wonderful?

What Is Freezer Cooking?

Get ready to embark on a fantastic journey into the world of freezer cooking. You'll be amazed at how easy it is to fill your freezer with pre-cooked and ready-to-cook meals that don't require a large amount of preparation time. Along the way, keep in mind that there are countless uses for freezer meals—they are not just for dinner.

Picture this: Your family is asking "what's for dinner?" As you stare into the freezer, your stress level rises while your energy plummets. With no ideas for dinner, you go out to eat. Sitting in the restaurant with your family, you feel renewed and energized. You no longer have to think about what is for dinner, and someone else is doing the cooking. All is well, but this is only a temporary fix to the dinner crisis. The good news is there is a simple solution: freezer cooking.

Most families find when switching to freezer cooking they are eating healthier meals because they eat more meals at home. The normally chaotic dinner time becomes organized and under control. Holidays and entertaining are simplified as you prepare appetizers, main dishes, and desserts ahead of time, giving you more time with your guests.

Uses for Freezer Meals

Here are some ideas on how you can use freezer meals:

- Freezer meals make planning a weekly meal schedule a breeze.
- Freezer meals provide a home-cooked meal for your family when you are unavailable to cook.
- Bring frozen meals with you on vacation and save money on eating out.
- Build up a supply of meals when you are pregnant so you won't have to cook once your baby is born.
- Deliver a home-cooked meal to your sick neighbor.
- If you get sick, don't worry about dinner—your family can heat a frozen meal.
- When unexpected company drops by, simply defrost a dessert from the freezer and start a pot of coffee.

- Give pies and cakes as gifts to teachers, caregivers, nurses, and others you appreciate.
- Bring a meal or two to a family who is struggling financially.
- Deliver a hot, home-cooked meal to a friend with a new baby.

Freezer meals are wonderful for planning ahead, as well as for dealing with the unexpected. Stock your freezer and be surprised at the uses you find for the meals.

ESSENTIAL

You can make and freeze baby food! If you like to make your own baby food, you can whip up large batches at one time and not worry about it going bad. Simply fill an ice cube tray with the homemade baby food, and freeze. Once frozen, transfer the cubes to a freezer bag and you can defrost as needed.

Mix and Match Meals

The Mix and Match chapter (Chapter 15) of this book contains basic elements that are common to multiple recipes. By having these basics on hand, you have the ability to create a variety of meals so you or your family won't get tired of the "same old thing." You get the benefits of prepackaged convenience food without the cost. Say you have 30 minutes to make dinner, no idea what to serve, and nothing is defrosted. From the freezer remove a frozen pizza crust, homemade pizza sauce you quickly defrost in the microwave, cooked shredded chicken you defrost in hot water, and mozzarella cheese you have on hand in the refrigerator. In minutes a homemade pizza is in the oven with very little time or effort on your part. Are you in the mood for stir-fry? Take out a package of cubed, seasoned chicken breast; a bag of vegetables; and a container of frozen sweet and sour sauce. With very little planning, you've just put together a healthy dinner.

The Benefits of Freezer Cooking

Consider the following questions:

- Would you like to simplify your life?
- Does dinnertime have you stressed because you never know what to cook?
- Would you like to find a way to save money on groceries?
- Do you never seem to have enough hours in the day?

If you answered yes to any of these questions, then freezer cooking is for you. By using the recipes in this cookbook to prepare freezer meals, you and your family benefit in numerous, sometimes surprising, ways.

Spend Less Time in the Kitchen

People lead busy lives, and therefore time is a precious commodity. By investing a small amount of time in freezer cooking, you reap great benefits. For example, it takes just as much time to make three batches of spaghetti sauce as does to make one. By simply tripling your recipe, you save cooking time for future dinners. Think of freezer cooking as banking time.

Since you (theoretically) have more time on the weekends, you can spend time making freezer meals. Then, when busy weeknights roll around and you are short on time, you're able to pull a meal out of the freezer and provide your family with a meal in minutes. You have just withdrawn time from that investment you made over the weekend.

Saves Money

When faced with a busy day and little or no time to prepare dinner, the fastest solution is to eat out. This might mean ordering pizza, swinging through a fast food drive-thru, or dinner in a restaurant. Regardless of how you eat out, every option available is more expensive than fixing a home-cooked meal. A middle-of-the-road approach is to purchase convenience food at the grocery store. This might be pre-cooked and packaged food, or full meals from the deli. While this solution isn't as expensive as eating out, it is still more expensive than cooking at home. The best solution is to heat up a prepared meal from your freezer. By planning ahead, you'll save a lot of money by not eating out because you have no other options.

FACT

Save money with freezer meals through controlled meal portions. Because you cook and freeze the amount of food your family eats in a given meal, you won't waste money by overcooking. The controlled meal portions also protect your family from overeating.

Simplifies Dinnertime and Helps Alleviate Stress

Imagine this scenario: it is late afternoon, you've had a busy day, and all you want to do is sit on the couch, take your shoes off, and lose yourself in a good book. But that can't happen because you forgot to take meat out of the freezer to defrost. If only you had a frozen meal already prepared, you could pop it into the oven. Then you remember last week when you doubled your lasagna recipe and froze half. Because lasagna is a freezer-to-oven meal, you don't have to defrost it first. With renewed energy, you put the frozen casserole in the oven. Dinner has been taken care of and you can now enjoy your book!

Brings Families Together

When you practice freezer cooking, you give yourself the opportunity to serve a home-cooked dinner to your family each night. Nightly family gatherings at the dinner table become a time for family members to talk about their day. Family members feel comfortable sharing with one another when they are able to have regular conversations. This may be the only time during the day everyone is together.

Meal Planning Made Easy

What's for dinner? Chances are you've heard those words a few times in your life because just about everyone likes to know what's for dinner. Including you! Freezer cooking makes meal planning a breeze.

The easiest way to plan your meals is to print off a monthly calendar. Next, make a list of the meals in your freezer. Assign a meal to each day and write it on the calendar. Hang your calendar on the refrigerator so that everyone knows, at a glance, what is for dinner each night.

Planning your meals in advance offers another benefit. Because many of the freezer meals need to be defrosted before cooking, you know what to remove from the freezer and put into the refrigerator so the meal will have a full 24 hours to defrost in the refrigerator.

Get Organized

A.A. Milne wrote, "Organizing is what you do before you do something, so that when you do it, it is not all mixed up." Sometimes the simplest ideas are the most insightful, and this quote certainly applies to freezer cooking because it isn't something that just happens; you get the best results when you plan and are prepared for cooking. A little time spent getting organized and planning your meals is time well spent.

Stocking Your Pantry

A well-stocked pantry is one that contains basic ingredients regularly used. Here are some basic suggestions:

- Baking supplies such as flour, cornstarch, sugar, baking powder, baking soda, yeast, vegetable shortening, brown sugar, vanilla extract, and chocolate chips.
- Staples such as rice, dried pastas and beans, canned beans, herbs and spices, mushrooms, canned tomatoes, chicken and beef stock, wines, bread crumbs, and cooking spray.
- Condiments such as ketchup, honey, mustard, vinegar, olive oil, Worcestershire sauce, hot pepper sauce, and soy sauce.

Kitchen Essentials

Like most jobs, freezer cooking is easier when you have the right tools. It is not necessary to have all the tools listed, but you benefit from having as many as possible.

- Utensils: measuring spoons, dry measuring cups, wet measuring cups, can opener, garlic press, spatula, tongs, cutting board, slotted spoons, colander, meat thermometer, whisk, zester, rolling pin, wooden spoons, rubber spatula, and a variety of knives.
- Dishes, pots and pans: mixing bowls, baking dishes, small and large skillets, sauté pans, sauce pans, baking sheets, loaf pans, muffin tins, rectangular and square baking pans, and a large stockpot.
- Electrical appliances: hand mixer, food processor, standing mixer, slow cooker, and a microwave oven.
- Freezing supplies: freezer bags (quart and gallon sized), wax paper, plastic wrap, heavy-duty aluminum foil, and a variety of containers made specifically for food storage in the freezer.

Meal Planning

Before you begin to freezer cook, plan which meals you want to cook according to what your family likes. If you are on a tight budget, choose recipes that contain common ingredients you will use in other recipes. There's no sense in buying a $10.00 bottle of a rare spice that is only used one time. Once you have a list of meals, decide how you are going to tackle freezer cooking. Review the methods found in this chapter, and select what is right for you.

Grocery Shopping

Nothing is worse than getting halfway through a recipe only to find you are missing a key ingredient, so an accurate grocery list can be the difference between success and failure in your freezer cooking. Go through each recipe and write down the items and quantities you need to buy. Check your list against what's in your pantry to ensure you are not buying items you already have. Do not forget to add quart- and gallon-sized freezer bags, aluminum foil, freezer wrap, and any disposable freezer containers you want to use for freezing. Another shopping preparation option reverses the process—refer to your coupons and store sale flyers and plan meals around which ingredients are on sale. Or plan meals according to what you have stockpiled.

ALERT

Remember to take precautions to protect your family from food-borne illnesses when you are grocery shopping. Because meat can potentially grow harmful bacteria, it is important to keep it at a safe temperature. Bring a cooler packed with ice with you when shopping and place meat in the cooler for safe traveling.

Freezer Inventory List

When you begin freezer cooking, start an inventory list and add to it as you freeze. A freezer inventory list is a list of everything you have in your freezer, and the date it was frozen. This list allows you to quickly see which freezer meals you have. Because you have a date next to each item, you can keep track of meals that need to be eaten first. A simple way to make a freezer inventory list is to hang a white board on the freezer and attach a marker with string. It is easy to erase meals as you take them out of the freezer.

How to Freeze a Meal

Properly freezing your meals is a major factor in whether a frozen meal tastes fantastic, or whether it comes out freezer burned. Each recipe in this cookbook has a suggested method of freezing. When you are ready to package your meal for the freezer, remove as much air as possible and provide sufficient protection from the freezer. This will guard your food from freezer burn.

Freezer Bag Method

Use either gallon- or quart-sized freezer bags to freeze meals. This method is often used with meals that contain a marinade, soup, gravy, or sauce. Wait until the food has cooled before adding it to the bag since putting hot food into a freezer bag can compromise the strength of the bag. In addition, putting hot food directly in the freezer raises the temperature of your freezer and makes it work too hard. Before sealing the bag, remove as much air as possible.

ESSENTIAL

To maximize freezer space when using the freezer bag method, try this idea: Place a cookie sheet in your freezer and lay the plastic bag flat on the cookie sheet. The cookie sheet helps the meal freeze flat, and frozen meals stack nicely on top of each other.

Casserole Method

This method of freezing is perfect for when you make meals in a casserole dish but do not want to tie up your dish in the freezer. The idea is to flash freeze the casserole in the shape of the pan so the pan doesn't need to stay in the freezer. Before adding food, line your casserole dish with aluminum foil, and on top of the aluminum foil layer add a layer of plastic wrap. Leave enough foil and plastic wrap hanging over the edges of the dish to completely cover and seal the dish. Add your food to the dish, wrap it tightly with the wrap and foil, and place the entire dish in the freezer. After several hours, remove the dish from the freezer, take the frozen, wrapped casserole out of the dish, and place the casserole back in the freezer. Your casserole is now frozen in the shape of the dish. When you are ready to defrost or reheat the meal, unwrap the frozen casserole by removing the foil and plastic wrap. Place the frozen casserole in the same dish used when freezing, and defrost or cook.

Plastic Wrap Method

Use this method for food items that do not fit into a freezer bag. The plastic wrap method is the best choice when freezing a loaf of bread. To use this method, completely wrap your food item with plastic wrap so no part of the food is directly exposed to the freezer. Because plastic wrap does not always stick as well as it should, use tape to secure the seams.

Tupperware Method

Tupperware and other sturdy plastic containers come in all shapes and sizes and are a great choice for freezing a variety of foods. The drawback is these containers take up a lot of space in your freezer, and can stain when used for spaghetti sauce, chili, and other tomato-based foods. Make sure you leave space at the top and don't fill these plastic containers to the rim.

Because food expands as it freezes, if you don't leave space, the top could pop off exposing your food to the freezer.

ESSENTIAL

To help prevent your plastic containers from staining and absorbing food odors when freezing, try this trick. Spray cooking oil over the surface of the container before filling it with food. The oil acts as a barrier and helps protect the porous container. To further prevent stains, never use plastic containers to heat tomato-based sauces in the microwave.

Flash Freezing Method

Flash freezing is a method used to freeze food items individually. Meatballs are a good example of when to use flash freezing. Once meatballs are formed, place them on a baking sheet that has been lined with wax paper and put the baking sheet in the freezer. Once the meatballs are frozen (1–2 hours), transfer them to a freezer bag. When you are ready to cook, remove as many individually frozen meatballs as needed.

Label with Name, Date, and Instructions

Always label your food before putting it in the freezer. It may be easy to tell what you're freezing before you put it in the freezer, but everything looks the same once frozen. By putting the date on your food, you know at a glance how long it has been in the freezer. For guidelines on how long food can be frozen, please refer to the Freezing Chart: Maximum Food-Storage Times in Appendix C. Although long-term freezing will not affect the safety of your meals, it will affect the quality and taste of your meals.

Take the time to write out the reheating instructions and attach them to the frozen meal; that way another family member can do the reheating or you can give the dish to someone in need.

How to Cook a Freezer Meal

Now that you have a freezer full of meals, it is time to reap the benefits of your labor! For health reasons, it is extremely important you follow proper defrosting procedures. Each recipe has instructions for reheating your meals, and these are different for each recipe. Some meals can go directly into the oven frozen, and others need to be defrosted first. Look for the "NO DEFROSTING NEEDED!" indication to see which recipes don't need to be defrosted first.

How to Safely Defrost Your Meals

Growing up, you may have watched your mother take meat out of the freezer and set it on the counter all day to defrost. While you have lived to tell the story, it is not safe practice to defrost meals this way. The safest way to defrost meals is in the refrigerator. The drawback is you need nearly 24 hours in the refrigerator to defrost some foods. Another option for safely defrosting is the microwave. Most microwaves have a defrost button to help you get the right setting. A third option is to defrost in cold water.

ALERT

Never use hot water to defrost your freezer meals, especially those containing raw meat. Raw meat should never go between 40–140°F for any length of time because harmful bacteria could rapidly multiply. Defrost in cold water, and refresh the water often to keep the temperature below 40°F.

How to Build Up Your Meal Inventory

There are many ways to get the most out of freezer cooking, so you'll need to pick the one that's best for you. Often the first that comes to mind is once a month cooking. Perhaps you've thought of doing once a month cooking, but the idea of preparing thirty meals in one day overwhelms you. Not to worry, there are many ways to have a freezer full of meals. Choose the method that is most convenient for you.

Double a Meal

Doubling a meal is an easy way to create an inventory of freezer meals. When cooking a meal, simply double the recipe and make two batches; one meal is to serve that night, and one to freeze. When you double a meal, choose a recipe you know your family loves. Doubling a meal is a simple way freezer cooking saves you time in the kitchen since it doesn't take twice as long to cook twice as much. For very little extra time and effort, you have cooked an extra meal for your family to serve in the future.

Bulk Cooking in Mini Sessions

When you bulk cook in mini sessions, you make 7–14 meals in one day by following these steps:

1. Consult your calendar and choose a shopping day and a cooking day. Ideally these should not be the same day. Plan to spend 3–6 hours cooking.
2. Choose a variety of recipes based on what your family likes to eat. They are not going to be happy if they have a chicken dish every day for the next 14 days, so mix it up.
3. Check which ingredients you have on hand and make a grocery list.
4. Read over each recipe and ensure you understand the instructions.
5. Plan your cooking session and write it out. Look for recipe steps you can combine. Do two of the recipes call for chopped onions? Chop them at the same time. When deciding the order of cooking, first do the steps that take the longest amount of time. If you need to boil a whole chicken, start this early in the day. Save dishes containing raw ingredients for last since they are the quickest to assemble and don't need cooking time.
6. On cooking day, begin with a clean and organized kitchen.

Stockpile Cooking

Stockpile cooking involves planning meals around ingredients you buy, often in bulk, at the best prices. Finding these best prices requires research, but the savings make it well worth your time. Stores often advertise loss leaders, or items stores sell at a great discount, to get you in the store. By making a weekly habit of checking the sales in your area, you can find items you need and can scoop them up in large quantities. Coupons are another way to save money on ingredients, but it is easy to fall into the trap of buying things you don't need. To get the most out of coupon shopping, make sure the brand name product with a coupon is less expensive than the store brand product without one. Maximize your savings with coupons by saving them until the item goes on sale.

QUESTION

What is a price book?
It is a notebook you build that keeps track of product prices. Each page of the notebook is dedicated to one product and lists the best prices found and the store you found them at. With this information, you can easily see if a sale price is a good price.

Shopping warehouse stores is another way to stockpile by buying in bulk. It is critical to know your prices, because warehouse stores don't necessarily have the best deal on every product. When comparing warehouse prices to grocery store prices, make sure to compare the price per unit (whether it is ounces, pounds, per item, etc.). A price book (see previous E-Question sidebar) is an invaluable tool in this scenario since it helps you recognize good prices and guides you as to which items to buy in bulk. Buying bulk and items on sale are two ways to help reduce your cost per meal.

Special Event and Holiday Cooking

Holidays bring to mind delicious food shared with friends and family. While these special occasions are fun, they can also be stressful. Many of us leave the cooking to the day of the event, a practice that robs you of time with friends and family. The solution is freezer cooking. Plan your menu, from appetizers to desserts, a month before the event with food you can make ahead and freeze. Defrost your food in the refrigerator the day before the event, and the next day it will be ready for the oven. You are spared the time of preparation and cleanup, leaving you more time to enjoy your day.

Swap Meals with Friends

A freezer meal swap is a fun and easy way to fill your freezer with a variety of meals. To start a freezer meal swap, find 3–6 friends interested in swapping. Put together a menu and assign each person one different meal to prepare. Each swap member cooks her assigned meal in his or her own kitchen, but makes the meal for every person participating in the swap instead of just one batch. In other words, if there are a total of 4 people in the swap, each person will quadruple the recipe and package four meals. Once each member has prepared the meals, arrange a time to get together and trade. Even though you only cooked one recipe, you come home with a variety of dining options.

Freezer Dos and Don'ts

Practically speaking, there are things you should and should not do when it comes to your freezer. By knowing how to best care for your freezer and which foods freeze well, you will get the best, most productive use out of your appliance. Try to keep your freezer full so it runs efficiently. If you have a lot of empty spaces, your freezer will have to work hard to fill those spaces with cold air.

Foods That Freeze Well

Being able to freeze food allows you to take advantage of store sales and stock up on items, but how do you know what you can freeze? Breads and buns freeze well, as does shredded cheese (block cheese will be crumbly when thawed), milk, butter, flour, lunch meat, tortillas, most fruits and vegetables (some need to be blanched first), nuts, dough, and spices. Your food will stay safe so long as the temperature is kept at a constant 0°F.

Foods That Should Not Be Frozen

It is easier to remember which foods do not freeze well since that list is shorter than those that *do* freeze well. Raw potatoes (especially when shredded) will turn black. Other foods that do not freeze well are sour cream (because it separates once defrosted), lettuce, and mayonnaise. Eggs in the shell should not be frozen. Gravies thickened with flour tend to defrost clumpy, so consider thickening with cornstarch if you plan to freeze this sauce. Fully cooked pasta does not freeze well—it becomes mushy and often disintegrates once defrosted. The secret to freezing pasta is to under-cook it before freezing.

FACT

Use this trick to freeze eggs. Spray a plastic ice cube tray with non-stick spray. In a bowl, mix 6 eggs, ¾ teaspoon sugar, and ¼ teaspoon salt. Pour egg mixture into ice cube trays and freeze. Transfer frozen cubes to freezer bag. One cube equals one egg.

Freezer Maintenance and Repair

If you've ever lost a freezer full of food due to a broken freezer, you understand the importance of maintaining your freezer. Repairs to your freezer can be costly, but most can be avoided by good maintenance. Follow these tips to keep your freezer in tip-top shape:

- Place a thermometer in your freezer to ensure the temperature is 0°F.
- Locate the coils in your freezer and dust them every six months.
- Clean spills immediately, and clean the inside shelves and compartments regularly to prevent odor. Use baking soda to tackle tough food odors in the freezer.
- To keep the door working properly, store the heaviest door items close to the hinge, and the lighter things close to the handle.
- If frost builds up greater than ½" thickness, defrost freezer.
- Do not place your freezer close to a heat source because it will need to work extra hard to keep cool.
- Leave room between the freezer and the wall so air can flow easily.

Customizing Your Freezer Meals

Did you know you can tailor your freezer meals to meet your needs? Maybe you have dietary restrictions and want meals on hand you can readily eat.

Maybe you are cooking for only one or two. Or maybe you want to create frozen diet meals. By customizing your freezer meals, you put your freezer to work for you.

Single-Serving Sizes

Single-serving-sized freezer meals are perfect for single people and for lunch at work. Lasagna is a great example of a dish that is easily made into single-serving sizes. Make the lasagna according to the recipe in Chapter 8 but instead of freezing it as an entire meal let it cool then cut into single portions for freezing. Single portions mean less waste and have the advantage of controlling your portions.

Homemade TV Dinners

Buy a variety of plastic containers shaped like traditional TV dinner trays. Make an entire dinner including main dish, sides, and dessert and then portion it out so each tray contains main dish, side dish, and dessert portion. Cover tightly and freeze. When you need something quick for dinner or would like to bring a hot lunch to work, heat it up in the microwave and enjoy a homemade TV dinner.

Diet Meals

You've no doubt seen the frozen diet meals in the grocery store. They look appetizing on the package, but the finished meal never seems to match the picture. What if you could create your own frozen diet meals that look delicious even after cooking? When you put together your own low-fat and low-calorie meals, you help yourself lose weight and eat healthy. You control the portions as well as the ingredients that go into the meal. Each recipe in this book includes nutritional information per serving so you can choose recipes based on calories or fat content.

Freezing Leftovers

How many times have you thrown away leftovers gone bad and felt guilty by the amount of wasted food? Instead of putting the leftovers into the refrigerator, next time label and freeze them. Get creative with your leftovers. Some cooks have containers in the freezer where they add leftover vegetables. When the container becomes full, they add broth and seasoning and have vegetable soup!

QUESTION

Can leftover rice be frozen?
Yes, leftover rice can be frozen as long as it isn't instant rice. A great idea for leftover rice is to start a rice bag in your freezer. Every time you have any left over, add it to the bag. When you gather enough for a meal, defrost, heat, and serve!

How to Turn Your Recipe into a Freezer Meal

Turning your favorite recipe into a freezer meal is easy:

1. Look through all ingredients and make sure everything can be frozen.
2. Decide if it is better to cook the meat before freezing or freeze it raw. Freezing meat raw allows it to soak up the flavors of marinades and sauces, making it more moist and flavorful. Generally speaking, meat cooked with a sauce is frozen raw, and meats cooked within a casserole should be cooked first.
3. Write out the recipe noting what is to be done on freezing day and what is to be done on reheating day. Check that you haven't missed any steps or ingredients.
4. Test your recipe and make changes as needed.

You'll learn what works and what doesn't as you convert your own recipes. With a little practice, you will become a pro at making freezer meals.

CHAPTER 2

Appetizers, Snacks, and Hors d'Oeuvres

Mushroom Croustades

NO DEFROSTING NEEDED!

INGREDIENTS | SERVES 4

17 ounces frozen puff pastry sheets
2 tablespoons butter
2 cups chopped mushrooms
1 small onion, chopped
Salt and pepper, to taste
1 small clove garlic, minced
4 tablespoons cooking sherry
Cooking spray

The Croustade

Croustade is a French term that most often describes a pastry in the shape of a bowl designed to hold a filling. For example, the croustade can hold a fruit filling, a vegetable mixture, or seafood. You can get creative when making your own croustades.

Freezing Day

Remove pastry sheets from box and lay on counter to defrost. In a medium skillet, add the butter, mushrooms, onions, and salt and pepper and sauté for 5–6 minutes. Add garlic and sauté an additional minute. Add cooking sherry and use a wooden spoon to stir in all particles from the sides of the pan. Remove from heat.

Spray mini muffin pan with cooking spray. Roll puff pastry out on a floured counter, and cut 6 (3") circles from each sheet. Put each pastry circle in muffin pan, ruffling the edges. Fill with mushroom mixture. Flash freeze in muffin pan, transfer to freezer bag.

Reheating Instructions

Place frozen croustades in original greased muffin pan. Bake at 400°F for 15–20 minutes until pastry is golden brown.

PER SERVING
Calories: 758 | Fat: 52g | Protein: 11g | Sodium: 367mg | Carbohydrates: 62g | Fiber: 3g

Cheese and Bacon Potato Skins

NO DEFROSTING NEEDED!

INGREDIENTS | SERVES 8

8 large potatoes
1 stick salted butter or margarine
½ pound bacon
½–1 cup shredded Cheddar cheese

Love Your Skins Crunchy?

If you like your potato skins extra crunchy, scoop out the potatoes and then rub both the inside and outside with canola oil. Broil the skins on both sides until browned. Potato skins taste delicious topped with chopped chives and dipped in ranch dressing or sour cream.

Freezing Day

Bake potatoes in a 400°F oven for 1 hour. Let cool completely. Cut potatoes lengthwise into quarters. Carve out the inside of each of the potato quarters and discard. In a small saucepan, melt the butter. Once melted, brush on the inside and outside of each potato quarters.

In skillet over medium heat, cook the bacon, turning frequently, 10–15 minutes until crispy. Crumble into small pieces. Top each potato quarter with grated Cheddar cheese and bacon. Flash freeze then transfer to freezer bag.

Reheating Instructions

Place frozen potato skins on a baking sheet and bake at 450°F for 15–25 minutes.

PER SERVING
Calories: 480 | Fat: 29g | Protein: 17g | Sodium: 624mg | Carbohydrates: 39g | Fiber: 2g

Buffalo Chicken Wings

Raw vegetables, especially celery, and bleu cheese or ranch dressing are the perfect complements to these spicy wings. Guests will also enjoy dipping their wings directly into the dressing.

INGREDIENTS | SERVES 8–12

1½ cups butter

1 (12-ounce) bottle hot sauce

2 tablespoons white vinegar

12 whole chicken wings

Freezing Day

In a small saucepan over medium heat, melt the butter. Remove from heat. Mix in hot sauce and vinegar. Remove from heat and let cool. When you buy your wings, they are large and need to be cut into smaller pieces by making two cuts. The first cut is made at the joint between the two meaty portions. After the first cut, the larger piece contains two sections, one being the tip of the wing. Make your second cut and discard the tip of the wing.

Place 1 inch of water in the bottom of a 6-quart saucepan. Put a steamer basket inside the pan and cover. Bring the water to a boil. Put wings in steamer basket and steam over medium heat for 10 minutes. Pat dry and cool. Put cooled wings in gallon-sized freezer bag and pour prepared sauce over wings. Seal the bag and freeze.

Reheating Instructions

Defrost chicken wings in refrigerator for 24 hours. Place wings and sauce in a 9" x 13" baking dish. Bake at 425°F for 40 minutes until wings are fully cooked.

PER SERVING
Calories: 390 | Fat: 34g | Protein: 21g | Sodium: 943mg | Carbohydrates: 0g | Fiber: 0g

Ham and Provolone Pinwheels

These pinwheels are versatile, so you can make a variety to suit your guests. Try substituting olives for the pickles, or turkey for the ham.

INGREDIENTS | SERVES 10

10 flour tortillas
2 (8-ounce) packages cream cheese, softened
½ cup shredded provolone cheese
20 slices of deli ham
1 jar sliced dill pickles

How to Soften Cream Cheese

When your recipe calls for softened cream cheese, you may not have time to wait for it to soften on its own. The solution is to soften it quickly, microwaving an 8 ounce package at 30 percent power for 2 minutes.

Freezing Day

Spread each tortilla with 3 tablespoons cream cheese. Layer with 2 slices of ham, 2 rounded teaspoons provolone cheese, and pickles to taste. Roll up the tortilla, and slice into ¾" thick pinwheels. Lay each pinwheel flat on a baking sheet and flash freeze. Once flash frozen, transfer to freezer bag.

Reheating Instructions

Defrost pinwheels in refrigerator overnight and serve cold.

PER SERVING
Calories: 415 | Fat: 28g | Protein: 14g | Sodium: 1068mg | Carbohydrates: 29g | Fiber: 1g

Spicy Crab Ball

The peppers in the cheese give this crab ball a spicy hot flavor. You may substitute Cheddar cheese for the pepper jack cheese to make it less spicy.

INGREDIENTS | SERVES 12

2 (6-ounce) cans crab meat, rinsed
2 (8-ounce) packages cream cheese
1 cup shredded pepper jack cheese
1 tablespoon lemon juice
1 teaspoon Worcestershire sauce
½ cup toasted almonds, chopped

Freezing Day

In a mixing bowl, combine all ingredients except almonds. Shape the resulting mixture into a large ball. Place chopped almonds onto a plate. Roll the crab ball in the almonds, covering completely. Wrap in plastic wrap and freeze.

Reheating Instructions

Defrost in refrigerator overnight. Serve cold with crackers for dipping.

PER SERVING
Calories: 144 | Fat: 12g | Protein: 8g | Sodium: 289mg | Carbohydrates: 2g | Fiber: 1g

Sesame Encrusted Teriyaki Chicken Bites

NO DEFROSTING NEEDED!

Teriyaki Sauce

Bottled teriyaki sauce is readily available at the grocery store, but you can also make a similar sauce. To make your own style of teriyaki sauce, mix the following in a food processor: ¼ cup soy sauce, ¼ cup water, 2 tablespoons honey, 1 clove minced garlic, ¼ teaspoon allspice, and ⅛ teaspoon ground ginger.

Freezing Day

Cut chicken into bite-sized cubes and marinate in teriyaki sauce for 1–3 hours in refrigerator. Gently pat chicken dry with paper towels. In separate bowl, mix soy sauce with honey. Put sesame seeds on a small plate. Dip each chicken bite into the soy sauce and honey mixture, fully coating the bite. Then dip one side of the coated chicken in the sesame seeds. Flash freeze on a baking sheet lined with wax paper, sesame seed side up. Transfer to freezer bag.

Reheating Instructions

Bake the frozen chicken on a lightly greased baking sheet at 400°F for 15–20 minutes, or until chicken is fully cooked. Do not overcook.

PER SERVING
Calories: 230 | Fat: 6g | Protein: 25g | Sodium: 1200mg | Carbohydrates: 22g | Fiber: 1.5g

Bruschetta Turnovers

NO DEFROSTING NEEDED!

INGREDIENTS | SERVES 4–5

1 (17-ounce) box frozen puff pastry

3 cloves garlic, minced

1 small tomato, chopped

4–6 fresh basil leaves, chopped

¼–½ cup shredded mozzarella cheese

2 tablespoons olive oil

4 tablespoons Parmesan cheese

A New Take on Classic Bruschetta

These turnovers are a variation of traditional Italian bruschetta. Traditional bruschetta is made by rubbing toasted bread with olive oil and garlic.

Freezing Day

Defrost puff pastry on the counter for about 30 minutes. Spread puff pastry sheet on a floured surface and roll it out a few times to flatten folds in pastry. Use a 3" diameter circle and cut out 9 circles. On half of each pastry circle put garlic, tomato, basil, and mozzarella cheese. Fold over half of each circle (making a half moon shape) and seal edges by pressing down. Place on baking sheet and flash freeze. Transfer to freezer bag.

Reheating Instructions

Place frozen pastries on baking sheet and bake at 400°F for 10 minutes. Brush each turnover with olive oil and sprinkle with Parmesan cheese. Return to oven for 10–15 additional minutes until pastry turns a golden brown.

PER SERVING
Calories: 532 | Fat: 35g | Protein: 11g | Sodium: 282mg | Carbohydrates: 46g | Fiber: 2g

Cheesy Artichoke and Spinach Spirals

When cutting the spirals, use a serrated knife.
You will get a clean cut and it will help prevent the bread from tearing.

INGREDIENTS | SERVES 4

1 (11-ounce) can refrigerated French
  bread loaf

1 (10-ounce) package frozen spinach

1 (14-ounce) jar artichoke hearts

1 (5-ounce) can sliced water chestnuts

2 tablespoons minced onion

1 (8-ounce) package cream cheese

2 cups Monterey jack cheese

¼ teaspoon red pepper flakes

Best Ways to Defrost and Squeeze Dry Spinach

Try these tips for defrosting and squeezing water out of spinach. One method is to defrost spinach in a microwave. Then fold a towel around the defrosted spinach and, holding the towel over the sink, twist one end of towel in one direction and the other end in the opposite direction squeezing out the water. A second way to accomplish this is to use a mesh strainer under running water to defrost the spinach, then press spinach against the mesh to squeeze out water.

Freezing Day

Unroll the dough and roll it out to a 12" x 13" rectangle. Defrost the spinach and squeeze out extra water. Drain the artichoke hearts and chop into pieces. In large mixing bowl, mix chopped artichoke hearts with the spinach. Add remaining ingredients to bowl and mix thoroughly.

Spread mixture on the dough, and roll up into a tight roll using wet fingers to seal the seam. Pinch and seal the ends closed. Bake at 375°F for 25–30 minutes or until it is golden brown. Cool, wrap with plastic wrap, and freeze.

Reheating Instructions

Defrost in the refrigerator overnight. Bake at 350°F for 15 minutes or until heated. Cut into 6–8 slices.

PER SERVING
Calories: 664 | Fat: 46g | Protein: 28g | Sodium: 1048mg | Carbohydrates: 40g | Fiber: 4.5g

Orange Cheese Sticks

NO DEFROSTING NEEDED!

INGREDIENTS | SERVES 5

1 cup flour plus additional tablespoons as needed

1 cup shredded Cheddar cheese

6 tablespoons margarine

½ teaspoon baking powder

¼ teaspoon salt

2 tablespoons orange zest

¼ cup orange juice

Orange Zest

Orange zest comes from the colorful outer part of the orange and is filled with delicious flavor. To remove the zest, first wash the orange, and then use a zester on the outer layer. Do not use the white pith that lies directly under the top layer because it has a bitter flavor. If you do not have a zester, use a fine cheese grater, a sharp knife, or a vegetable peeler.

Freezing Day

Mix all ingredients to form a dough. If dough is too wet, add additional flour one tablespoon at a time. Roll out dough on a floured surface. Roll to ⅛" thick and 5" wide. Cut rolled dough into 15 strips. Flash freeze on a baking sheet lined with wax paper. Transfer to a freezer bag once fully frozen.

Reheating Instructions

Lay frozen dough sticks in a single layer on a greased baking sheet. Bake at 400°F for 16–20 minutes or until edges and bottom turn golden brown.

PER SERVING
Calories: 245 | Fat: 14g | Protein: 9g | Sodium: 334mg | Carbohydrates: 21g | Fiber: 1g

Italian Pastry Roll-ups

NO DEFROSTING NEEDED!

INGREDIENTS | SERVES 12

1 (17-ounce) box frozen puff pastry
1 cup ricotta cheese
1 cup jarred spaghetti sauce
1 cup mozzarella cheese, shredded

Freezing Day

Defrost pastry sheets and lay flat. Spread ricotta cheese on sheets, then sauce, and top with mozzarella. Starting on the long side, roll up pastry. Wet the tips of your fingers with water and seal edge of pastry down. Using a serrated knife, cut each roll into 6–8 slices. Lay slices on a baking sheet lined with wax paper and flash freeze. Transfer to freezer bag.

Reheating Instructions

Place the frozen slices on a baking sheet and bake at 400°F for 15–20 minutes.

PER SERVING
Calories: 368 | Fat: 22g | Protein: 9g | Sodium: 499mg | Carbohydrates: 33g | Fiber: 3.5g

Asiago Baked Olives

NO DEFROSTING NEEDED!

INGREDIENTS | SERVES 10

2 cups grated Asiago cheese
1¼ cups flour
½ cup butter, plus 2 tablespoons if needed
1 teaspoon Worcestershire sauce
⅛ teaspoon cayenne pepper
40 green olives

Freezing Day

In a large mixing bowl, combine all but the olives to make dough. Add more flour or butter to dough as needed. Roll dough into balls a little larger than the size of your olives. Push an olive into each ball so it is covered completely with the dough. Place olives on a baking sheet lined with wax paper and flash freeze. Transfer to freezer bag.

Reheating Instructions

Place frozen olives on baking sheet and cook 20–25 minutes at 400°F.

PER SERVING
Calories: 240 | Fat: 17g | Protein: 9g | Sodium: 705mg | Carbohydrates: 12g | Fiber: 1.5g

Dijon Kielbasa Bites

NO DEFROSTING NEEDED!

A Simple Puff Pastry Solution

Puff pastry is a layered pastry made by a time consuming and repetitive process of folding layers of dough and butter, and then letting the pastry rest in a temperature controlled environment. Frozen puff pastry is readily available and is a huge time saver.

Freezing Day

Defrost puff pastry on counter for about 30 minutes. Cut kielbasa into bite-sized pieces and brown in skillet for 10–15 minutes. Once defrosted, roll out puff pastry on floured surface to smooth out the folds in the pastry. Cut pastry into 3" circles. In the center of each circle, put ¼ teaspoon of Dijon mustard (or more to taste) and a piece of kielbasa on top of the Dijon. Pull up the edges of the circles so it looks like a Hershey's Kiss. Use water on your fingers to seal the top together. Flash freeze and transfer to freezer bag.

Reheating Instructions

Place frozen Dijon Kielbasa Bites on a greased baking sheet and bake at 400°F for 15–20 minutes or until golden brown.

PER SERVING
Calories: 557 | Fat: 28g | Protein: 12g | Sodium: 800mg | Carbohydrates: 29g | Fiber: 1g

Sausage Rolls

NO DEFROSTING NEEDED!

INGREDIENTS | SERVES 6

1 pound sausage

1 small onion, minced

½ teaspoon minced garlic

1 teaspoon sage

1 (15-ounce) box refrigerated pie crust

1 egg

1 tablespoon milk

Bake Beautiful Rolls

When you brush them with an egg and milk mixture before baking, the rolls bake shiny with a beautiful golden color.

Freezing Day

In skillet, brown sausage and onion for 7–10 minutes until sausage is no longer pink. Add garlic and sage. Roll out the pie crust to about half its original thickness and form a rectangle. Spread the sausage mixture along the long end of the rectangle. Beginning at the end with the sausage, roll the pie crust up like a jelly roll.

In a small bowl, mix the egg and milk. Brush around the outside of the roll with the egg mixture. Cut into 2-inch pieces and flash freeze. Transfer to a freezer bag.

Reheating Instructions

Bake frozen sausage rolls at 400°F for 15–20 minutes, or until they are golden brown.

PER SERVING
Calories: 384 | Fat: 29g | Protein: 16g | Sodium: 640mg | Carbohydrates: 14g | Fiber: 1g

Sweet and Savory Mini Meatballs

NO DEFROSTING NEEDED!

INGREDIENTS | SERVES 6–8

1 batch Basic Meatballs (Chapter 15)
1 cup ketchup
½ cup brown sugar
½ teaspoon yellow mustard

Meatball Making Tips

No time to make meatballs? Try buying frozen mini meatballs and adding your own sauce. If you do make your own meatballs, use a melon scoop for mini meatballs or an ice cream scoop for larger ones. Your meatballs will be uniform in size and your hands are spared the mess!

Freezing Day

Make meatball recipe and form into 2" balls. In separate bowl, mix ketchup, brown sugar, and mustard. Roll each meatball in prepared sauce and place on a baking sheet. Flash freeze and transfer to freezer bag.

Reheating Instructions

Place frozen meatballs in oven at 350°F and bake for 30 minutes.

PER SERVING
Calories: 624 | Fat: 31g | Protein: 49g | Sodium: 879mg | Carbohydrates: 35g | Fiber: 1g

Sweet Smokin' Smokies

These little sausages are always a hit. Vary this recipe a bit by wrapping each Little Smokie in half of a refrigerated crescent roll and spreading the sauce on the dough. Follow package directions for baking.

INGREDIENTS | SERVES 8–10

2 (16-ounce) packages cocktail smokies
1 cup barbecue sauce
¼ cup brown sugar
½ teaspoon liquid smoke

Dress Up Your Platters

Are your appetizer trays looking a little bare? Try dressing them up with some color! Add fluffy greens around the outside of the tray or underneath the appetizers. Put cherry tomatoes with complementary appetizers. Cheese is a simple way to brighten up any appetizer tray and remains a favorite.

Freezing Day

In skillet, brown cocktail smokies over medium-high heat for 5–7 minutes. In separate bowl, mix the barbecue sauce, brown sugar, and liquid smoke. Put sauce in freezer bag, add cocktail smokies, and mix. Freeze.

Reheating Instructions

Defrost cocktail smokies in refrigerator overnight. Put in saucepan and heat for 25–30 minutes over medium heat, or in slow cooker on low for 2 hours. Serve with toothpicks.

PER SERVING
Calories: 131 | Fat: 5g | Protein: 2g | Sodium: 418mg | Carbohydrates: 19g | Fiber: 0g

Sesame Shrimp Toast

NO DEFROSTING NEEDED!

INGREDIENTS | SERVES 6

6 slices white bread

8 ounces cooked shrimp, peeled

2 tablespoons water chestnuts, finely chopped

1 egg white

½ teaspoon garlic, minced

½ teaspoon sesame oil

½ teaspoon fresh ginger, minced

2 tablespoons scallions, minced

1 tablespoon sesame seeds

Dim Sum

Shrimp Toast is a Chinese dish often included in Dim Sum. Dim sum (which means "heart warmers") consists of a variety of both sweet and savory snacks that are shared with pots of tea. In restaurants, the freshly cooked dim sum selections are brought to the tables, stacked on rolling carts and often served in steaming bamboo baskets.

Freezing Day

Remove crusts from bread, cut diagonally into 4 pieces and toast lightly. In a food processor, combine shrimp, water chestnuts, egg white, garlic, sesame oil, and ginger. Pulse 5–10 times, but do not purée. Stir in scallions.

Spread shrimp mixture on the toasted bread slices, and sprinkle with sesame seeds. Flash freeze and transfer to a Tupperware container.

Re-heating Instructions

Cook frozen Shrimp Toast at 400°F for 10–15 minutes.

PER SERVING
Calories: 170 | Fat: 2.8 g | Protein: 10 g | Sodium: 202 mg | Carbohydrates: 25g | Fiber: 1g

Mini Chicken Turnovers

NO DEFROSTING NEEDED!

INGREDIENTS | YIELDS APPROXIMATELY 30 TURNOVERS

FILLING:

2 tablespoons onion, minced

4 tablespoons mushrooms, diced

¼ teaspoon garlic, minced

1½ cups cooked chicken

3 ounces cream cheese

¼ teaspoon salt

¼ teaspoon pepper

3 tablespoons white wine

PASTRY:

1½ cups flour

¾ teaspoon salt

½ cup shortening

3 tablespoons water, as needed

2 tablespoons butter

Puff Pastry Chicken Turnovers

If you prefer a simpler route, purchase frozen puff pastry. You need 2 (17-ounce) boxes. Defrost the pastry on the counter for about 30 minutes, and roll it out on a floured surface. Cut out 3-inch circles and fill with the chicken mixture. Fold, seal the edges with a fork, and flash freeze. To bake, defrost and bake at 400°F for 5 minutes or until pastry is golden brown.

Freezing Day

Make the filling: In skillet over medium heat, sauté onions and mushrooms in butter for 5–6 minutes. Add the garlic and sauté 1–2 more minutes. Add chicken, cream cheese, salt, pepper, and wine. Heat over medium-low heat 5–7 minutes until cream cheese melts. Remove from heat and set aside.

Make the pastry: Sift the flour and salt. Cut in the shortening until it is crumbly. Add water, a tablespoon at a time, until the dough holds together. Make dough into a ball and roll out on a floured surface to ⅛"-thick. Cut into 2 half-inch circles. Line a baking sheet with wax paper. Put a spoonful of chicken mixture on one half of each pastry circle, and fold it over. Moisten the edge of the turnover to help seal the dough. Press around the outside with a fork. Put on baking sheet and flash freeze. Transfer to freezer bag once flash frozen.

Reheating Instructions

Place frozen turnovers on a baking sheet and bake at 400°F for 15–20 minutes or until turnovers are golden brown.

PER SERVING
Calories: 80 | Fat: 5g | Protein: 3g | Sodium: 94mg | Carbohydrates: 5g | Fiber: 0g

Ham and Pineapple Bites

These appetizers are sweet and spicy. The red pepper flakes give the bites a spicy kick, while the honey gives them a sweet flavor.

INGREDIENTS | SERVES 12

¼ cup honey

25 cubes of cooked ham

25 pineapple chunks

Red pepper flakes to taste

Freezing Day

Coat one side of each cube of ham with honey. Sprinkle a small amount of red pepper flakes on top of the honey, and top that with a pineapple chunk. Hold it together with a toothpick. Flash freeze and transfer to a freezer bag.

Reheating Instructions

Defrost Ham and Pineapple Bites overnight in refrigerator and serve cold.

PER SERVING
Calories: 160 | Fat: 3.5g | Protein: 17g | Sodium: 600mg | Carbohydrates: 14g | Fiber: 1g

Basil and Mozzarella Stuffed Tomatoes

Basil can be expensive to buy out of season, but it is easily grown at home. This herb needs about seven hours of sunlight a day, and can be grown indoors or outdoors after the last frost.

INGREDIENTS | SERVES 6–8

10 ounces cherry tomatoes (about 18)

½ cup mozzarella cheese

1 tablespoon olive oil

1–3 tablespoons fresh basil, chopped (according to taste)

¼ teaspoon salt

1 small clove garlic, minced

Freezing Day

With a paring knife, remove the tops and insides of tomatoes. In a large mixing bowl, combine the cheese, olive oil, basil, salt, and garlic. Mix well. Spoon the stuffing into each tomato. Flash freeze on a baking sheet and transfer to freezer bag.

Reheating Instructions

Defrost in refrigerator overnight and serve cold.

PER SERVING
Calories: 45 | Fat: 3g | Protein: 3g | Sodium: 5mg | Carbohydrates: 2g | Fiber: 1g

Spicy Beef Kabobs with Cucumber Dipping Sauce

Fresh ginger should be kept in the refrigerator, but will last longer if you freeze it.
When using frozen ginger, there is no need to defrost.
Simply grate however much ginger you need, and return the rest to the freezer.

INGREDIENTS | SERVES 6–8

¼ cup lime juice

2 cloves garlic, minced

1 cup soy sauce

2 teaspoons fresh ginger, grated

1 teaspoon crushed red pepper flakes

2 pounds lean steak, cut into cubes

2 red bell peppers (used on reheating day)

2 green bell peppers (used on reheating day)

2 yellow bell peppers (used on reheating day)

Cucumber Dipping Sauce (Chapter 14) (used on reheating day)

Freezing Day

In bowl, combine lime juice, garlic, soy sauce, ginger, and red pepper flakes. Put marinade in a freezer bag, add cubed steak, and freeze.

Reheating Instructions

Defrost meat and marinade in refrigerator overnight. Cut red, green, and yellow peppers into 1½-inch pieces. Place meat and vegetables on skewers and grill over medium-high heat 8–12 minutes, or until desired doneness. Serve with Cucumber Dipping Sauce.

PER SERVING
Calories: 270 | Fat: 8g | Protein: 40g | Sodium: 1500mg | Carbohydrates: 7g | Fiber: 2g

CHAPTER 3

Beef

Mushroom Beef Stroganoff

Serve the Mushroom Beef Stroganoff over egg noodles or rice.
Don't forget to serve bread so you can soak up every last bit of the delicious sauce.

INGREDIENTS | SERVES 4

½ cup flour

½ teaspoon salt

¼ teaspoon pepper

1 pound top round steak or equivalent, cut into cubes

2 tablespoons cooking oil

1 (10.75-ounce) can cream of mushroom soup

1 cup water

2 (8-ounce) cans sliced mushrooms

¼ cup white wine

1 cup sour cream (used on reheating day)

Make It Last

One of the benefits of owning a freezer is the ability to stock up on meat when it goes on sale. To help your meat taste as fresh as possible for as long as possible, rewrap it when you come home from the grocery store. Rather than put it directly in the freezer, repackage it in freezer bags or freezer wrap.

Freezing Day

In a 1-gallon sized plastic bag, put flour, salt, and pepper. Add beef and shake to coat completely. Heat oil in skillet. Add beef and brown on all sides, about 7–10 minutes. In separate bowl, mix soup and water. Slowly add soup and water to skillet, scraping the bottom as you mix with beef. Add mushrooms and wine.

Cook over medium-low heat for 1 hour, stirring frequently. Scrape the bottom of the skillet when you stir. Cool and freeze in freezer bag.

Reheating Instructions

Defrost Stroganoff overnight, stir in sour cream, and heat on medium-low 30–45 minutes or until it is thoroughly heated.

PER SERVING
Calories: 507 | Fat: 29g | Protein: 39g | Sodium: 690mg | Carbohydrates: 22g | Fiber: 1g

Ricotta and Beef Stuffed Shells

NO DEFROSTING NEEDED!

INGREDIENTS | SERVES 6

1 pound ground beef

1 small onion, chopped

1 clove garlic, minced

3 slices white bread

1 cup mozzarella cheese

½ cup ricotta cheese

1 egg

½ cup milk

1 teaspoon Italian seasoning

1 (12-ounce) box jumbo pasta shells, uncooked

2 (24-ounce) jars spaghetti sauce (to be used on reheating day)

1 cup mozzarella cheese (to be used on reheating day)

Stuffed Shells Two Ways

An alternative preparation of this dish is to prepare and freeze it as an entire casserole rather than flash freezing the shells and assembling the casserole on serving day.

Freezing Day

In a skillet, brown ground beef and onion for 7–10 minutes or until meat is thoroughly cooked. Add garlic and cook 1 more minute. Drain if needed. Put ground beef mixture in large mixing bowl. Add bread (torn into small pieces), mozzarella cheese, ricotta, egg, milk, and Italian seasoning to the mixing bowl. Mix well. Carefully stuff each shell with meat mixture. Flash freeze shells and transfer to freezer bag.

Reheating Instructions

Put frozen shells in a 9" x 12" baking dish. Pour up to 2 jars of sauce over the top of shells, depending on your taste. Spread 1 cup mozzarella cheese over shells. Cover with aluminum foil. Bake at 375°F for 1 hour 45 minutes–2 hours until shells are tender.

PER SERVING

Calories: 911 | Fat: 31g | Protein: 46g | Sodium: 1300mg | Carbohydrates: 114g | Fiber: 13g

Grilled Sirloin Wraps

An alternative to grilling your steak is to stir-fry it. On freezing day, cut steak into ½" strips and put into freezer bag with marinade. On cooking day, defrost steak, discard marinade, and stir-fry in a wok or skillet.

INGREDIENTS | SERVES 6

2 pounds sirloin steak

½ cup butter

⅓ cup onion, minced

3 teaspoons dried parsley

2 tablespoons Worcestershire sauce

½ teaspoon yellow mustard

¼ teaspoon pepper

½ teaspoon salt

12 flour tortillas (used on reheating day)

½ cup lettuce, shredded (used on reheating day)

2 tomatoes, chopped (used on reheating day)

⅓ cup Vidalia onions, chopped (used on reheating day)

½ cup sour cream (used on reheating day)

½ cup shredded Cheddar cheese (used on reheating day)

Freezing Day

Score the top of the steak by cutting slits across the grain. In saucepan, melt butter. Add onion, parsley, Worcestershire sauce, mustard, pepper, and salt. Cook on low heat 5–10 minutes. Remove marinade from heat and cool. Put the steak in a freezer bag and pour in the marinade. Freeze.

Reheating Instructions

Defrost steak and marinade overnight in the refrigerator, then discard marinade. Grill the steak over high heat until desired doneness. Let rest for 5 minutes. Cut steak into ½" strips. To serve, layer each tortilla with steak, lettuce, tomato, onion, cheese, and sour cream. Roll like a burrito.

PER SERVING
Calories: 687 | Fat: 34g | Protein: 53g | Sodium: 629mg | Carbohydrates: 39g | Fiber: 3g

Let Your Steak Rest

Ever wondered why chefs let steak rest before cutting? During grilling, the juices flow inward and saturate the middle of the steak. When cut immediately after cooking, the juices flooding the middle have nowhere to go but out. By allowing it to rest, the juices have time to be reabsorbed evenly throughout the meat.

Steak and Tomatoes

This hearty, rib-sticking dish tastes delicious served with mashed potatoes.
It is a simple dish to prepare, but tastes like you spent hours in the kitchen.

INGREDIENTS | SERVES 4

1 pound top round steak

⅓ cup flour

Salt and pepper to taste

2 tablespoons cooking oil

1 onion, sliced

1 (29-ounce) can chopped tomatoes

Freezing Day

Dredge steak in flour, salt, and pepper. In a skillet, brown steak for 3–4 minutes per side in cooking oil. Remove steak from skillet and sauté sliced onion in same skillet for 3–4 minutes. Return steak to skillet and add chopped tomatoes, then remove from heat and allow to cool. Freeze steak, onions, and tomatoes in a freezer bag.

Reheating Instructions

Defrost in refrigerator for 20–24 hours. Cook covered over medium-low heat, stirring occasionally, for 1 hour or until steak is tender.

PER SERVING
Calories: 447 | Fat: 27g | Protein: 27g | Sodium: 507mg | Carbohydrates: 24g | Fiber: 3g

Pepper Steak

Flank steak is full of flavor, but it can be tough.
Slice it thin and diagonally across the grain when you cut it into strips.

INGREDIENTS | SERVES 4–6

1½-pound flank steak

1 green bell pepper

1 yellow bell pepper

1 red bell pepper

1 large onion

Stir-fry Sauce (Chapter 14)

Water, as needed (used on reheating day)

3 tablespoons cornstarch (used on reheating day)

How to Thicken Sauce with Cornstarch

Cornstarch is a great solution any time you have a sauce you want to thicken. Simply mix 3 tablespoons of cornstarch with ¼ cup cold water. Stir until the cornstarch is completely dissolved, and add to sauce. Stir until the sauce thickens. To multiply your sauce, you can also add 1 cup of beef or chicken broth.

Freezing Day

Cut steak, peppers, and onions into thin strips. Place into a mixing bowl. Add the Stir-fry Sauce to the bowl and mix well. Put meat, vegetables, and sauce in freezer bag and freeze.

Reheating Instructions

Defrost in the microwave. Put in skillet and stir-fry over medium-high heat for 7–10 minutes or until meat reaches desired doneness and vegetables are tender. Add water as needed. Use cornstarch to thicken sauce if desired. Serve over rice.

PER SERVING
Calories: 154 | Fat: 7g | Protein: 12g | Sodium: 27mg | Carbohydrates: 10g | Fiber: 1g

Spicy Beef and Penne Pasta

This hearty stew is a great choice when you have a crowd to feed.
It is popular with the kids, and goes well with a loaf of crunchy French bread.

INGREDIENTS | SERVES 6–8

1 pound ground beef

2 tablespoons minced onion

1 clove garlic, minced

1 teaspoon red pepper flakes

6 cups plus ¾ cups water, separated

5 beef bouillon cubes

9 tablespoons cornstarch

1 (16-ounce) bag frozen corn

1 (16 ounce) box penne pasta (used on reheating day)

Freezing Day

In large skillet, brown ground beef. Add minced onion, garlic, and red pepper flakes. Cook until all pan juices have evaporated, approximately 10 minutes. In separate saucepan, bring 6 cups of water to a boil. Dissolve bouillon cubes in boiling water. Add to ground beef.

In a measuring cup, mix ¾ cup water with cornstarch. Mix well. Add cornstarch mixture to skillet. Cook over medium heat 10–12 minutes, stirring frequently until mixture thickens. Add corn. Remove from heat and cool. Freeze in a freezer bag.

Reheating Instructions

In large pot, defrost beef mixture and heat over medium-low heat for 30 minutes until it is fully heated. Cook penne pasta according to package directions. Drain and add to beef mixture. Serve.

PER SERVING
Calories: 413 | Fat: 8.5g | Protein: 25g | Sodium: 440mg |
Carbohydrates: 61g | Fiber: 3g

Rolled Burgundy Flank Steak

In this recipe you will be making two batches of the marinade. One will be used on cooking day to marinate the flank steak, and the second batch will be frozen and used on the day you cook the steak.

INGREDIENTS | SERVES 6

2 pounds flank steak

½ cup burgundy wine

4 tablespoons Worcestershire sauce

2 teaspoons thyme

1 teaspoon rosemary

2 teaspoons salt

1 teaspoon pepper

1 (6-ounce) box Stove Top Savory Herb Stuffing Mix

1 cup chopped mushrooms

Easy Marinating

A simple way to marinate is to put the meat and the marinade in a plastic bag, and put the bag in the refrigerator. Turning the meat is easy; just flip over the bag. And cleanup takes no time at all—just throw away the plastic bag!

Freezing Day

With mallet, pound steak to ¼" thickness. Combine wine, Worcestershire sauce, thyme, rosemary, salt, and pepper in bowl. Pour half the marinade into a quart-size freezer bag and freeze. Pour the other half into a shallow dish. Marinate flank steak in dish for 3–5 hours in refrigerator, turning twice. Discard marinade.

Prepare the stuffing according to directions on the box. Stir in mushrooms. Lay flank steak out on counter and spread stuffing mixture over top. Starting at one long side, tightly roll steak up like a jelly roll and secure it with string. Tightly rap rolled steak with a layer of plastic wrap, followed by a layer of aluminum foil. Freeze.

Reheating Instructions

Defrost the rolled steak in the refrigerator for a minimum of 24 hours. Defrost marinade in cold water for about 30 minutes, or in the microwave. Place steak in a 9" x 13" dish and pour marinade in the bottom of the pan. Baste the steak with the marinade. Cook steak in a 400°F oven for 50–60 minutes (until meat thermometer reaches 160°F). Baste frequently.

PER SERVING
Calories: 417 | Fat: 12g | Protein: 50g | Sodium: 659mg | Carbohydrates: 24g | Fiber: 1g

Skillet Beef with Black Beans

Worcestershire sauce is so named because it was first made in Worcester, England. It is a popular condiment made up of vinegar, molasses, various spices, and anchovies.

INGREDIENTS | SERVES 4–6

1 pound ground beef

1 small onion, chopped

1 green pepper, chopped

1 clove garlic, minced

2 teaspoons lemon juice

2 teaspoons yellow mustard

2 tablespoons Worcestershire sauce

½ teaspoon cumin

1 cup tomato sauce

1 (16-ounce) can black beans

Freezing Day

In skillet, brown ground beef, onion, green pepper, and garlic. Add remaining ingredients except black beans. Mix well. Gently stir in black beans. Freeze in freezer bag.

Reheating Instructions

Defrost in the refrigerator overnight. Heat over medium-low heat for 20 minutes, or until desired temperature is reached, and serve over rice.

PER SERVING
Calories: 433 | Fat: 10g | Protein: 37g | Sodium: 131mg | Carbohydrates: 49g | Fiber: 11g

Zesty Breakfast Burritos

NO DEFROSTING NEEDED!

INGREDIENTS | SERVES 20–24

2 pounds ground beef

1 onion, diced

1 green bell pepper, diced

1 tablespoon butter

12 eggs

2 cups shredded Cheddar cheese

1 (15-ounce) jar salsa

24 flour tortillas

Freezing Day

In skillet brown ground beef, onion, and bell pepper. Drain. In a mixing bowl, whisk the eggs. Melt butter in a clean skillet, add eggs, and scramble. Assemble each burrito by putting meat, egg, cheese, and a spoonful of salsa inside each tortilla. Flash freeze and transfer to freezer bag, or wrap individually in plastic wrap and freeze.

Reheating Instructions

Heat frozen burrito in microwave for 2 minutes. Serve.

PER SERVING
Calories: 318 | Fat: 15g | Protein: 23g | Sodium: 358mg | Carbohydrates: 21g | Fiber: 2g

Sweet Ginger Sloppy Joes

Although ground ginger may be substituted for fresh ginger in the correct proportion,
tt does have a different flavor. Ground ginger is much stronger, so substitute
¼ teaspoon ground ginger for every 4 teaspoons fresh ginger.

INGREDIENTS | SERVES 4–6

1 pound ground beef

1 onion, chopped

1½ cups ketchup

¾ cup brown sugar

½ cup soy sauce

4 teaspoons fresh ginger, grated

½ cup water

8 hamburger buns (used on reheating day)

Freezing Day

In skillet, brown ground beef and onion. Drain. Add remaining ingredients and cook over medium heat for 5 minutes. Freeze mixture in a freezer bag.

Reheating Instructions

Defrost meat. Heat in a saucepan over medium heat for 20 minutes, or until desired temperature is reached. Make sandwiches using hamburger buns.

PER SERVING
Calories: 627 | Fat: 12g | Protein: 35g | Sodium: 2300mg | Carbohydrates: 96g | Fiber: 3.5g

Lemon Pepper Grilled Steak

Instead of grilling, you may prefer to broil the steak.
Preheat the broiler, and then place the steak on a broiler pan 6 inches from the heat.
Broil for 10 minutes, turn, and broil an additional 10–15 minutes until steak reaches desired doneness.

INGREDIENTS | SERVES 4–6

2-pound top round steak

2 cloves garlic, sliced thin

2 tablespoons lemon zest

1 tablespoon butter, room temperature

1 teaspoon black pepper

1 teaspoon salt

Freezing Day

Cut small slits on both sides of the steak. Push a thin slice of garlic into each slit. In separate bowl, mix lemon zest, butter, black pepper, and salt. Spread the mixture over all sides of the steak. Freeze in a freezer bag.

Reheating Instructions

Defrost steak in refrigerator for up to 24 hours. Grill over medium heat until desired doneness.

PER SERVING
Calories: 313 | Fat: 13 g | Protein: 46g | Sodium: 500mg | Carbohydrates: 0g | Fiber: 0g

Chestnut Stuffed Cube Steaks with Mushroom Gravy

Chestnuts have a sweet nutty flavor and although they can be eaten raw, they taste better when boiled or roasted. They are a seasonal nut and are most often available October through December.

INGREDIENTS | SERVES 4

¾ pound chestnuts

4 tablespoons butter

½ onion, chopped

1 rib celery, chopped

½ pound mushrooms, sliced

¼ cup cream sherry

4 cups soft bread cubes (5–6 slices bread, toasted)

1 teaspoons sage

½ teaspoon thyme

1 to 1½ cups chicken broth

4 cube steaks

1 (12-ounce) jar mushroom gravy (used on reheating day)

Freezing Day

In pan, cover chestnuts with water and heat to boiling. Reduce heat to medium and cook 10 minutes. Remove 3 chestnuts at a time from water, cut in half lengthwise, and peel each one. In a skillet, melt butter and sauté onions and celery. Add mushrooms and sherry. Cook over medium-low heat for 10 minutes.

In large bowl, combine vegetables with bread cubes and herbs. Add chestnuts and mix well. Moisten the stuffing with chicken broth, adding a little at a time, until the desired consistency is reached. Lay out steaks and cover each with stuffing. Fold steak over the stuffing, and secure with a toothpick. Flash freeze on a cookie sheet lined with wax paper. Transfer to freezer bag.

Reheating Instructions

Defrost steak in refrigerator for 24 hours. Place in a baking dish and pour mushroom gravy over the top. Cover with aluminum foil. Bake at 350°F for 30–45 minutes, or until steaks are tender.

PER SERVING
Calories: 617 | Fat: 25g | Protein: 44g | Sodium: 1123mg | Carbohydrates: 54g | Fiber: 3g

Stuffed Peppers with Sunflower Seeds

Stuffed Peppers is a dish that can be found around the globe, with each country having its own version. The classic American stuffed peppers contain meat and rice and are served with tomato sauce, although there are quite a few variations.

INGREDIENTS | SERVES 8

2 pounds ground beef

Ground Beef Seasoning Mix (Chapter 13)

2 (15-ounce) cans tomato sauce

2 cups cooked rice (not minute rice)

½ cup sunflower seeds

8 green peppers

1 (15-ounce) can seasoned diced tomatoes (used on reheating day)

How to Freeze Green Peppers

Many vegetables need to be blanched before they can be frozen, but not green peppers. So before you throw away another rotten pepper from your crisper drawer, freeze them instead. Simply cut the peppers in half, and remove the membrane, seeds, and stem. You can chop them, or cut them into strips. Flash freeze on a baking sheet, and transfer to a freezer bag.

Freezing Day

In skillet, brown ground beef with the Ground Beef Seasoning Mix. Stir in the 2 cans of tomato sauce. Let simmer for 10 minutes. Stir in rice and sunflower seeds. Cut each pepper in half lengthwise, and remove the stem and seeds. Steam peppers by placing them, cut side up, in ½" of water. Bring to a boil, cover, and simmer for 5 minutes. Remove from heat. Lay each pepper half on a baking sheet and fill with meat filling. Flash freeze and transfer to a freezer bag.

Reheating Instructions

Defrost peppers in refrigerator for 24 hours and lay them in a baking dish. Pour the diced tomatoes over the top of the peppers and around the bottom of the pan. Bake at 350°F for 30–45 minutes until the peppers are hot and start to brown.

PER SERVING

Calories: 425 | Fat: 18g | Protein: 37g | Sodium: 536mg | Carbohydrates: 29g | Fiber: 4.5g

Goulash

Goulash has evolved over the years, but authentic Hungarian Goulash was cooked in a large cast-iron kettle over an open fire. The hearty soup was used to feed the herdsmen working in the fields.

INGREDIENTS | SERVES 8–10

2 cups uncooked macaroni

1 pound ground beef

1 pound ground sausage

1 onion, chopped

2 cloves garlic, minced

2 (29-ounce) cans tomato sauce

2 (15-ounce) cans corn, drained

2 tablespoons dried Italian seasoning

Parmesan cheese (used on reheating day)

Freezing Day

In large saucepot, cook macaroni 8–9 minutes until it is just under-done. Drain and return to saucepot. In skillet, brown the ground beef, ground sausage, and onion for 15 minutes, or until the meat is thoroughly cooked. Add garlic and cook an additional 1–2 minutes. Drain off fat. Add all remaining ingredients to the saucepot, remove from stove, and cool. Cool and freeze in a freezer bag.

Reheating Instructions

Defrost goulash in refrigerator for 24 hours. In skillet, bring goulash to a boil, turn heat down, and simmer for 20 minutes. Serve with Parmesan cheese sprinkled over the top.

PER SERVING
Calories: 432 | Fat: 19g | Protein: 27g | Sodium: 357mg | Carbohydrates: 38g | Fiber: 3g

Glazed Meatloaf

When you bake your meatloaf, put 2 pieces of bread underneath it to soak up the grease while it cooks. When you are ready to serve, simply throw the pieces of bread away.

INGREDIENTS | SERVES 4–6

2 pounds lean ground beef

4 eggs, lightly beaten

1 onion, chopped

¼ cup celery, chopped

2 teaspoons seasoning salt

1 teaspoon pepper

1 cup Saltine crackers, finely crumbled

2 cups ketchup

⅔ cup ketchup (used on reheating day)

½ cup brown sugar (used on reheating day)

1½ teaspoons prepared yellow mustard (used on reheating day)

Freezing Day

Combine beef and eggs. Blend in onions, celery, seasonings, cracker crumbs, and ketchup. Mixture will be smooth and moist. Flash freeze in a 9" x 5" loaf pan. Once frozen, remove meatloaf from pan, wrap well, and return to freezer.

Reheating Instructions

Defrost in refrigerator for 24 hours. Cook at 350°F for 1 hour. In a small bowl, mix ketchup, brown sugar, and mustard. Spread on meatloaf during last 20 minutes of cooking time.

PER SERVING
Calories: 590 | Fat: 23g | Protein: 50g | Sodium: 1800mg | Carbohydrates: 47g | Fiber: 1.5g

Loose Meat Sandwiches

The secret to the perfect loose meat sandwich is to crumble the ground beef as small as possible. When browning it, use your spatula and break up the chunks.

INGREDIENTS | SERVES 4–6

2 pounds ground beef

2 green bell peppers, finely chopped

1 onion, finely chopped

1 clove garlic, minced

½ cup celery, finely chopped

1 cup water

1 cup chili sauce

2 teaspoons Dijon mustard

2 tablespoons barbecue sauce

1 teaspoon salt

Kaiser rolls (used on reheating day)

Dill pickles (used on reheating day)

Dijon or yellow mustard (used on reheating day)

Freezing Day

In skillet, brown ground beef, bell peppers, onion, and garlic. Drain. To the skillet add celery, water, chili sauce, mustard, barbecue sauce, and salt. Remove from heat and cool. Freeze in a freezer bag.

Reheating Instructions

Defrost in the refrigerator for 24 hours. Heat in a saucepan over medium-low heat for 25 minutes. Serve on kaiser rolls with dill pickles and mustard.

PER SERVING
Calories: 380 | Fat: 10g | Protein: 35g | Sodium: 1043mg | Carbohydrates: 48g | Fiber: 3g

Teriyaki Beef and Vegetable Kabobs

Fresh grilled pineapple is delicious when paired with the teriyaki marinated sirloin steak and vegetables. Serve the kabobs over rice.

INGREDIENTS | SERVES 6–8

1 cup Teriyaki Marinade (Chapter 14)

2 pounds sirloin steak cut into 1½" cubes

2 green bell peppers, cut into 2" pieces

1 sweet onion, cut into 2" pieces

½ cup Teriyaki Marinade (Chapter 14) (used on reheating day)

1 fresh pineapple, cut into 2" pieces (used on reheating day)

Skewers

Freezing Day

Prepare a double batch of Teriyaki Marinade, or defrost if it is already prepared. Put steak, peppers, and onions in a freezer bag. Pour 1 cup marinade over the top and freeze.

Reheating Instructions

Defrost steak, peppers, and onions in refrigerator overnight, or in microwave, and discard the marinade. Prepare the skewers by threading on each a combination of steak, peppers, onions, and pineapple. Prepare another batch of Teriyaki Marinade. This will be used for basting during grilling. Grill the skewers over high heat for approximately 10 minutes. Baste with Teriyaki Marinade.

PER SERVING
Calories: 380 | Fat: 29g | Protein: 38g | Sodium: 624mg | Carbohydrates: 27g | Fiber: 3g

Blue Ribbon Chili

This award-winning chili tastes fantastic served over rice.
Have toppings such as grated Parmesan cheese, shredded Cheddar cheese, sliced jalapeño peppers,
sour cream, and oyster crackers available for even more flavor.

INGREDIENTS | SERVES 20

5 pounds 80/20 or 75/25 ground beef

1 large sweet onion, diced

3 tablespoons jalapeños, diced

3 cloves garlic, minced

4 tablespoons cumin

3 tablespoons cocoa

5 tablespoons chili powder

2 tablespoons salt

2 cups beef broth

3 tablespoons oregano

8 tablespoons minced, dried onion

½–1 teaspoon cayenne pepper, according to taste

2 (6-ounce) cans tomato paste

4 (14.5-ounce) cans diced tomatoes with green chilies

⅛ cup ketchup

2 tablespoons dark brown sugar

Freezing Day

In skillet, brown ground beef with the diced onion, jalapeño, and garlic. Drain. Transfer meat to stockpot, and add all other ingredients. Mix well. Simmer on low 60–90 minutes. Add water as necessary to achieve desired thickness. Remove from heat, cool, and freeze using freezer bags, or plastic containers.

Reheating Instructions

Defrost chili in the refrigerator for 24 hours (less time for small portions). Heat chili in a saucepan over medium-low heat for 20–30 minutes, or until it reaches desired temperature.

PER SERVING
Calories: 348 | Fat: 20g | Protein: 32g | Sodium: 1157mg | Carbohydrates: 9g | Fiber: 1.5g

Thoughts on Chili

Cooking chili is all about getting the right balance between the heat of the chili and the savory of the meat and spices. Purists will maintain that real chili does not have beans and that it should make you sweat, even if it's just a little bit! Chili is a great food to experiment with to develop your own personal recipe.

Beef and Broccoli Stir Fry

Sirloin is the preferred choice of beef for this dish because it is tender when cooked. If you use a tougher cut of steak, be sure to cut it thin and tenderize it with a meat mallet before freezing.

INGREDIENTS | SERVES 6–8

4 cups fresh broccoli, chopped

2 cloves garlic, minced

3 cups beef bouillon

2 tablespoons sugar

4 tablespoons soy sauce

½ teaspoon ground ginger

1 teaspoon oyster sauce

¼–½ teaspoon red pepper, to taste

1 pound beef sirloin, sliced thinly across the grain

3 tablespoons oil (used on reheating day)

1 green onion, sliced (used on reheating day)

1 tablespoon cornstarch (used on reheating day)

2 tablespoons cold water (used on reheating day)

Why Blanch the Broccoli?

There are two reasons why the broccoli is blanched. First, fresh broccoli must always be blanched before freezing. Second, the 3-minute blanch shortens the time the broccoli needs to cook with the steak in the skillet, thus protecting the steak from overcooking.

Freezing Day

Blanch the broccoli: Bring 6 cups of water to a boil. Prepare a large bowl filled with ice and water. Put the broccoli in the boiling water for 3 minutes. Remove and put in the ice water for 3 minutes. Drain well and put in a freezer bag. Set aside.

In a mixing bowl, whisk together garlic, beef bouillon, sugar, soy sauce, ginger, oyster sauce, and red pepper. Put sliced beef in a freezer bag and pour sauce over the top. Freeze with the bag of broccoli.

Reheating Instructions

Defrost the bag of beef with sauce, and the bag of broccoli in the refrigerator overnight. Pour the sauce into a saucepan. Bring to a boil for 1 minute, then reduce heat to medium-low for 2–3 minutes. Heat skillet over high heat. Add oil and arrange the sirloin in the skillet in a single layer. Cook for 1 minute and turn beef over. Cook on second side for 1 minute. Add onions and sauce to the skillet and bring to a low boil. Add the broccoli and cook 1 minute, stirring constantly. Mix the cornstarch with 2 tablespoons of cold water. Add to skillet and stir for 1–2 minutes until sauce thickens. Serve over rice.

PER SERVING
Calories: 184 | Fat: 10g | Protein: 16g | Sodium: 719mg | Carbohydrates: 8g | Fiber: 1.4g

Poultry

Chicken Verde Wraps
53

Chicken Cordon Bleu
54

Grilled Citrus Chicken
55

Apricot Walnut Stuffed Chicken
56

Turkey Fricassee in Mushroom
and Wine Sauce
57

Broiled Garlic and Tarragon
Chicken Breasts
58

Braised Italian Chicken
59

White Chili
60

Grilled Hawaiian Chicken
61

Chicken Breast with Creamy
Tarragon Sauce
62

Braised Southwestern Chicken
63

Lemon Chicken
64

Raspberry Glazed Chicken Breasts
65

Mini Turkey Meatballs
65

Grilled Honey Mustard Chicken
66

Curried Chicken
67

Chicken and Mushroom
Fettuccine Alfredo
68

Turkey Breast with Buttery Citrus
Sauce
69

Rosemary and Pineapple
Chicken
70

Paprika Chicken
71

Chicken Tacos
72

Orange Chicken
73

Mustard Chicken
73

Sweet and Sour Chicken
74

Breaded Chicken Breast with
Muenster Cheese Bake
75

Chicken Verde Wraps

Tomatillos are a popular ingredient in many traditional Mexican dishes.
They are covered with an inedible husk, but once peeled look like a small green tomato.
You can buy them fresh, or you can use jarred tomatillos for this recipe.

INGREDIENTS | SERVES 2–4

3 cups cubed chicken, uncooked

3 tablespoons olive oil

1 onion, coarsely diced

1½ cups green tomatillo (jarred)

Salt and pepper to taste

1 package flour tortillas (used on reheating day)

Grated Cheddar cheese (used as a topping on reheating day)

Sour cream (used as a topping on reheating day)

Freezing Day

In a large skillet over medium-high heat, sauté the chicken in oil for 4–6 minutes until white in color. Add the onion and sauté until most of the juices have disappeared. Drain any remaining juices. Add the tomatillo and cook over low heat until the mixture thickens. Season the mixture with salt and pepper. Freeze using a freezer bag.

Reheating Instructions

Defrost chicken mixture in the refrigerator overnight, in the microwave, or in cold water. Place in saucepan and heat over medium heat. Serve burrito-style with flour tortillas. Top with Cheddar cheese and sour cream as desired.

PER SERVING
Calories: 264 | Fat: 13g | Protein: 14g | Sodium: 178mg | Carbohydrates: 22g | Fiber: 1.5g

Chicken Cordon Bleu

Cordon bleu is a French phrase meaning "blue ribbon."
The term has come to stand for food or chefs that are distinguished and of the highest quality.

INGREDIENTS | SERVES 8

6 skinless, boneless chicken breasts

6 slices of deli ham

¾ pound Swiss cheese, grated

2 eggs

¼ cup milk

¾ cup flour

¾ teaspoon salt

1 cup plain breadcrumbs

1 cup grated Parmesan cheese

1–2 tablespoons finely chopped fresh basil or dried basil

1 teaspoon garlic powder

½ teaspoon salt

½ teaspoon black pepper

4–6 tablespoons olive oil, as needed

Chicken Cordon Bleu Sauce

Put this sauce in a gravy boat on the table so it can be poured over chicken on individual plates. To make, melt 1 tablespoon butter. Whisk in 1 tablespoon flour. Slowly stir in 1 cup milk and continue to whisk until sauce thickens. Stir in ½ cup shredded Swiss cheese and 3 tablespoons chicken broth. Heat until cheese melts.

Freezing Day

Lay each piece of chicken between 2 sheets of plastic wrap. With a meat mallet, flatten the chicken until it is ¼" thick. Cover each piece of chicken with a slice of ham, and sprinkle the Swiss cheese on top of the ham. Fold in each long side of chicken breast, beginning at a short end and rolling it up jelly-roll style. Secure with a toothpick.

In a small bowl, mix together eggs and milk. Set aside. In a shallow plate, mix together flour and ¾ teaspoon salt. Set aside. In a separate shallow plate, mix together breadcrumbs, Parmesan cheese, basil, garlic powder, and ½ teaspoon each salt and pepper. Dip chicken pieces in flour mixture to coat. Next dip in egg mixture to coat. Lastly, dredge in breadcrumb mixture.

Heat oil in large skillet over medium heat. Brown chicken for 2–3 minutes on all sides until golden brown. Drain on paper towels. Lay the chicken on a baking sheet lined with wax paper and flash freeze. Once frozen, transfer to a freezer bag.

Reheating Instructions

Defrost chicken in the refrigerator for 24 hours and put in a 9" x 13" baking dish. Pour 2 cups chicken broth into the pan. Bake chicken at 400°F for 30–40 minutes until chicken is fully cooked.

PER SERVING
Calories: 393 | Fat: 23g | Protein: 32g | Sodium: 412mg | Carbohydrates: 13g | Fiber: 0g

Grilled Citrus Chicken

This chicken may be broiled instead of grilled, although you won't get the smoky flavor that comes from grilling if you choose that route. To broil, place chicken on a broiler pan in a preheated oven with chicken 6 inches from heat. Broil on both sides until chicken reaches 170°F.

INGREDIENTS | SERVES 4

4 skinless chicken breast halves

⅔ cup orange juice

4 tablespoons lemon juice

4 teaspoons orange zest

2 cloves garlic, minced

4 tablespoons honey

Freezing Day

Place chicken in a gallon-sized freezer bag. In mixing bowl, whisk together the remaining ingredients. Divide the marinade in half. Pour one half of marinade over chicken and freeze. Pour the second half of marinade in a quart-sized freezer bag and freeze.

Reheating Instructions

Defrost chicken in the refrigerator overnight, in the microwave, or in cold water, and discard included marinade. Defrost quart-sized bag of marinade. This will be used to brush over chicken during grilling. Over medium heat, grill chicken breasts 12–15 minutes or until no longer pink. Brush chicken with marinade throughout cooking.

PER SERVING
Calories: 195 | Fat: 2g | Protein: 21g | Sodium: 49mg | Carbohydrates: 23g | Fiber: 0g

Apricot Walnut Stuffed Chicken

Basmati rice is grown in India, and gets its name from a Hindu word meaning "full of aroma." It has a sweet and slightly nutty flavor, and goes well with many savory dishes.

INGREDIENTS | SERVES 4

¾ cup dried apricots

1 cup chicken broth

1 sprig fresh thyme

½ cup uncooked basmati rice

¼ cup walnuts, chopped

¼ teaspoon cinnamon

4 boneless, skinless chicken breast halves

1 tablespoon butter (used on reheating day)

⅓ cup apricot preserves (used on reheating day)

¼ teaspoon salt (used on reheating day)

¼ cup flour (used on reheating day)

4 tablespoons vegetable oil (used on reheating day)

Freezing Day

Place dried apricots in a saucepan with the chicken broth and thyme. Bring to a gentle boil. Turn heat down to medium-low and cover for 10–15 minutes until apricots are soft. Cook the rice in a separate saucepan according to package directions. When apricots are soft, remove from pan and discard broth and thyme. Chop apricots and place in a large bowl. Add cooked rice, walnuts, and cinnamon. Mix well. Cut a slit in the side of each chicken breast, and widen it to make a pouch. Stuff each breast with the apricot-walnut mixture. Secure closed with a toothpick. Flash freeze and transfer to freezer bag.

Reheating Instructions

Defrost chicken breasts in the refrigerator for 24 hours. In a shallow dish, melt butter in microwave. Stir in the apricot preserves and salt. Put flour in a second shallow dish. Dip each chicken breast in the apricot preserves, then the flour. In a large skillet over medium heat, sauté the chicken in oil until fully cooked, approximately 10 minutes per side. For an alternative to frying, bake chicken at 375°F for 40 minutes, or until juices run clear.

PER SERVING
Calories: 400 | Fat: 10g | Protein: 25g | Sodium: 230mg | Carbohydrates: 54g | Fiber: 1g

Turkey Fricassee in Mushroom and Wine Sauce

Fricassee is a French term that refers to a process of cooking. It involves browning white meat in butter, adding flour, and then adding liquids to make a sauce. The end result is often compared to a stew.

INGREDIENTS | SERVES 4

1 pound boneless, skinless turkey breast

8–10 tablespoons butter, divided use

8 ounces fresh mushrooms, sliced

1 small onion, diced

1 clove garlic, minced

3 tablespoons flour

1 cup chicken broth

½ cup dry white wine (used on reheating day)

¾ cup sour cream (used on reheating day)

Freezing Day

Cut the turkey breast into bite-sized cubes. In a skillet, melt 4 tablespoons butter over medium-high heat being careful not to burn it. Add the turkey and cook 4–6 minutes until golden brown on all sides. Remove turkey from skillet and set aside on a plate. Add more butter to the skillet if necessary, and sauté mushrooms and onion over medium heat for 5 minutes. Add garlic and sauté 1 more minute. Remove the vegetables from the skillet and place on the plate with the turkey.

In a clean skillet, melt 4 tablespoons butter. Stir in 3 tablespoons flour and mix together. Add the chicken broth to the skillet and stir until mixture begins to thicken, approximately 3–5 minutes. Add the turkey and vegetables to the skillet, mix well, and immediately remove from heat to cool. Put the turkey and sauce into a freezer bag and freeze.

Reheating Instructions

Defrost turkey in the refrigerator overnight, in the microwave, or in cold water, and put into a skillet. Stir in the wine and sour cream. Cover and cook on medium for 10 minutes.

PER SERVING
Calories: 508 | Fat: 39g | Protein: 27g | Sodium: 1500mg | Carbohydrates: 15g | Fiber: 1g

Broiled Garlic and Tarragon Chicken Breasts

*Tarragon vinegar is easy to make and enhances the flavor of vegetables,
as well as poultry and fish dishes. To make it, place a sprig of tarragon
in a jar with distilled white vinegar. Steep for a few days, and then remove the sprig.*

INGREDIENTS | SERVES 4

4 boneless, skinless chicken breast
halves

1 clove garlic, sliced thin

5 tablespoons olive oil

4 teaspoons dried tarragon, crushed

¼ teaspoon pepper

¼ teaspoon salt

How to Flash Freeze Herbs

One method for freezing fresh herbs is accomplished by freezing the entire sprig of leaves. First wash the herbs, then fully dry them and remove all the moisture. Lay the herbs out on a baking sheet and flash freeze. Transfer them into a small freezer bag. To use, simply crumble frozen herbs into your dish.

Freezing Day

Using a paring knife cut 2 small slits in the top of each chicken breast. Insert a slice of garlic in each slit. In a small saucepan, combine the olive oil, tarragon, pepper, and salt and heat on medium-low for 5 minutes. Brush the olive oil mixture on all sides of each chicken breast and freeze in a freezer bag.

Reheating Instructions

Defrost chicken breasts in the refrigerator overnight and place on a broiler pan. Broil about 6 inches from heat for 7–8 minutes. Turn chicken and broil another 7–10 minutes or until chicken is fully cooked.

PER SERVING
Calories: 256 | Fat: 19g | Protein: 20g | Sodium: 194mg | Carbohydrates: 0g | Fiber: 0g

Braised Italian Chicken

Braising is a method of cooking where meat is first seared in a hot skillet, then finishes cooking in liquid, in a covered pan. It works well for cuts of meat that tend to be tough because the process tenderizes the meat.

INGREDIENTS | SERVES 6

1½ pounds boneless chicken thighs

2 tablespoons oregano

½ teaspoon garlic powder

¼–½ teaspoon black pepper, according to taste

½ teaspoon salt

2 tablespoons olive oil

1 seasoning packet from chicken flavored ramen noodles

2 cups hot water

1 (6-ounce) can tomato paste

1 tablespoon minced onion

1 large zucchini, sliced

Freezing Day

Season both sides of the chicken with oregano, garlic, pepper, and salt. Heat olive oil in a large skillet over medium-high heat. Brown the chicken thighs, 3–4 minutes per side. During the browning time, do not move the thighs or scrape underneath them. You want the yummy brown crunchies to cook under the chicken. Once thighs are browned, remove them to a platter.

In a medium bowl, add the seasoning packet to the water, mix, and add to the skillet. Bring to a boil. Use a spatula to scrape the bottom of the skillet and mix everything together. Add tomato paste and minced onion. Mix well. Return thighs to the sauce, add sliced zucchini, and remove from heat to cool. Freeze the meal in a freezer bag.

Reheating Instructions

Defrost chicken and sauce in refrigerator for 24 hours. Put in a skillet, cover, and cook at a simmer for 1 hour. Turn chicken halfway through cooking time.

PER SERVING
Calories: 356 | Fat: 20g | Protein: 33g | Sodium: 129mg | Carbohydrates: 9g | Fiber: 2g

White Chili

This spicy chili, made with chicken and cannellini beans, is a twist on traditional chili. If you prefer, you may substitute Northern beans for the cannellini beans.

INGREDIENTS | SERVES 4

1 pound boneless chicken thighs

1 tablespoon olive oil

1 onion, chopped

2 cups chicken broth

1 teaspoon cumin

1½ teaspoons chili powder

3 jalapeño peppers, chopped

1 (15-ounce) can cannellini beans, rinsed and drained

1 tablespoon lime juice

Sour cream (used as a topping on reheating day)

Monterey jack cheese (used as a topping on reheating day)

Fresh cilantro (used as a topping on reheating day)

Frozen Herb Butter

Flavor butter with fresh parsley, basil, or dill. Put 2 tablespoons of one herb in the food processor to purée. Add ½ cup softened butter and blend. Add more butter according to taste. Spoon the butter into ice cube trays and freeze. Once frozen, put cubes into a freezer bag. Use to season vegetables, on bread, or in recipes.

Freezing Day

Cut chicken into bite-sized cubes and stir-fry them in oil with the onion for 4–5 minutes. Add chicken to a large saucepan along with the chicken broth, cumin, chili powder, and chopped jalapeños. Bring to a boil, reduce heat, and simmer for 15 minutes. Add beans and lime juice and cook an additional 5 minutes. Cool chili and freeze in a Tupperware container or freezer bag.

Reheating Instructions

Defrost in the refrigerator 24 hours. Heat chili in a saucepan over medium heat for 20–30 minutes until desired temperature is reached. Serve with desired toppings.

PER SERVING

Calories: 490 | Fat: 23g | Protein: 42g | Sodium: 459mg | Carbohydrates: 27g | Fiber: 6g

Grilled Hawaiian Chicken

Give each of your dinner guests a small bowl filled with Sweet and Sour Sauce for dipping chicken. Serve with grilled pineapple slices and rice for a meal everyone will love.

Freezing Day

In saucepan over medium heat, melt butter. Add pineapple juice, honey, soy sauce, and ginger. Divide sauce into two equal parts. Put chicken into a freezer bag. Pour one half of sauce over the chicken and freeze. Pour the other half of sauce into a quart-sized freezer bag and freeze separately.

Reheating Instructions

Defrost the chicken and the separate marinade bag in the refrigerator for 24 hours. The separate bag of marinade is to baste chicken during grilling. Grill the chicken over medium heat for 30 minutes with bone side down, and 15–20 minutes on the other side, or until the breast reaches 165°F. Baste with reserved marinade during the last 15 minutes of grilling only.

PER SERVING
Calories: 708 | Fat: 48g | Protein: 39g | Sodium: 2000mg | Carbohydrates: 35g | Fiber: 0g

Chicken Breast with Creamy Tarragon Sauce

*Not only does tarragon taste delicious, but it can help your body as well.
It is healthy for your digestive system, eases stomach cramps, and even stimulates your appetite.
And, if you have high blood pressure, try substituting tarragon for salt!*

INGREDIENTS | SERVES 6

6 boneless, skinless, chicken breast halves

½ teaspoon salt

¼ teaspoon pepper

¼ cup flour plus 2 tablespoons flour, divided

3 tablespoons olive oil

½ small onion, chopped

½ cup dry white wine

2 teaspoons tarragon

½ cup chicken broth

½ cup heavy cream (used on reheating day)

2 tablespoons butter (used on reheating day)

How to Deglaze

This recipe calls for you to deglaze the skillet. *Deglaze* is a culinary term that means to remove the brown pieces and drippings that stuck to the bottom of the skillet during browning. A liquid such as wine is poured into the skillet and, over high heat, the bottom of the skillet is scraped so the browned pieces can flavor the sauce.

Freezing Day

Sprinkle the chicken breasts with salt and pepper, and coat them in the ¼ cup of flour. In large skillet, heat the olive oil over medium-high heat. Add the chicken and brown 3 minutes on both sides. Remove chicken from skillet to cool. Sauté onions in skillet 5–10 minutes until the onion is translucent. Over high heat, deglaze the skillet with the wine. Add 2 tablespoons flour and mix well. A thick paste should form. Add tarragon and chicken broth, mix well, and immediately remove from heat to cool. Put chicken in a freezer bag and pour the skillet ingredients over the chicken. Freeze.

Reheating Instructions

Defrost chicken and sauce in refrigerator overnight and put in a large skillet. Cover. Sauté approximately 30 minutes until chicken is fully cooked. Remove chicken from skillet. Add the heavy cream and 2 tablespoons butter to the skillet. Stir 5–7 minutes until sauce is fully heated. Serve chicken with sauce spooned over the top.

PER SERVING
Calories: 276 | Fat: 13g | Protein: 36g | Sodium: 287mg | Carbohydrates: 5g | Fiber: 0g

Braised Southwestern Chicken

This hearty chicken dish is best served over rice. If you want to add heat to your dish, include chopped jalapeño peppers, or put a bottle of hot sauce on the table and season to taste.

INGREDIENTS | SERVES 6–8

2 pounds chicken breast tenders

3 tablespoons olive oil

⅓ cup white wine

2 (10-ounce) cans cream of chicken soup

2 (16-ounce) cans black beans with liquid

2 (16-ounce) cans corn with liquid

1 (6-ounce) can tomato paste

1 cup milk

Salt and pepper to taste

Freezing Day

Brown chicken 2–3 minutes per side, in olive oil, over medium-high heat. Deglaze pan with wine. Refer to sidebar "How to Deglaze" for instructions on how to deglaze the pan. Stir in remaining ingredients and immediately remove from heat. Pour into a freezer bag and freeze.

Reheating Instructions

Defrost chicken and sauce in refrigerator overnight. Put into saucepan and bring to a low boil. Cover pan, turn down heat, and simmer for 20–30 minutes until chicken is fully cooked.

PER SERVING
Calories: 496 | Fat: 13g | Protein: 38g | Sodium: 925mg | Carbohydrates: 61g | Fiber: 11g

Lemon Chicken

With each piece of lemon chicken wrapped in its own foil pouch, whether you are cooking for one or cooking for ten, you'll know exactly how many packets to bake.

INGREDIENTS | SERVES 4

4 (12" x 12") pieces aluminum foil

4 boneless, skinless chicken breast halves

2 lemons

¼–½ teaspoon lemon pepper, according to taste

½ teaspoon basil

Frozen Lemon Slices

If you enjoy drinking water, or any other drink with a fresh slice of lemon, try freezing lemon slices! When you freeze the slices, you don't have to worry about using up your entire lemon before it goes bad. Slice lemon into wedges and flash freeze. Once frozen, put lemons in a small freezer bag. Enjoy freshening your drink with a cold slice.

Freezing Day

Lay the pieces of aluminum foil on the counter and put a chicken breast in the center. Pierce each chicken breast 3 or 4 times with a fork. Squeeze the juice from ½ of lemon over each breast. Fold up sides of foil to keep juice from running out if needed. Sprinkle each breast with lemon pepper and basil. Fold and secure foil over chicken. Place all chicken packets in a freezer bag and freeze.

Reheating Instructions

Keep chicken wrapped and defrost in refrigerator overnight. Place foil packet(s) in a baking dish and bake at 350°F for 35–40 minutes or until chicken is fully cooked.

PER SERVING
Calories: 161 | Fat: 2g | Protein: 35g | Sodium: 2mg | Carbohydrates: 6g | Fiber: 3g

Raspberry Glazed Chicken Breasts

This dish uses only five ingredients and is simple to put together.
Vary the cooking method by cooking in a covered skillet over medium heat.

INGREDIENTS | SERVES 4–6

1½ cups raspberry preserves

½ cup balsamic vinegar

½ cup soy sauce

2 cloves garlic, minced

2 pounds boneless, skinless chicken
 breasts

Freezing Day

In saucepan, combine all ingredients except chicken. Bring to a boil, reduce heat, and simmer for 10 minutes. Cool. Put chicken breasts in a freezer bag and pour sauce over chicken. Freeze.

Reheating Instructions

Defrost chicken in refrigerator overnight. Put chicken and sauce into a baking dish. Bake chicken at 350°F, covered, for 30–40 minutes or until chicken is fully cooked.

PER SERVING
Calories: 373 | Fat: 2g | Protein: 30g | Sodium: 1252mg |
Carbohydrates: 61g | Fiber: 1g

Mini Turkey Meatballs

These mini meatballs taste wonderful on rolls with red sauce and mozzarella cheese,
or with Alfredo Sauce (Chapter 14) and served over noodles.

INGREDIENTS | SERVES 4

1 pound ground turkey

½ cup Italian breadcrumbs

1 clove garlic, minced

1 egg

½ teaspoon Italian seasoning

1 tablespoon Worcestershire sauce

1 tablespoon olive oil

Freezing Day

In large mixing bowl, combine all ingredients except olive oil. Mix well and form into small meatballs. Place meatballs in pan and bake at 350°F for 20–30 minutes, or until they are fully cooked. Flash freeze and transfer to freezer bag.

Reheating Instructions

Defrost meatballs in refrigerator for 24 hours. Put meatballs in a saucepan with your favorite sauce and heat over medium heat for 30 minutes.

PER SERVING
Calories: 196 | Fat: 6g | Protein: 30g | Sodium: 272mg |
Carbohydrates: 11g | Fiber: 1 g

Grilled Honey Mustard Chicken

The honey mustard sauce in this recipe tastes delicious on hamburgers, and you can use it with pork chops or sliced ham.

INGREDIENTS | SERVES 6

6 boneless, skinless split chicken breasts

1 cup honey

½ cup Dijon mustard

2 tablespoons Worcestershire sauce

Use Tongs When Grilling

When you are grilling chicken or steak and it is time to turn the meat, use a pair of tongs instead of a fork that will pierce the meat. The delicious juices inside the meat can escape through the fork puncture and cause the meat to be dry and chewy.

Freezing Day

Place the chicken breast in a freezer bag. In food processor, mix honey, Dijon mustard, and Worcestershire sauce until smooth consistency is reached. Put ⅓ of honey mustard sauce in small freezer bag or plastic container. Pour remaining ⅔ of sauce over chicken and seal the bag. With your hands on the outside of the bag, move chicken around so it is coated with sauce. Freeze.

Reheating Instructions

Defrost chicken and separate container of sauce in refrigerator overnight. Over high heat, grill chicken 2 minutes per side. Decrease grill temperature to medium-low and cook an additional 5–10 minutes until chicken reaches an internal temperature of 165°F. Use separate container of sauce to baste chicken during last few minutes of cooking.

PER SERVING
Calories: 349 | Fat: 2g | Protein: 35g | Sodium: 79mg | Carbohydrates: 48g | Fiber: 0g

Curried Chicken

Made from the meat of the coconut, coconut milk is created through a multistep process of steeping grated coconut in hot water, straining out the pulp, and repeating this process up to three times. Thankfully, canned coconut milk is readily available in grocery stores.

INGREDIENTS | SERVES 4–6

1 whole chicken, cooked

1 onion, chopped

2 tablespoons butter

2 tablespoons flour

1 teaspoon curry powder (or to taste)

1 (14-ounce) can coconut milk

4 drops hot sauce (or to taste)

Freezing Day

Remove cooked chicken from bone and set aside. Over medium-high heat, sauté onions in butter 5–10 minutes until onions are soft and translucent. Stir in flour and curry powder. Slowly pour in coconut milk, stirring until mixture thickens. Add hot sauce and mix well. Simmer for 10 minutes. Add chicken to the sauce, mix, and immediately remove from heat to cool. Freeze in a freezer bag.

Reheating Instructions

Defrost chicken mixture in the refrigerator overnight, in the microwave, or in cold water. Heat in a saucepan over medium heat for 15–20 minutes or until desired temperature is reached. Serve over rice.

PER SERVING
Calories: 445 | Fat: 32g | Protein: 32g | Sodium: 216mg | Carbohydrates: 4g | Fiber: 0g

Chicken and Mushroom Fettuccine Alfredo

Offer your guests fresh ground pepper with this meal. To add variety, stir in broccoli florets or peas.

INGREDIENTS | SERVES 8

1 pound boneless, skinless chicken
 breasts, cubed

½ teaspoon poultry seasoning

3 tablespoons olive oil

8 ounces fresh mushrooms, sliced

1 clove garlic, minced

Alfredo Sauce (Chapter 14)

1 pound fettuccini pasta (used on
 reheating day)

Salt and pepper to taste (used on
 reheating day)

Vacuum Sealer for Freezing

A vacuum sealer is a great way to seal food before freezing, but be careful how you use it. Some of the softer foods like pasta, sauces, some fruits, or rice will need to be flash frozen before being vacuum sealed. When you flash freeze first, you prevent the vacuum sealer from squishing the soft food.

Freezing Day

Season the cubed chicken with poultry seasoning. In hot skillet with the olive oil, cook chicken 4–5 minutes until no longer pink. Add mushrooms and sauté 5–6 minutes. Add garlic and sauté 1 minute. Remove from heat. Prepare Alfredo Sauce and mix with chicken and mushrooms. Freeze in a freezer bag.

Reheating Instructions

Defrost Chicken and Mushroom Alfredo in the refrigerator overnight. Heat in a saucepan over medium heat for 15–20 minutes or until it reaches desired temperature. Prepare fettuccine according to package directions. Serve fettuccine on a plate with sauce and chicken spooned over the top.

PER SERVING
Calories: 289 | Fat: 7g | Protein: 17g | Sodium: 20mg | Carbohydrates: 42g | Fiber: 2g

Turkey Breast with Buttery Citrus Sauce

Make a second batch of the buttery citrus sauce to serve with the turkey on reheating day, and pour over the cutlets before serving.

INGREDIENTS | SERVES 2–4

1 pound boneless, skinless turkey breast
Salt and pepper to taste
½ cup scallions, minced
½ cup orange juice
1 teaspoon orange zest
1 tablespoon lemon juice
½ cup butter, softened

Freezing Day

With a meat mallet, flatten turkey breast. Season with salt and pepper on each side. In saucepan, over medium-low, heat scallions and orange juice for 5 minutes. In food processor, add orange zest, lemon juice, and butter. Slowly pour in orange juice and scallions and process until smooth. Put turkey breast in freezer bag and add butter mixture. Seal the bag, and squish it with your hands to cover turkey with butter sauce. Freeze.

Reheating Instructions

Defrost turkey in the refrigerator overnight. Discard marinade. In a skillet over medium-high heat, brown the turkey approximately 3 minutes on each side until fully cooked.

PER SERVING
Calories: 314 | Fat: 24g | Protein: 18g | Sodium: 1497mg | Carbohydrates: 8g | Fiber: 0g

Rosemary and Pineapple Chicken

Did you know that studies show rosemary can increase the blood flow to your brain-increasing concentration? Now that is something to think about!

INGREDIENTS | SERVES 6–8

2 pounds boneless, skinless chicken breast

Salt and pepper to taste

1–2 teaspoons dried rosemary, to taste

2 tablespoons olive oil

½ cup chicken broth

1 (20-ounce) can pineapple chunks

2 small peeled apples, sliced (used on reheating day)

3 tablespoons cornstarch (used on reheating day)

¼ cup cold water (used on reheating day)

½ cup milk (used on reheating day)

3 tablespoons butter (used on reheating day)

Getting the Most Flavor During Browning

When browning the chicken breasts, it may be tempting to peek under the chicken to see how it is doing, or scoot it around inside the skillet. Resist the urge to move it at all. You will get a better flavor in the skillet for your sauce if you allow the chicken to stay in one place and brown.

Freezing Day

Sprinkle one side of the chicken breasts with salt, pepper, and rosemary. Add olive oil to the skillet. Brown the chicken over medium-high heat, rosemary side down first. Brown each side approximately 3 minutes, then remove chicken from skillet.

Add the chicken broth to the empty skillet. Scrape the browned pieces off the bottom of the skillet. Add the pineapple chunks and juice from the can to the skillet. Mix with broth and set aside to cool. Put chicken pieces in a freezer bag, and pour the broth and pineapple chunks over the chicken. Freeze.

Reheating Instructions

Defrost chicken mixture in refrigerator overnight. Put the mixture into a skillet and cook covered over medium to medium-low heat for 30 minutes or until chicken is fully cooked. Add sliced apples during the last 5 minutes of cooking time. Remove chicken and fruit from the skillet.

In small bowl, mix cornstarch with ¼ cup cold water. Add the cornstarch mixture, milk, and butter to the sauce in the skillet. Stir over medium heat until sauce thickens, 5–10 minutes. Serve sauce spooned over chicken.

PER SERVING
Calories: 193 | Fat: 9g | Protein: 21g | Sodium: 52mg | Carbohydrates: 8g | Fiber: 1g

Paprika Chicken

Paprika is a spice most often associated with Hungary, where in Kalocsa you can visit the Paprika Museum or enter the cooking contest at the annual Paprika Days Festival. It is sometimes used as a garnish to add color to a dish, but the flavor is not released until the paprika is heated.

INGREDIENTS | SERVES 2–4

⅛ teaspoon garlic powder

1 cup chicken stock

¼ cup white wine

1 pound boneless, skinless chicken breasts

1 cup fresh mushrooms, sliced (used on reheating day)

1 teaspoon salt (used on reheating day)

1 teaspoon paprika, or according to taste (used on reheating day)

1½ cups sour cream (used on reheating day)

Freezing Day

In bowl, mix together garlic powder, chicken stock, and white wine. Put chicken breasts in bottom of a freezer bag. Pour liquid over the top. Freeze.

Reheating Instructions

Defrost chicken in the refrigerator overnight. Pour chicken and liquid into a pot. Add the mushrooms. Simmer for 45 minutes or until chicken is fully cooked and tender. Stir in salt, paprika, and sour cream. Heat the chicken and sauce for 5–10 minutes. Serve over rice.

PER SERVING
Calories: 177 | Fat: 7g | Protein: 23g | Sodium: 683mg | Carbohydrates: 5g | Fiber: 1g

Homemade Dumplings

Paprika Chicken can be served with dumplings instead of rice. To make dumplings, combine 2½ cups flour, 3 eggs, and ⅓ cup water. Mix well. Start a pot of water boiling. Add 1–2 teaspoons salt to the water. Once boiling, fill a teaspoon with batter and drop into water. Once the dumpling floats to the top, remove it from the water.

Chicken Tacos

Add toppings to these soft tacos such as Monterey jack cheese, diced tomatoes and onions, lettuce, guacamole, sour cream, and Garden Salsa (Chapter 13).

INGREDIENTS | SERVES 4–5

Juice of 1 lime

1 teaspoon lime zest

½ cup apple cider vinegar

1 teaspoon sugar

½ teaspoon salt

½ teaspoon black pepper

3 tablespoons fresh cilantro

1½ pounds chicken breast, cut into strips

10 flour tortillas (used on reheating day)

Freezing Day

In a food processor, combine lime juice, lime zest, apple cider vinegar, sugar, salt, pepper, and cilantro. Process until smooth. Put strips of chicken in a freezer bag. Pour the marinade over the chicken and freeze.

Reheating Instructions

Defrost chicken in the refrigerator overnight and discard marinade. Sauté chicken in skillet 5–6 minutes over medium-high heat, or until fully cooked. Heat flour tortillas according to package directions. Fill each tortilla with chicken and add your favorite toppings.

PER SERVING
Calories: 327 | Fat: 5g | Protein: 20g | Sodium: 384mg | Carbohydrates: 46g | Fiber: 2.5g

Orange Chicken

Serve this chicken and sauce over a bed of rice. You can also pair it with a salad containing mandarin oranges and almonds, with a vinaigrette dressing.

INGREDIENTS | SERVES 2–4

1 pound boneless, skinless chicken breasts

3 tablespoons soy sauce

2 tablespoons honey

¼ cup orange juice concentrate

¼ cup orange juice

1 clove garlic, minced

1 package onion soup mix

Freezing Day

Put chicken in a freezer bag. In a food processor, mix remaining ingredients. Process until smooth. Pour over chicken and freeze.

Reheating Instructions

Defrost chicken and sauce in the refrigerator overnight. Put in a 9" x 13" baking dish. Bake at 350 degrees, uncovered, for 1 hour or until chicken is fully cooked.

PER SERVING
Calories: 200 | Fat: 3g | Protein: 29g | Sodium: 296mg | Carbohydrates: 13g | Fiber: 0g

Mustard Chicken

Not only can you bake this chicken, but you can grill it or even bread and fry it. It is really easy to prepare and proves to be very elegant.

INGREDIENTS | SERVES 6–8

1 (8-ounce) jar Grey Poupon

2 cups heavy cream

2 dashes balsamic vinegar

4 tablespoons dried tarragon

Salt and pepper to taste

2 pounds boneless chicken breasts

Freezing Day

In a medium bowl, mix together the mustard, cream, vinegar, tarragon, salt, and pepper. Put chicken into a freezer bag and pour sauce over the top of it. Freeze.

Reheating Instructions

Defrost chicken in refrigerator overnight and put in a baking dish with the sauce. Bake at 350°F for 1 hour or until chicken is fully cooked.

PER SERVING
Calories: 385 | Fat: 25g | Protein: 28g | Sodium: 761mg | Carbohydrates: 5g | Fiber: 0g

Sweet and Sour Chicken

This recipes calls for a fryer, but you can use the pieces you like best. Try chicken breasts only, or boneless chicken thighs. Suit it to whatever you have on hand!

INGREDIENTS | SERVES 4–6

2½-pound fryer, cut into pieces

2 tablespoons cornstarch

3 tablespoons cold water

1 cup brown sugar

1 cup soy sauce

½ cup apple cider vinegar

2 cloves garlic, minced

1 teaspoon ginger

¼–½ teaspoon red pepper flakes, to taste

1 (20-ounce) can pineapple rings (used on reheating day)

Freezing Day

Put chicken pieces in the bottom of a freezer bag. In a small bowl, mix the cornstarch and water until the cornstarch is completely dissolved. In a saucepan add brown sugar, soy sauce, vinegar, garlic, ginger, and pepper flakes. Stir in the cornstarch and water. Bring sauce to a boil, stirring constantly for 3–5 minutes. Once mixture thickens, remove from heat and let cool. Pour half the sauce over chicken in freezer bag and freeze. Pour the other half of sauce in a separate freezer bag and freeze.

Reheating Instructions

Defrost chicken in refrigerator for at least 24 hours and discard marinade. Defrost bag of extra sauce—this is used for basting during cooking. Bake chicken in a greased casserole dish for 1 hour (or until chicken is fully cooked) at 400°F, turning halfway through cooking time. Baste chicken with extra sauce every 15 minutes. Add pineapple rings to the top of chicken during the last 10 minutes of baking.

PER SERVING

Calories: 616 | Fat: 23g | Protein: 51g | Sodium: 568mg | Carbohydrates: 45g | Fiber: 1g

Breaded Chicken Breast with Muenster Cheese Bake

This is a great choice for serving to guests for dinner.
The chicken is moist, full of flavor, and the Muenster cheese is the perfect topping.

INGREDIENTS | SERVES 6

2 eggs

¼ cup milk

¾ cup flour

¾ teaspoon salt

1 cup plain breadcrumbs

1 cup grated Parmesan cheese

1–2 tablespoons finely chopped fresh basil or dried basil

1 teaspoon garlic powder

½ teaspoon salt

½ teaspoon black pepper

6 boneless chicken breasts, cut into 2–3 pieces

½ cup olive oil for frying

Slices of Muenster cheese; ½ of a slice for each piece of chicken

1–2 cups chicken broth (used on reheating day)

Freezing Day

In a small bowl, mix together eggs and milk. Set aside. In a shallow plate, mix together flour, and ¾ teaspoon salt. Set aside. In a separate shallow plate, mix together breadcrumbs, Parmesan cheese, basil, garlic powder, and salt and pepper. Dip chicken pieces in flour mixture to coat. Next dip in egg mixture to coat. Lastly dredge in breadcrumb mixture.

Heat oil in large skillet over medium heat. Fry chicken for 2–3 minutes on each side until golden brown. Drain on paper towels. Top each piece of chicken with half of a slice of Muenster cheese. Flash freeze the chicken, then transfer to a freezer bag.

Reheating Instructions

Defrost chicken in refrigerator overnight. Lay chicken pieces in a 9" x 13" inch baking dish. Pour 1–2 cups of chicken broth over the chicken. Use enough broth so it comes halfway up the sides of the chicken breasts. Broth should not cover chicken. Bake at 425°F for 20 minutes until cheese melts.

PER SERVING
Calories: 310 | Fat: 9g | Protein: 29g | Sodium: 417mg | Carbohydrates: 26g | Fiber: 29g

Pork and Seafood

Parmesan Crusted Pork Chops

NO DEFROSTING NEEDED!

INGREDIENTS | SERVES 6

Salt and pepper to taste

6 pork chops

1 tablespoon vegetable oil

2 tablespoons butter

⅓ cup flour

⅔ cup milk

1 egg

1 small onion, finely chopped

½ cup Parmesan cheese

Portion-Control Pork Chops

With pork chops it's easy to control portion size. Instead of freezing them all together in a casserole dish, flash freeze the pork chops then transfer them to a freezer bag. You may remove as many chops as needed from the bag on reheating night.

Freezing Day

Salt and pepper pork chops to taste. In a skillet over medium-high heat, brown pork chops in oil, 3–4 minutes per side, then arrange them in a single layer on a baking sheet. In a saucepan, melt the butter. Gradually stir in flour and milk and mix with a whisk to remove all lumps. Add the egg and mix well. Cook 5–10 minutes, stirring often, until mixture turns shiny. Stir in onion and cheese. Spread the mixture over the top of each pork chop. Flash freeze the pork chops then transfer to a freezer bag.

Reheating Instructions

Fully defrost chops in refrigerator for approximately 24 hours. Bake pork chops at 350°F for 30–45 minutes or until pork chops are fully cooked.

To cook pork chops straight from the freezer, bake at 350°F for 1 hour–1 hour 15 minutes or until pork chops are fully cooked. Cooking time will depend upon the thickness of the pork chops.

PER SERVING

Calories: 426 | Fat: 27g | Protein: 39g | Sodium: 270mg | Carbohydrates: 5g | Fiber: 1g

Shrimp Creole

Bacon drippings add instant flavor to your dishes. After cooking bacon, pour the grease into a jar, secure the lid, and store in the refrigerator. Now you'll have bacon drippings available anytime you need them.

INGREDIENTS | SERVES 6

3 tablespoons bacon drippings (or vegetable oil)

1 small onion, chopped

1 small bell pepper, chopped

2 cloves garlic, minced

1½ teaspoons chopped parsley

2 teaspoons sugar

2 teaspoons seasoned salt

¼ teaspoon pepper

1 (14-ounce) can seasoned diced tomatoes

1 (8-ounce) can tomato paste

1 tablespoon hot sauce

2 pounds cooked shrimp

Freezing Day

In bacon drippings, sauté onion and bell pepper for 8–10 minutes until vegetables are soft. Add garlic and sauté 1 minute. Add remaining ingredients, mix, and immediately remove from heat. Pour into a freezer bag and freeze.

Reheating Instructions

Defrost in refrigerator 12–24 hours and put into saucepan. Simmer over medium heat for 20 minutes. Serve over rice.

PER SERVING
Calories: 241 | Fat: 9g | Protein: 25g | Sodium: 687mg | Carbohydrates: 15g | Fiber: 2.5g

Marinated Red Snapper

When you purchase red snapper, make sure you ask for fillets with the skin. The skin helps to hold in the flavor of the fish, and also holds the fillet together so it doesn't fall apart during cooking.

INGREDIENTS | SERVES 4

2 tablespoons teriyaki sauce

4 tablespoons olive oil

4 tablespoons lime juice

4 red snapper fillets

Freezing Day

In food processor, mix teriyaki sauce, olive oil, and lime juice. Place snapper in a freezer bag. Pour in marinade and freeze.

Reheating Instructions

Defrost fish in refrigerator overnight and discard marinade. Place snapper skin side down on broiler pan. Broil 6 inches from heat 8–10 minutes until the fish is done cooking, or starts to flake.

PER SERVING
Calories: 309 | Fat: 15g | Protein: 41g | Sodium: 496mg | Carbohydrates: 3g | Fiber: 0g

Pork Ragout

Ragout (pronounced ra-GOO) is a French term that refers to a stew that is slowly cooked over a low heat. It can contain a wide variety of meat and vegetables that are often heavily seasoned.

INGREDIENTS | SERVES 6

2 tablespoons olive oil

1 large onion, sliced

1 clove garlic, minced

Salt and pepper to taste

1½ pounds pork, cubed

Flour for dredging pork

1 (16-ounce) can diced tomatoes

1½ cups fresh mushrooms, sliced

4 medium carrots, sliced

¼ cup port wine

Freezing Day

In stockpot or Dutch oven, heat oil. Sauté onions 5–10 minutes until tender. Add garlic and sauté 1 more minute, then remove from heat. Salt and pepper the pork then dredge it in flour. Brown the pork for 5–10 minutes in the stockpot where onions were cooked. Add more olive oil if necessary. Return onions to stockpot and add all remaining ingredients. Put into a freezer bag and freeze.

Reheating Instructions

Defrost in a pan in the refrigerator 12–24 hours and cook on medium-low heat for 45 minutes–1 hour.

PER SERVING
Calories: 306 | Fat: 16g | Protein: 24g | Sodium: 257mg | Carbohydrates: 16g | Fiber: 4g

Shrimp and Sausage Jambalaya

Creole jambalaya is tomato based and originated in New Orleans. There is also a Cajun-style jambalaya which is darker in color and does not contain tomatoes.

INGREDIENTS | SERVES 6

½ pound ground sausage

2 tablespoons butter

1 onion, chopped

1 large green pepper, chopped

2 cloves garlic, minced

2 tablespoons parsley

½ teaspoon thyme

¼ teaspoon cayenne pepper

1 (14-ounce) can diced tomatoes

1 chicken bouillon cube

½ teaspoon salt

1 bay leaf

1½ cups rice

1 pound large shrimp, raw, shelled, deveined

How Jambalaya Got Its Name

As folklore has it, the name *jambalaya* came about when a traveler stopped at an inn for dinner. There was nothing prepared so Jean, the cook, was told to *balayez*, which in French Creole means to "throw something together." The new dish was named *Jean balayez* which evolved to *jambalaya*.

Freezing Day

In large skillet (or stockpot), brown sausage over medium-high heat. Remove sausage and drain if needed. Melt butter in skillet, and sauté onion and pepper 5–10 minutes until vegetables are tender. Add garlic and sauté 1 more minute. Add cooked sausage, parsley, thyme, and cayenne and sauté an additional 5 minutes.

Drain diced tomatoes into a measuring cup, reserving liquid. Add enough water to the liquid from the tomatoes to make 2½ cups of liquid. Pour liquid into the skillet. Add tomatoes, bouillon cube, salt, bay leaf, and rice. Cover and lightly boil for 35 minutes. Add the shrimp, cover, and cook an additional 20–25 minutes until rice is tender. Cool, then freeze in a freezer bag or plastic container.

Reheating Instructions

Defrost in the refrigerator for 24 hours and heat over low heat for 20–30 minutes or until heated through.

PER SERVING

Calories: 324 | Fat: 16 g | Protein: 21g | Sodium: 737mg | Carbohydrates: 24g | Fiber: 2g

Grilled Curry Shrimp

Shrimp can be grilled individually, or you can put them on skewers. Threading the shrimp on skewers makes them easier to turn and control on the grill.

INGREDIENTS | SERVES 6

2 pounds large shrimp, peeled and deveined with tails attached

2 tablespoons butter

¼ cup green onions, minced

½ teaspoons salt

2½ teaspoons curry powder

1 teaspoon sugar

⅛ teaspoon ginger

⅛ teaspoon cinnamon

2 tablespoons flour

1 cup half and half

Skewers

How to Devein Shrimp

To devein a shrimp, remove the outer shell and legs from the shrimp. Next, make a long cut along the back of the shrimp to expose the vein. Flare out the shrimp on each side, further exposing the vein. Drag your finger along the vein, removing it completely, and rinse the shrimp with water.

Freezing Day

Put shrimp in a freezer bag. In skillet, melt butter over medium-high heat and sauté the green onions for 5–10 minutes until tender. Add the salt, curry powder, sugar, ginger, and cinnamon. Stir the flour into the skillet mixing it well with onions and spices. Pour in the half and half. Stir 5–10 minutes until mixture thickens. Pour curry sauce over shrimp and freeze.

Reheating Instructions

Defrost shrimp in refrigerator overnight. Thread shrimp onto skewers. Lightly oil the grill. Over high heat, grill the shrimp for 2–3 minutes per side.

PER SERVING
Calories: 219 | Fat: 11g | Protein: 24g | Sodium: 417mg | Carbohydrates: 6g | Fiber: 0g

Sausage and Biscuit Breakfast Sandwiches

Keep a supply of these sandwiches in your freezer for those mornings when you don't have time for breakfast. They are quick to heat up and make for a great morning breakfast on the run.

INGREDIENTS | SERVES 8

1 package Pillsbury Grands refrigerator biscuits—8 count

8 sausage patties

8 eggs

8 slices of American cheese

Freezing Day

Cook biscuits according to package directions. Split down middle to separate the tops from the bottoms. In skillet, cook sausage patties. Drain pan, then scramble the eggs. Put sausage, egg, and a slice of cheese on each of the biscuits. Wrap individually in plastic wrap, or in quart-sized freezer bags, and freeze.

Reheating Instructions

Wrap frozen sandwich in a paper towel and microwave at 30% for 1 minute 15 seconds, then microwave on high for 1 minute or until desired temperature.

PER SERVING
Calories: 373 | Fat: 22g | Protein: 21g | Sodium: 933mg | Carbohydrates: 22g | Fiber: 0g

Honey Mustard Baked Pork Chops

NO DEFROSTING NEEDED!

INGREDIENTS | SERVES 4

2 tablespoons honey

2 tablespoons Dijon mustard

1 tablespoon fresh tarragon

4 pork chops

Pan Fry Your Pork Chops

If you like a nice sear on the outside of your pork chops, use a combination of skillet and oven. Heat a cast-iron skillet to medium-high with 1 tablespoon of oil. Fry seasoned chops 5 minutes on one side (do not move them!) then 5 minutes on the other side. Put skillet in oven preheated to 400°F for 5 minutes, or until pork reaches 170°F.

Freezing Day

In a bowl, mix honey, mustard, and tarragon. Brush mixture on both sides of pork chops and flash freeze on a baking sheet lined with wax paper. Transfer to freezer bag.

Reheating Instructions

To cook defrosted pork chops, bake 45 minutes–1 hour at 350°F or until pork chops reach an internal temperature of 170°F. Cooking time will depend upon the thickness of the pork chops. Turn halfway through cooking time.

To cook frozen pork chops, bake 1 hour–1 hour 15 minutes at 350°F or until pork chops reach an internal temperature of 170°F. Turn halfway through cooking time.

PER SERVING
Calories: 194 | Fat: 9g | Protein: 17g | Sodium: 45mg | Carbohydrates: 9g | Fiber: 0g

Shrimp Pesto

Most Italian chefs consider putting Parmesan cheese on seafood pastas a faux pas. But you have permission to do so, because it is delicious over this Shrimp Pesto! You may also substitute chicken for the shrimp if you have a shellfish allergy.

INGREDIENTS | SERVES 2–4

½ pound shrimp, shells and tails removed

1 onion, chopped

3 cloves garlic, diced

2 tablespoons olive oil

1 pound box rotini or farfalle pasta

1 tomato, diced

3–4 tablespoons Basil and Pine Nut Pesto, to taste (Chapter 13)

Freshly grated Parmesan cheese (used on reheating day)

Freezing Day

Start water boiling for pasta. Cut shrimp into pieces. In a skillet, sauté the onion in olive oil for 5–10 minutes until onions are translucent. Add garlic and sauté 1 minute. Add shrimp and sauté 2 minutes on each side or until shrimp turns pink. Cook pasta al dente; be careful not to overcook. Drain pasta and put in large mixing bowl. Add the shrimp, onion, garlic, and tomatoes to the pasta. Add enough pesto to lightly cover the pasta. Toss together and freeze in a freezer bag.

Reheating Instructions

Defrost pasta in refrigerator overnight and heat in saucepan on medium-low until it is heated through, approximately 15–20 minutes or until desired temperature is reached. If desired, add more pesto or butter to the dish. Sprinkle with Parmesan cheese to taste.

PER SERVING
Calories: 451 | Fat: 31g | Protein: 17g | Sodium: 449mg | Carbohydrates: 30g | Fiber: 3g

Pork Tenderloin with Bacon

The juices made from deglazing the pan with the sherry and cola after searing the pork are absolutely delicious. Serve with any leftover juices for pouring on meat.

INGREDIENTS | SERVES 8–10

3 tablespoons Italian seasoning

3 tablespoons paprika

1 teaspoon salt

4–5 pounds pork tenderloin

4 tablespoons olive oil

¼ cup cooking sherry

½ cup cola

¾ pound bacon

The Secret to Braising

When browning meat for braising recipes, don't be afraid to turn up the heat. You want a good dark-brown sear that can only come from medium-high heat. You also want to get some well-cooked bits in the pan that will deglaze into a nice sauce, so don't be too quick to turn the meat.

Freezing Day

Mix Italian seasoning, paprika, and salt. Rub seasoning around the outside of the pork. In skillet, heat oil. Sear the pork on each side for 3–4 minutes until it is golden brown and crispy all around. Remove pork from skillet and put in roasting pan. Deglaze the skillet with the sherry and cola. For instructions on how to deglaze, see sidebar "How to Deglaze." Pour over roast. Lay strips of bacon across the pork (perpendicular to the length), slightly overlapping. Tuck ends under the pork. Wrap the pan tightly with aluminum foil, tenting it in so it does not touch the bacon. Cook at 375°F for 30 minutes per pound. Remove pork from oven, and pour juices into a bowl to cool. Double wrap the pork tightly with foil, and freeze. Put juice in a freezer bag and freeze.

Reheating Instructions

Remove 1 layer of foil from the roast; keep the second layer around the roast and defrost in the refrigerator for approximately 24 hours. Once defrosted, put the foil-wrapped pork in a roasting pan and heat for 45 minutes at 325°F, or until it reaches an internal temperature of 170°F. Unwrap the pork and broil on middle rack for about 5 minutes until the bacon is crisped and browned. Let rest 10–15 minutes before slicing. Heat up juices in a saucepan over medium heat for 5–10 minutes, or until desired temperature is reached. Pour over meat, then serve.

PER SERVING
Calories: 561 | Fat: 39g | Protein: 48g | Sodium: 787mg | Carbohydrates: 2g | Fiber: 0g

Pot Stickers with Sesame Ginger Dipping Sauce

NO DEFROSTING NEEDED!

INGREDIENTS | SERVES 4–6

1 pound ground pork

½ head of cabbage, finely chopped

¼ cup finely chopped green onion

1 tablespoon soy sauce

2 teaspoons sesame oil

1 teaspoon sugar

½ teaspoon fresh gingerroot, minced

2 (14-ounce) packages round pot sticker wrappers (wonton wrappers)

2 tablespoons cooking oil (used on reheating day)

½ cup chicken broth (used on reheating day)

Sesame Ginger Dipping Sauce (Chapter 14)

Chinese Dumplings

A pot sticker is a Chinese dumpling that can be stuffed with a variety of ground meats and vegetables. When cooked, the dumpling is browned on one side, then simmered in a liquid.

Freezing Day

In a skillet, brown the ground pork. Drain and crumble the pork so it is in very small pieces. In mixing bowl, mix the cooked pork, cabbage, green onion, soy sauce, sesame oil, sugar, and ginger. Mix thoroughly. Line a baking sheet with wax paper. To make the pot stickers, lay a wrapper flat and put about a teaspoon of filling on it. Wet the edges, fold it over, and seal tightly. Flash freeze the pot stickers, and then transfer to freezer bag.

Reheating Instructions

Add 2 tablespoons oil to a skillet. Put frozen pot stickers in the skillet (12 at a time) and cook 5 minutes on one side until golden brown. Reduce the heat to low, add chicken broth, and cover. Let them steam until they soak up most of the chicken broth, about 10 minutes. Uncover and cook an additional 2–3 minutes until wrappers have shrunk down over filling. Serve with Sesame Ginger Dipping Sauce.

PER SERVING
Calories: 411 | Fat: 18g | Protein: 21g | Sodium: 626mg | Carbohydrates: 41g | Fiber: 2g

Braised Apple Stuffed Pork Chops

The fruity apple flavor complements the pork chops wonderfully. Serve this with Creamy Leek Soup (Chapter 11) and Dinner Rolls (Chapter 12).

INGREDIENTS | SERVES 2–4

4 apples
4 thick center-cut pork chops
1 teaspoon cumin
1 teaspoon salt
½ teaspoon pepper
6 tablespoons olive oil
1 tablespoon butter
1 cup apple juice
½ teaspoon cinnamon
2 teaspoons dark brown sugar

Cook Seasonally

Visit your local farmer's market, find out what is in season, and plan your cooking around those foods. Not only will your food be fresh and at the peak of its flavor, but you will able to buy it at a great price and freeze it so you can enjoy it year round.

Freezing Day

Core, peel, and slice apples into eighths. Set aside. In the side opposite the bone, cut a pocket in each pork chop large enough for 3 apple slices. Season pork chops with cumin, salt, and pepper. Over medium-high heat in the oil and ½ the butter, sear the pork chops for 3–4 minutes on each side until well browned. Remove the chops from the pan and reduce heat to medium-low. Deglaze by adding ½ cup apple juice and scraping loose all the cooked bits that have stuck to the pan and mixing these into the sauce. Add remaining butter. Add apples to the skillet. Cover the apples, turn heat to low, and cook for 5 minutes. Remove half of the apple slices to a plate, add remaining apple juice, cinnamon, and brown sugar. Continue to cook the apples and sauce mix.

Stuff 3 slices or more of the reserved apple into each chop. Mash remaining apples in the sauce mix. Prepare a casserole dish for freezer according to instructions in Chapter 1. Place pork chops in a single layer in dish, pour apple sauce mixture over chops, wrap tightly, and freeze according to casserole dish freezing instructions.

Reheating Instructions

Defrost completely in refrigerator for 24 hours. Preheat oven to 350°F. Place chops in oven and reduce temperature to 325°F. Cook, tightly covered, for 45 minutes.

PER SERVING
Calories: 461 | Fat: 32g | Protein: 17g | Sodium: 652mg | Carbohydrates: 27g | Fiber: 2.5g

Honey Sesame Pork Tenderloin

Use an oven-proof meat thermometer every time you cook, and eliminate the guesswork involved with knowing when your meat is safe to eat. Insert the thermometer into the thickest part of the meat before putting it into the oven. You'll know pork is ready once the internal temperature reaches 160°F.

INGREDIENTS | SERVES 4–6

2 pounds pork tenderloin

4 tablespoons olive oil

¼ cup water

3 tablespoons sesame oil

½ teaspoon ground ginger

1 clove garlic, minced

½ cup soy sauce

⅓ cup sesame seeds

½ cup honey

¼ cup packed brown sugar

⅛ teaspoon cayenne pepper

3 tablespoons soy sauce

Freezing Day

Brown pork loin in 4 tablespoons of olive oil on medium high heat for 3–4 minutes per side or until well browned. Reduce to medium-low, add water, and let most of water cook off. Add sesame oil to pan. Cook pork loin 90 seconds on each side and remove to deep baking dish. Mix ginger, garlic, and soy sauce in cup and brush onto pork loin. Cook at 350°F for 20 minutes. Remove the pork from oven and cool.

Reduce oven temp to 325°F, place sesame seeds in a single layer on a baking sheet, and bake 15 minutes or until golden brown. Combine honey, brown sugar, cayenne, and soy sauce. Brush on pork and sprinkle with cooked sesame seeds. Put on baking sheet lined with wax paper and flash freeze. Spray a sheet of plastic wrap with cooking spray and wrap around frozen pork. Finish wrapping with aluminum foil.

Reheating Instructions

Defrost pork in refrigerator for about 24 hours. Bake uncovered at 350°F for about 20–30 minutes or until a meat thermometer reads 160°F. Let stand for at least 10 minutes before slicing.

PER SERVING
Calories: 586 | Fat: 35g | Protein: 34g | Sodium: 1300mg | Carbohydrates: 34g | Fiber: 1g

Walnut Tarragon Pork Cutlets

Fresh tarragon can be used in place of dried tarragon.
Use 1 tablespoon of fresh tarragon in place of 1 teaspoon of dried tarragon.

INGREDIENTS | SERVES 4

2 teaspoons olive oil

4 boneless pork loin chops

Salt and pepper to taste

½ cup dry white wine

½ cup chopped walnuts

½ teaspoon cinnamon

1 teaspoon dried tarragon

½ cup unsweetened applesauce (used on reheating day)

Freezing Day

Heat olive oil in a large skillet over medium-high heat. Season pork chops with salt and pepper, and cook in the hot oil until lightly browned on both sides, about 4 minutes per side. Add the wine, walnuts, cinnamon, and tarragon, and bring to a simmer. Reduce heat to medium-low, cover and simmer, stirring occasionally, 10–15 minutes, until the pork is no longer pink in the center. Remove the pork chops from the skillet, set aside to cool, and freeze. Freeze sauce separately.

Reheating Instructions

Defrost chops and sauce overnight in the refrigerator. Place chops in pan with sauce and cook covered over medium-low heat for 30 minutes or until chops are warmed through. Remove the pork chops from the skillet, and keep warm. Add applesauce to the sauce, and heat an additional 5 minutes. Pour sauce over the pork chops and serve.

PER SERVING
Calories: 442 | Fat: 37g | Protein: 20g | Sodium: 47mg | Carbohydrates: 6g | Fiber: 2g

Hot and Spicy Shrimp Kabobs

Vary this recipe by adding pieces of chicken with the vegetables on some kabobs, and pieces of pork on other kabobs!

INGREDIENTS | SERVES 4–6

2 pounds jumbo shrimp

2 large sweet onions

16 large fresh mushrooms

4 large banana peppers, cut into 1½-inch pieces

16 cherry tomatoes

⅛ cup soy (used on reheating day)

½ cup honey (used on reheating day)

1 tablespoon red pepper flakes (used on reheating day)

Tips for Grilling Kabobs

When cooking kabobs, try to cut all ingredients about the same size so they cook evenly. If using bamboo skewers, make sure to soak them in water for 30 minutes prior to use. For foods (like shrimp) that can curl on the skewer, it will help to use two skewers inserted parallel to each other.

Freezing Day

Peel and devein the shrimp. Cut each onion into eight wedges. On eight metal or soaked wooden skewers, alternately thread the shrimp and vegetables. Grill kabobs, covered, over medium heat for 3 minutes on each side or until shrimp begin to get pink. Remove from heat, cool, and freeze on the skewers by wrapping kabobs in plastic wrap first, followed by aluminum foil.

Reheating Instructions

Defrost shrimp kabobs in refrigerator overnight. Mix soy, honey, and red pepper flakes to make a glaze. Place kabobs on foil-lined tray and coat well with glaze, using all the sauce. Cook for 10 minutes at 375°F. Remove, spoon extra sauce over kabobs, and serve warm.

PER SERVING
Calories: 262 | Fat: 3g | Protein: 26g | Sodium: 496mg | Carbohydrates: 36g | Fiber: 2g

Sweet and Spicy Pork Chops

The honey adds the sweet and the cayenne pepper adds the spice in this recipe.
Need more heat? Up the amount of cayenne pepper in the sauce a pinch at a time.
Be careful—the heat can really sneak up on you!

INGREDIENTS | SERVES 2–4

2 tablespoons olive oil

4 pork chops

Salt and pepper to taste

1 teaspoon cumin

⅓ cup honey

¼ cup hickory barbecue sauce

4 tablespoons soy sauce

⅓ teaspoon cayenne pepper

Freezing Day

Heat olive oil in a large skillet over medium-high heat. Season pork chops with salt, pepper, and cumin. Cook in the hot oil until well browned on both sides, about 4 minutes per side. Remove from pan, cool, and freeze. In a small bowl mix together honey, barbecue sauce, soy sauce, and cayenne pepper. Freeze in a freezer bag or Tupperware.

Reheating Instructions

Defrost pork chops and sauce in refrigerator for 12–24 hours. Place the chops in a casserole dish. Pour the sauce evenly over chops. Cover dish with aluminum foil and bake at 325 degrees for 1 hour.

PER SERVING

Calories: 459 | Fat: 28g | Protein: 20g | Sodium: 1112mg | Carbohydrates: 32g | Fiber: 0g

Grilled Orange Salmon

When selecting salmon, purchase the freshest fish available.
The salmon should smell like the ocean, and should not have a fishy smell.

INGREDIENTS | SERVES 6

½ cup orange juice

2 teaspoons orange zest

½ cup honey

1 tablespoon teriyaki sauce

2½ pounds salmon fillet

Freezing Day

In a small bowl, mix together orange juice, zest, honey, and teriyaki sauce. Put salmon in a freezer bag and pour in marinade. Freeze.

Reheating Instructions

Defrost salmon in the refrigerator overnight and discard marinade. Grill over medium heat, skin side down, just until it flakes.

PER SERVING

Calories: 356 | Fat: 9.5g | Protein: 44g | Sodium: 870mg | Carbohydrates: 26g | Fiber: 2g

Clam Spaghetti

Want to spice it up? Add ½ teaspoon red pepper flakes to the sauce to add a bit of a kick.

INGREDIENTS | SERVES 4–6

¼ cup butter or margarine

3 tablespoons flour

3 cloves garlic, minced

1 tablespoon dried parsley

¼ teaspoon dried oregano

¼ teaspoon dried basil

¼ teaspoon ground black pepper

3 tablespoons olive oil

¼ cup white wine plus 1 tablespoon

2 (6.5-ounce) cans minced clams, with juice

1 pound linguine (used on reheating day)

Grated Parmesan cheese (used on reheating day)

Freezing Day

In saucepan, melt butter. Stir in flour, making a paste. Add garlic, herbs, pepper, olive oil, wine, and juice from clams. Stir for 5 minutes over low heat. Remove from heat and stir in clams. Transfer to a freezer bag and freeze.

Reheating Instructions

Defrost in refrigerator overnight. Heat over medium-low 5–10 minutes. Cook linguine according to package directions. Toss the linguine with the clam sauce. Serve with grated Parmesan cheese.

PER SERVING

Calories: 411 | Fat: 16g | Protein: 10g | Sodium: 170mg | Carbohydrates: 59g | Fiber: 3g

Sausage and Peppers

Sausage and Peppers tastes wonderful served as a sub on a toasted, crunchy roll, or over your favorite pasta.

INGREDIENTS | SERVES 4–5

4 tablespoons olive oil

2 cloves garlic, minced

⅛ teaspoon salt

⅛ teaspoon pepper

4 large leaves fresh basil, minced

1 (15-ounce) can diced tomatoes, drained

1½ pounds sweet (or hot) Italian sausage links, diagonally sliced

1 large green bell pepper, sliced

1 large red bell pepper, sliced

1 large yellow bell pepper, sliced

2 large sweet onions, thinly sliced

Freezing Day

Add 2 tablespoons olive oil, garlic, salt, and pepper to hot skillet. Sauté garlic 1–2 minutes until it becomes golden brown. Add basil and tomatoes. Cook over medium-high heat stirring for about 5 minutes. Transfer everything from skillet to a bowl and allow to cool. In the same skillet, brown sausage over medium-high heat for about 5 minutes. Remove sausage from skillet and set aside to cool. Add 2 tablespoons olive oil to skillet, and cook peppers and onions 5–10 minutes over medium-high heat until the vegetables are tender. Set aside to cool. Put all parts of the meal into a freezer bag: the tomatoes, sausage, peppers, and onions. Freeze.

Reheating Instructions

Defrost sausage and peppers in refrigerator for 24 hours. Put into a skillet, cover, and simmer for approximately 15 minutes until the sausage is fully cooked.

PER SERVING
Calories: 604 | Fat: 49g | Protein: 26g | Sodium: 1135mg | Carbohydrates: 13g | Fiber: 2.5g

Baked Barbecue Pork Chops

Want to take a short cut with this recipe? Instead of making the sauce, use your favorite bottled barbecue sauce and pour it over the pork chops in the freezer bag.

INGREDIENTS | SERVES 4–6

2 pounds pork chops

Salt and pepper to taste

2 tablespoons olive oil

1 onion, finely chopped

2 ribs celery, finely chopped

2 cups water

1 tablespoon lemon juice

¼ cup Worcestershire sauce

½ cup ketchup

½ cup barbecue sauce

¼ cup vinegar

¼ cup brown sugar

1 teaspoon chili powder

1 teaspoon salt

The Picky Eater

Is someone in your home a picky eater? Dinnertime can be a time of frustration for someone who is hungry, but doesn't like what is being served. Consider keeping a few backup meals in the freezer that can be quickly cooked in the microwave. It may be a single serving of macaroni and cheese or a cup of soup.

Freezing Day

Season the pork chops on both sides with salt and pepper. In a skillet over medium-high heat, brown the chops 3–4 minutes on both sides in olive oil. Remove from heat to cool. In a saucepan, mix together the remaining ingredients. Bring to a boil, reduce heat, and simmer for 10 minutes. Remove from heat to cool. Place pork chops in a freezer bag and pour the sauce over the top. Freeze.

Reheating Instructions

Defrost pork chops and sauce in refrigerator for 12–24 hours and put in baking dish. Bake at 350°F for 1 hour or until chops are fully cooked.

PER SERVING
Calories: 651 | Fat: 43g | Protein: 34g | Sodium: 1009mg | Carbohydrates: 31g | Fiber: 1g

Tuna Bake

This classic dish has stood the test of time.
Add variety to the casserole by stirring in a cup of cooked peas, carrots, or broccoli.

INGREDIENTS | SERVES 6–8

8 ounces elbow macaroni

4 tablespoons butter

3 tablespoons flour

2 cups heavy cream

½ teaspoon salt

½ teaspoon pepper

2 cups Cheddar cheese, shredded

1½ teaspoons prepared yellow mustard

4 (9-ounce) cans tuna, drained

½–1 cup milk, as needed (used on reheating day)

2 cups crushed cornflakes (used on reheating day)

1 stick butter, melted (used on reheating day)

Freezing Day

Cook elbow macaroni to al dente (cooked but still firm) and drain. In a large saucepan, melt the butter over medium heat. Add flour and mix well. Slowly add the cream to the butter mixture, stirring as you pour. Bring to just under a boil, stirring constantly for about 5 minutes until the sauce thickens. Add salt, pepper, cheese, and mustard. Continue to stir until all of the cheese is melted. Gently stir in macaroni and tuna and remove from heat to cool. Freeze in a freezer bag.

Reheating Instructions

Defrost in the refrigerator overnight. Grease a large baking dish and put tuna mixture in it. Add milk as needed to reach a creamy consistency. Cover the casserole with crushed cornflakes and pour the melted butter over the cornflakes. Bake at 375°F for 30–40 minutes.

PER SERVING
Calories: 709 | Fat: 55g | Protein: 42g | Sodium: 1028mg | Carbohydrates: 23g | Fiber: 2g

Cranberry Apricot Pork Chops

The flavors of cranberry and apricot beautifully meld into a delicious sauce that perfectly complements the pork chops. Serve with a side of rice and your favorite vegetable.

INGREDIENTS | SERVES 4

4 center-cut pork chops

Salt and pepper to taste

2 tablespoons vegetable oil

4 teaspoons honey

1 cup fresh cranberries

½ cup apricot marmalade

How to Freeze Fresh Cranberries

Fresh cranberries are only available in the fall and early winter. Fortunately, fresh cranberries will freeze very well so you can enjoy this healthy, delicious fruit year round. Do not wash the berries before freezing. Sealed in an airtight container, fresh cranberries will freeze well for almost a whole year. Freeze in small batches of 1–2 cups, so you'll only have to thaw what you need for a given recipe.

Freezing Day

Prepare a casserole dish for freezing according to the casserole method in Chapter 1. Season pork chops with salt and pepper, then in a skillet over medium-high heat, brown both sides of chops in vegetable oil for 3–4 minutes. Remove pork chops from pan and lay them in bottom of casserole. Spread 1 teaspoon honey on top of each pork chop. In separate bowl, mix cranberries with the marmalade. Spoon over pork chops. Following the casserole method for freezing, wrap well and freeze.

Reheating Instructions

Defrost casserole in the refrigerator for 24 hours, according to the casserole method. Bake at 350°F for 35–45 minutes until pork is fully cooked.

PER SERVING
Calories: 463 | Fat: 28g | Protein: 18g | Sodium: 69mg | Carbohydrates: 36g | Fiber: 2g

CHAPTER 6

Slow Cooker

Minestrone

*Minestrone is a hearty Italian soup loaded with vegetables and beans.
You can substitute any of the vegetables in this recipe with ones you have on hand.
Pasta has been omitted since fully cooked pasta gets mushy when frozen.*

INGREDIENTS | SERVES 6–8

2 tablespoons tomato paste

2 (14-ounce) cans beef broth

1 (10-ounce) package of frozen chopped spinach, thawed

1 onion, chopped

2 carrots, cut into bite-sized pieces

1 red bell pepper, cut into bite-sized pieces

1 zucchini, sliced

4 teaspoons dried parsley

2 cloves garlic, minced

1 teaspoon dried basil

½ cup grated Parmesan cheese

2 (15-ounce) cans kidney beans with juice

1 (28-ounce) can chopped tomatoes with juice

Freezing Day

In a mixing bowl mix tomato paste and beef broth. Set aside. Put all other ingredients into slow cooker. Pour beef broth mixture over the top. Cook on low 8–10 hours. Cool and freeze in freezer bag, or in individual portions in Tupperware containers.

Reheating Instructions

Defrost soup in the microwave or refrigerator overnight. Warm on stovetop for 20–25 minutes over medium heat or microwave individual portions 2–3 minutes in the microwave, and serve.

PER SERVING
Calories: 390 | Fat: 3g | Protein: 28g | Sodium: 841mg | Carbohydrates: 68g | Fiber: 21g

Italian Beef

This beef makes awesome sandwiches, especially when served with a side of steak fries. Don't forget to keep a bowl of the sauce next to your plate; you'll love dipping your sandwich and fries in it! You can also use the beef to make Beef Taquitos (Chapter 9).

INGREDIENTS | SERVES 6

3 pounds chuck roast

Salt and pepper to taste

Garlic powder to taste

2–3 tablespoons vegetable oil

2 (.7-ounce) envelopes dry Italian salad dressing mix

3 cups beef broth

2 green peppers, sliced

1 large onion, sliced

5 hoagie rolls (used on reheating day)

1 cup provolone cheese, shredded (used on reheating day)

Sliced banana peppers (used on reheating day)

Freeze Individual Sandwiches

You can also make up individual sandwiches to freeze. Buy fresh rolls and layer them with the beef and any desired toppings. Wrap the sandwich tightly in plastic and freeze. Don't forget to freeze portions of the sauce for dipping. To serve, simply defrost and bake in the oven until hot!

Freezing Day

Season roast with salt, pepper, and garlic powder. In a skillet over high heat, sear roast in oil for 2–3 minutes on each side. Transfer roast to the slow cooker. Mix 2 packages of dry seasoning mix with the beef broth and pour over the top of the roast. Cook on low for 8 hours. Remove the roast from the slow cooker and shred it. Put it back into the slow cooker, add the green pepper and onion slices, and cook an additional hour. Let cool and transfer meat, vegetables, and all liquid to a freezer bag.

Reheating Instructions

Defrost in the refrigerator overnight. Heat in a saucepan over medium heat for 15–20 minutes, or until desired temperature is reached. Toast the hoagie rolls. Top each roll with meat, Provolone cheese, and banana peppers. Put under broiler and toast until cheese is melted.

PER SERVING
Calories: 677 | Fat: 35g | Protein: 58g | Sodium: 1081mg | Carbohydrates: 28g | Fiber: 2g

San Francisco Ginger Pork Chops

*This is a variation of the classic San Francisco recipe.
The subtle hint of ginger goes very well with the tangy red wine sauce.*

INGREDIENTS | SERVES 4

4 center-cut pork chops
2 tablespoons olive oil
1 clove garlic, chopped
1 onion, cut into rings
½ cup soy sauce
½ cup red wine
¼ teaspoon crushed red pepper flakes
1 teaspoon ground ginger
3 tablespoons brown sugar
1 tablespoon honey

Freezing Day

In skillet, brown pork chops in olive oil over medium-high heat for 3–4 minutes per side. Remove chops to cool. In same skillet, sauté the chopped garlic for 1–2 minutes until garlic is a light golden brown. Place pork chops and garlic in a freezer bag. Layer onion rings on top of chops. In a food processor, mix soy sauce, red wine, red pepper flakes, ginger, brown sugar, and honey. Blend well and pour over pork chops. Freeze.

Reheating Instructions

Defrost pork chops and sauce in the refrigerator for 24 hours and place in slow cooker. Cook on low for 7–8 hours.

PER SERVING
Calories: 408 | Fat: 28g | Protein: 23g | Sodium: 1801mg | Carbohydrates: 15g | Fiber: 0g

Pineapple Pork Chops

Start these in the slow cooker in the morning, and don't give the "what's for dinner?" question another thought. Just add some rice and a vegetable and dinner is ready.

INGREDIENTS | SERVES 6

6 pork chops
2 tablespoons vegetable oil
1 (20-ounce) can pineapple chunks with juice
¼ cup brown sugar
2 teaspoons soy sauce

Freezing Day

In skillet, brown pork chops in oil over medium-high heat for 3–4 minutes per side. Cool and place in freezer bag. In food processor, add pineapple chunks with juice, brown sugar, and soy sauce. Pulse until pineapple chunks are in small pieces. Pour sauce over pork chops and freeze.

Reheating Instructions

Defrost pork chops and sauce in the refrigerator for 24 hours. Place in slow cooker and cook on low for 7–8 hours.

PER SERVING
Calories: 261 | Fat: 14g | Protein: 18g | Sodium: 143mg | Carbohydrates: 16g | Fiber: 1g

Sweet and Sour Meatballs

NO DEFROSTING NEEDED!

INGREDIENTS | SERVES 6

1 batch Basic Meatballs (Chapter 15)
1 batch Sweet and Sour Sauce (Chapter 14)

Freezing Day

Prepare Basic Meatballs and Sweet and Sour Sauce. Freeze separately.

Reheating Instructions

Put the frozen Basic Meatballs in the slow cooker, and pour the Sweet and Sour Sauce over the top of them. Cook on low for 7–8 hours. Meatballs should be fully cooked.

PER SERVING
CALORIES: 687 | Fat: 31g | Protein: 48g | Sodium: 714mg | Carbohydrates: 50g | Fiber: 2g

Homestyle Beef Stew

Your home will be filled with delicious aromas as this stew simmers all day in the slow cooker.
Serve this stew over mashed potatoes for a hearty dinner.

INGREDIENTS | SERVES 6–8

2½ pounds beef stew meat, cubed

4 tablespoons flour

3 tablespoons olive oil

4 carrots

2 onions

2 beef bouillon cubes

4 cups water

½ cup red wine

2 tablespoons Worcestershire sauce

1 bay leaf

Portion Control

Beef stew is a delicious meal to have on a cold wintery day, and with portion-control freezing you can make it into a delicious lunch. Once stew has cooled, divide it up into lunch-sized portions and freeze in individual Tupperware containers. Defrost overnight in the refrigerator and you now have an easy meal you can heat up in the microwave in minutes.

Freezing Day

Dredge meat in flour. In skillet with olive oil, brown the beef on all sides, 7–10 minutes. Put beef in slow cooker. Cut carrots into 1-inch pieces, and peel and quarter the onions. Add to the slow cooker. Dissolve bouillon cubes in 4 cups boiling water. Add to slow cooker. Add remaining ingredients, cover, and cook in slow cooker on low for 7–8 hours or until beef is fork tender. Cool, portion, and freeze.

Reheating Instructions

Defrost in the refrigerator overnight. Heat stew in a saucepan, over medium heat, for 20–25 minutes or until fully heated.

PER SERVING
Calories: 412 | Fat: 22g | Protein: 38g | Sodium: 341mg | Carbohydrates: 12g | Fiber: 2g

Beef Roast

When your roast freezes and defrosts with the marinade, the meat soaks up all the juices. This technique makes for an extra delicious meal, especially after it has cooked all day in your slow cooker.

INGREDIENTS | SERVES 4–6

2 pounds lean roast

2 cloves garlic, sliced thin

3 tablespoons balsamic vinegar

¼ cup soy sauce

2 tablespoons Worcestershire sauce

1 teaspoon Dijon mustard

Salt and pepper to taste

Freezing Day

Make small slits around the roast and push thin slices of garlic into them. In bowl combine vinegar, soy sauce, Worcestershire sauce, Dijon mustard, and salt and pepper. Put roast into a freezer bag and pour in marinade. Freeze.

Reheating Instructions

Defrost roast in refrigerator 24 hours, and cook in slow cooker on low for 8–10 hours.

PER SERVING
Calories: 288 | Fat: 15g | Protein: 31g | Sodium: 743mg | Carbohydrates: 3g | Fiber: 0g

Chunky Applesauce

When selecting apples for applesauce, choose the sweetest you can find because the sweeter the apple, the less sugar you will need. Gala and Fuji apples will need very little, if any, sugar, whereas Golden Delicious, Jonathan, or Rome apples will need more.

INGREDIENTS | YIELDS APPROXIMATELY 1 QUART

10 large apples

½ cup water

1 teaspoon cinnamon

½ teaspoon vanilla

¼–1 cup sugar, to taste

Freezing Day

Peel, core, and dice the apples. Add apples to slow cooker and mix in water, cinnamon, and vanilla. Stir in sugar. The amount of sugar you use depends upon how sweet you want your applesauce, as well as the variety of apples you are using. Begin with ¼ cup and add up to 1 cup. Cook on low 8–10 hours, or on high 3–4 hours. Cool and freeze.

Reheating Instructions

Defrost applesauce in the refrigerator overnight and serve.

PER SERVING
Calories: 460 | Fat: 0.5g | Protein: 0g | Sodium: 0mg | Carbohydrates: 122g | Fiber: 5g

Chicken Cacciatore

Chicken Cacciatore is an Italian dish that was once called hunter's stew because it was something hunters could easily make in the field. Try using boneless chicken thighs for an even richer taste.

INGREDIENTS | SERVES 4

1½ pounds boneless, skinless chicken breasts

1 onion, sliced into rings

1 green bell pepper, sliced

½ pound mushrooms, sliced

2 cloves garlic, minced

2 (6-ounce) cans tomato paste

¼ cup red wine

1 cup water

1 (14.5-ounce) can stewed tomatoes with liquid

1 teaspoon dried oregano

½ teaspoon dried basil

½ teaspoon salt

¼ teaspoon pepper

Freezing Day

Put chicken, onions, peppers, and mushrooms in a freezer bag. In a separate bowl mix the remaining ingredients and pour over the chicken. Freeze.

Reheating Instructions

Defrost chicken in refrigerator overnight. Put in slow cooker and cook 7–9 hours on low. Add additional water if needed.

PER SERVING
Calories: 361 | Fat: 5g | Protein: 48g | Sodium: 737mg | Carbohydrates: 34g | Fiber: 8g

Butternut Squash Soup

When serving the soup, ladle into bowls and then drizzle additional cream over the surface of the soup. Drag a toothpick through the cream to create a marbled effect.

INGREDIENTS | SERVES 6

1 medium apple

4 cups butternut squash, cooked and puréed

3 cups chicken broth

2 tablespoons mild onion, grated

¼ teaspoon dried ginger

1 tablespoon dark brown sugar, packed

1 teaspoon fresh sage, minced

½ cup heavy cream (to be used on reheating day)

Freezing Day

Peel, core, and finely chop the apple. To the slow cooker add the apple, squash, chicken broth, onion, ginger, and brown sugar. Cook on low for 6 hours. Add sage during the last 30 minutes of cooking. Put soup in blender and purée. Freeze in a freezer bag.

Reheating Instructions

Defrost soup in refrigerator overnight. Heat soup on medium for 15–20 minutes. Pour cream in before serving.

PER SERVING
Calories: 207 | Fat: 11g | Protein: 4g | Sodium: 434mg | Carbohydrates: 26g | Fiber: 3g

Barbecue Brisket

This brisket turns out moist and tender as it is slow cooked in the sauce.
Serve on sandwich buns or sliced on a platter.

INGREDIENTS | SERVES 15–18

5-pound beef brisket (not corned beef)
4 teaspoons liquid smoke
½ teaspoon salt
¼ teaspoon pepper
1 cup chili sauce
½ cup barbecue sauce

Freezing Day

Season the brisket with liquid smoke, salt, and pepper. Place in the slow cooker. Combine chili sauce and barbecue sauce and pour over the brisket. Cover and cook 8–10 hours or until brisket is tender. Thinly slice meat against the grain and freeze in a freezer bag. Pour the sauce into a large measuring cup and let it sit several minutes. Pour off and discard any oil that rises to the top of the sauce, then freeze sauce separately in a freezer bag.

Reheating Instructions

Defrost brisket and sauce in the refrigerator overnight. Place brisket slices in a baking dish and pour sauce over the top. Bake at 350°F for 20–25 minutes or until meat is heated through.

PER SERVING
Calories: 384 | Fat: 22g | Protein: 37g | Sodium: 194mg | Carbohydrates: 8g | Fiber: 0g

Pulled Pork

Serve this pork with Sweet Barbecue Sauce (Chapter 14),
Garlic Toast (Chapter 12), and a salad for a delicious meal.

INGREDIENTS | SERVES 6–8

3-pound lean pork roast
Salt and pepper to taste
1 teaspoon onion powder
2 medium onions, sliced
3 cloves garlic, minced
Water to cover

Gravy in the Slow Cooker

Once you remove the pork from the cooker, you can make gravy out of the juices. Remove the onions and set aside. In a small bowl, combine ½ cup cold water with 3 tablespoons cornstarch. Stir until cornstarch is completely dissolved. Pour into the slow cooker and stir until mixture thickens. Add onions to gravy, cool, and freeze in a plastic container or freezer bag.

Freezing Day

Season pork with salt, pepper, and onion powder and set aside. Lay ⅔ of sliced onions in bottom of slow cooker, and add ½ of minced garlic evenly over onions. Place seasoned pork roast on top of onions, and lay remaining onion and garlic on top of roast. Cover with water. Cook on low for 8 hours and remove to a plate. Remove any fat and pull meat apart using two forks. Freeze using a freezer bag.

Reheating Instructions

Defrost pork in the refrigerator overnight, heat in a saucepan over medium heat (or microwave), and serve.

PER SERVING
Calories: 345 | Fat: 21g | Protein: 35g | Sodium: 78mg |
Carbohydrates: 2g | Fiber: 0 g

Split Pea and Ham Soup

Divide and freeze this soup into single-serving portions to create a delicious homemade option you can pair with a sandwich or salad for lunch or a light dinner.

INGREDIENTS | SERVES 8

4 strips bacon

1 cup sweet onion, chopped

1 clove garlic, minced

1 cup carrots, shredded

1 pound dried split peas

2 cups cooked, lean ham

1 ham bone (optional)

10 cups water

Salt and pepper to taste

Freezing Day

In a skillet, cook bacon until crisp. Sauté onions in 1 tablespoon bacon grease for 5–6 minutes. Add garlic and sauté 1 more minute. To the slow cooker add the bacon, onions, garlic, carrots, dried split peas, ham, and ham bone. Add water and season with salt and pepper. Cover, and cook on high 4–5 hours. Remove ham bone and let soup cool. Freeze in a freezer bag or plastic container.

Reheating Instructions

Defrost soup in refrigerator overnight and heat in saucepan over medium heat for 15–20 minutes, or until desired temperature is reached.

PER SERVING
Calories: 295 | Fat: 7g | Protein: 20g | Sodium: 405mg | Carbohydrates: 38g | Fiber: 15g

Cabbage Rolls

Did you know you can freeze cabbage? You should never freeze the entire head of cabbage, but remove the leaves and freeze them whole, or cut into coarse shreds. And there's no need to blanch the cabbage first!

INGREDIENTS | SERVES 6

1 head cabbage

1 cup cooked rice

1 pound extra-lean ground beef

1 egg

¼ cup milk

½ cup onion, finely chopped

1 teaspoon paprika

2 cloves garlic, minced

¼–½ teaspoon pepper to taste

Salt to taste (used on reheating day)

1 (32-ounce) jar sauerkraut (used on reheating day)

2 cups V8 juice (used on reheating day)

Alternate Cooking Methods

To prepare this recipe on the stovetop, follow these directions but use a stockpot instead of the slow cooker: Cover the stock-pot and simmer for 1½–2 hours. To prepare in the oven, use a casserole dish instead of the slow cooker. Bake at 350°F, covered, for 2 hours.

Freezing Day

Remove core of cabbage. Separate about 12–15 large leaves and put in boiling water for 2 minutes to soften the leaves. Drain leaves. In a bowl, combine rice, ground beef, egg, milk, onion, paprika, garlic, and pepper. Put 3–4 tablespoons of mixture in the center of each leaf. Fold in sides of leaf, then roll from the bottom. Use a toothpick to fasten bottom if necessary. Flash freeze each roll on a baking sheet lined with wax paper. Transfer to freezer bag once frozen.

Reheating Instructions

Defrost cabbage rolls in the refrigerator overnight. Lightly salt the top of each roll. Put the sauerkraut in the bottom of the slow cooker. Place cabbage rolls seam side down on top of the sauerkraut. Pour V8 juice over the top of everything. Cover the slow cooker and cook on low for 8–9 hours.

PER SERVING
Calories: 323 | Fat: 14g | Protein: 25g | Sodium: 407mg | Carbohydrates: 23g | Fiber: 6g

Cola Roast

This roast is comfort food and will become one of your family's regular meals. Serve with Mashed Potatoes (Chapter 11), Dinner Rolls (Chapter 12), and a vegetable for the perfect dinner.

INGREDIENTS | SERVES 6–8

3-pound chuck roast

Salt and pepper to taste

Powdered garlic to taste

3 tablespoons olive oil

¼ cup red wine

2 (12-ounce) cans cola

2 (10.75-ounce) cans cream of mushroom soup

1 package dry onion soup mix

Freezing Day

Dry the meat with a paper towel before seasoning. Season the meat with salt, pepper, and garlic powder on all sides. In a skillet over medium-high, sear the roast 1–2 minutes in hot olive oil on each side until the roast is brown and crisp. Once seared, put the roast in the slow cooker. Deglaze the skillet as follows: Pour the red wine into the skillet with the heat on high. Bring it to a boil as you scrape the bottom of the pan removing the browned bits from the roast. Once the browned bits have mixed in with the wine, remove from heat. To the skillet add cola, cream of mushroom soup, and dry onion soup mix. Mix well and pour over roast in the slow cooker. Cover the slow cooker and cook on low for 6–8 hours. Remove and cool. Slice the roast and freeze with the sauce.

Reheating Instructions

Defrost in the refrigerator overnight. Place slices in a baking dish. Pour the juice over the top and cover tightly. Put in oven at 300°F for 30–40 minutes until meat reaches 200°F.

PER SERVING
Calories: 529 | Fat: 33g | Protein: 37g | Sodium: 1002mg | Carbohydrates: 19g | Fiber: 0g

Taco Soup

Serve this soup with a variety of toppings, just like a taco! Cheddar cheese, sour cream, jalapeño peppers, and tortilla chips all taste delicious paired with this soup.

INGREDIENTS | SERVES 8

1½ pounds ground beef

1 (15-ounce) can whole kernel corn, with liquid

1 (15-ounce) can cream corn

1 (15-ounce) can hominy, with liquid

1 (15-ounce) can kidney beans, with liquid

1 (15-ounce) can pinto beans, with liquid

2 (14.5-ounce) cans diced tomatoes, with liquid

1 (1.25-ounce) package taco mix

1 (1-ounce) package dry ranch dressing mix

Portion Control Your Soup

Line your favorite microwavable soup mug with a quart-sized freezer bag. Pour the soup into the lined mug and flash freeze. Once the soup is frozen, lift the bag of soup from the mug, and return the soup to the freezer. Now you have a perfectly shaped portion of soup that can go from the freezer straight to your mug. To heat, defrost, microwave, and serve soup in the same cup!

Freezing Day

Brown ground beef in skillet. Drain. Add beef and remaining ingredients to the slow cooker and mix well. Cover and cook on low for 6–7 hours. Cool and freeze in a freezer bag.

Reheating Instructions

Defrost in the refrigerator overnight. Heat over medium for 15–20 minutes or until desired temperature is reached, and serve.

PER SERVING

Calories: 665 | Fat: 17g | Protein: 47g | Sodium: 550mg | Carbohydrates: 85g | Fiber: 21g

Sweet and Sour Pork Roast

This pork roast comes out of the crock pot full of flavor, and tastes even better after being frozen with the sauce. Serve this tangy roast with Flavored White Rice (Chapter 11), and green beans.

INGREDIENTS | SERVES 6–8

4-pound lean pork roast
Salt and pepper to taste
Sweet and Sour Sauce (Chapter 14)
1 (20-ounce) can pineapple chunks

Freezing Day

Season the pork with salt and pepper and put in the bottom of the slow cooker. Prepare the Sweet and Sour Sauce and pour over the top of the roast. Cook on low for 7–8 hours. Remove pork from slow cooker and shred. Return shredded pork to the slow cooker and stir in can of pineapple chunks. Cook additional 30 minutes. Remove from slow cooker, put meat and sauce in freezer bag, and freeze.

Reheating Instructions

Defrost pork in the refrigerator overnight. Heat in saucepan on medium for 15–20 minutes until desired temperature is reached.

PER SERVING
Calories: 416 | Fat: 22g | Protein: 45g | Sodium: 108mg | Carbohydrates: 4g | Fiber: 0.5g

Meatless Dishes

Spinach and Cheddar Quiche

NO DEFROSTING NEEDED!

INGREDIENTS | SERVES 4

1 (9") unbaked pastry shell

1 tablespoon butter, softened

4 eggs

2 cups heavy cream

½ teaspoon salt

1 cup Cheddar cheese, shredded

½ cup chopped spinach

Portion Control

This recipe calls for the quiche to be slightly undercooked before freezing. To fully cook it and cut into single-serving pieces before freezing, cook for 30 minutes or until a knife inserted into center comes out clean. Individually wrap each slice of quiche in plastic wrap for the freezer. To cook a frozen piece of quiche, unwrap and heat in microwave.

Freezing Day

Spread the pastry shell with the softened butter and put it in the refrigerator. In a large bowl, whisk eggs, cream, and salt. Stir in cheese. Remove shell from refrigerator and line the bottom with spinach. Pour egg mixture over the top. Bake quiche for 20 minutes at 375°F. It should be a bit undercooked. Cool, wrap tightly with plastic wrap, and freeze.

Reheating Instructions

Bake frozen quiche at 350°F for 50 minutes, or until it is fully heated.

PER SERVING

Calories: 710 | Fat: 67g | Protein: 18g | Sodium: 665mg | Carbohydrates: 10g | Fiber: 0.5g

Chocolate Chip Pancakes

NO DEFROSTING NEEDED!

INGREDIENTS | SERVES 6

1¼ cups flour

2 tablespoons sugar

2 teaspoons baking powder

½ teaspoon salt

1 cup milk

3 tablespoons vegetable oil

1 egg

½ cup chocolate chip morsels

Freezing Day

In a large mixing bowl, combine flour, sugar, baking powder, and salt. Stir in milk, oil, and egg. Mix batter. Gently stir in chocolate chips. Make pancakes in a skillet, and transfer to a baking sheet. Flash freeze and transfer to a freezer bag.

Reheating Instructions

Heat frozen pancakes in the microwave and serve.

PER SERVING
Calories: 283 | Fat: 14g | Protein: 5g | Sodium: 229mg | Carbohydrates: 34g | Fiber: 0.5g

Gazpacho

This refreshing summer soup is served chilled.
Spice it up by adding sliced jalapeño peppers and cayenne pepper to suit your tastes.

INGREDIENTS | SERVES 2–4

4 cups tomato juice

2 seedless cucumbers, peeled and
 chopped

½ green bell pepper, chopped

2 green onions, chopped

¼ teaspoon Worcestershire sauce

1 clove garlic

1 tablespoon fresh basil

2 tablespoons wine vinegar

1 tablespoon plus 1 teaspoon olive oil

Freezing Day

Place all ingredients into a blender or food processor and mix until smooth. Freeze in a freezer bag.

Reheating Instructions

Defrost gazpacho in the refrigerator overnight. Serve chilled and topped with diced onions, green peppers, and tomatoes.

PER SERVING
Calories: 116 | Fat: 3g | Protein: 4g | Sodium: 32mg | Carbohydrates: 22g | Fiber: 3g

Spinach Stuffed Shells

If you prefer to freeze this meal as a casserole, simply prepare a casserole dish for freezing and build the casserole according to the reheating instructions. Cover the casserole tightly and flash freeze.

INGREDIENTS | SERVES 4–5

16 large pasta shells

1 (10-ounce) package frozen spinach, thawed

1 cup ricotta cheese

½ cup Parmesan cheese

1 (28-ounce) jar spaghetti sauce (used on reheating day)

1 cup shredded mozzarella cheese (used on reheating day)

How to Freeze Fresh Spinach

Only select young and tender spinach to freeze. Wash the spinach and cut off the stems. Blanch the spinach by putting into boiling water for 2 minutes, then into ice-cold water for 2 minutes. Drain and freeze in a freezer bag. You may flash freeze the leaves before putting in the freezer bag if desired.

Freezing Day

Cook shells for half the recommended cooking time. Squeeze excess water out of the spinach. In a large bowl, mix together the spinach, ricotta cheese, and Parmesan cheese. Stuff the shells with the spinach mixture and flash freeze. Transfer to freezer bag.

Reheating Instructions

Defrost shells completely in the refrigerator for 24 hours. Pour a small amount of spaghetti sauce on the bottom of a casserole dish. Arrange shells in the pan and cover with remaining spaghetti sauce. Top with mozzarella cheese. Cook for 30 minutes at 350°F.

PER SERVING
Calories: 690 | Fat: 29g | Protein: 29g | Sodium: 2095mg | Carbohydrates: 83g | Fiber: 5g

Bean Burritos

NO DEFROSTING NEEDED!

INGREDIENTS | SERVES 20

2 (16-ounce) cans refried beans

2 (10-ounce) cans enchilada sauce

20 flour tortillas

2 cups shredded Cheddar cheese

Assembly-Line Burritos

Set up a burrito-making station in your kitchen and get the whole family to help! The kids will have a great time building and freezing the burritos with you.

Freezing Day

In a large bowl, combine refried beans with enchilada sauce. Mix well. Spread 3 tablespoons of bean mixture down the center of each tortilla, and sprinkle Cheddar cheese on top. Fold the burritos by first folding the bottom of the tortilla about ⅓ of the way up. Next fold the right side of the tortilla over the filling, then fold the left side of the tortilla so it overlaps the right side. Flash freeze on a baking sheet, folded side down. Once frozen, transfer the burritos to a freezer bag.

Reheating Instructions

Microwave frozen burrito for 1 minute, turn over, and microwave an additional minute.

PER SERVING
Calories: 214 | Fat: 7g | Protein: 9g | Sodium: 584mg | Carbohydrates: 27g | Fiber: 4g

Easy Baked Ziti

NO DEFROSTING NEEDED!

INGREDIENTS | SERVES 6–8

1 (16-ounce) box ziti

1 (15-ounce) container ricotta cheese

1 egg

1 (24-ounce) jar spaghetti sauce

¼ cup freshly grated Parmesan cheese
  (used on reheating day)

Pasta Tips

When you buy ziti, look for ziti with ridges, rather than a smooth pasta. The ridges help hold the sauce to the pasta. When cooking the pasta, use a large pot with lots of water and salt—the water keeps the pasta from sticking together—and never rinse your pasta after draining (unless making pasta salad). The rinsing washes away the delicious pasta flavor.

Freezing Day

Cook the ziti according to package directions, but only boil the noodles 8 minutes. In a large mixing bowl, combine ricotta cheese with egg. Prepare a casserole dish for freezing according to the casserole method found in Chapter 1. Add the cooked ziti and spaghetti sauce to the ricotta cheese mixture. Mix well. Put the ziti mixture in the baking pan and flash freeze.

Reheating Instructions

Defrost casserole in the refrigerator for 24 hours following the casserole method, cover, and bake 30–45 minutes at 350°F. To bake the casserole frozen, add 45 minutes–1 hour to the defrosted cooking time. Uncover casserole and sprinkle with fresh Parmesan cheese during last 30 minutes of baking.

PER SERVING
Calories: 350 | Fat: 9g | Protein: 15g | Sodium: 128mg | Carbohydrates: 54g | Fiber: 4g

Lasagna Florentine

NO DEFROSTING NEEDED!

INGREDIENTS | SERVES 6–8

1 (16-ounce) box lasagna noodles

1 onion, diced

1 pound fresh mushrooms, coarsely chopped

1 teaspoon basil

2 cloves garlic, minced

2 tablespoons olive oil

2 (10-ounce) boxes frozen spinach, defrosted and squeezed of excess water

2 (6-ounce) cans tomato paste

2 cups hot water

1 teaspoon Italian seasoning

Salt and pepper to taste

3 cups ricotta cheese

1½ cups Parmesan cheese, freshly grated, divided

2 eggs, beaten

4 cups shredded mozzarella

Vegetarian Lasagna

Lasagna Florentine is similar to Mom's Lasagna Chapter 8, but spinach is substituted for the beef. This vegetarian dish is a nice alternative for your guests who do not enjoy meat.

Freezing Day

Cook lasagna noodles according to the directions on the package. In skillet, sauté onions, mushrooms, and basil in olive oil for 5–8 minutes until the onions have softened. Add garlic and spinach and sauté 2–3 minutes more. Remove from heat. In saucepan, mix the tomato paste with 2 cups of hot water, Italian seasoning, salt, and pepper. Cook over medium heat for 15 minutes. In mixing bowl, combine the ricotta cheese, ½ cup Parmesan cheese, and eggs. Add the spinach mixture to the cheese mixture and mix well. In small mixing bowl combine remaining Parmesan cheese with the mozzarella cheese.

In a casserole dish prepared for the freezer according to the casserole method in Chapter 1, put a thin layer of tomato sauce. Add alternating layers of noodles, then spinach mixture, then mozzarella and Parmesan cheese, then tomato sauce. Top with mozzarella and Parmesan layer. Wrap tightly following the casserole method of freezing, and flash freeze casserole.

Reheating Instructions

Cover frozen lasagna with foil, and bake it at 375°F for 1 hour 30 minutes–1 hour 45 minutes, or until it is fully heated. Remove foil during the last 15 minutes of baking.

PER SERVING

Calories: 721 | Fat: 31g | Protein: 51g | Sodium: 532mg | Carbohydrates: 65g | Fiber: 7g

Macaroni and Cheese Bake

This baked casserole is one you will make over and over again.
Kids love it and it is a good choice for potluck suppers.

INGREDIENTS | SERVES 6–8

8 ounces elbow macaroni

4 tablespoons butter

3 tablespoons flour

2 cups heavy cream

½ teaspoon salt

½ teaspoon pepper

1½ teaspoons yellow or Dijon mustard

2 cups Cheddar cheese, shredded

½–1 cup milk, as needed (used on reheating day)

2 cups crushed cornflakes (used on reheating day)

1 stick butter, melted (used on reheating day)

Freezing Cheese

It is often less expensive to buy a large block of cheese than it is to buy grated cheese. Take advantage of the lower price, and do the grating yourself with a food processor. Divide the grated cheese into 1-cup portions and freeze in a freezer bag.

Freezing Day

Undercook elbow macaroni by 5 minutes and drain. In a large saucepan, melt the butter over medium heat. Add flour and mix well. Slowly add the cream to the butter mixture, stirring as you pour. Bring to just under a boil, stirring constantly until sauce thickens, approximately 5 minutes. Add salt, pepper, mustard, and cheese. Continue to stir until all of the cheese is melted. Gently stir in macaroni and remove from heat to cool. Freeze in a freezer bag.

Reheating Instructions

Defrost macaroni and cheese in the refrigerator overnight. Grease a large baking dish and put macaroni and cheese in it. Stir the milk into the macaroni and cheese to give it a creamy (not soupy) texture. Top the macaroni and cheese with crushed cornflakes and pour the melted butter over the cornflakes. Bake at 375°F for 30–40 minutes.

PER SERVING
Calories: 554 | Fat: 51g | Protein: 12g | Sodium: 557mg | Carbohydrates: 19g | Fiber: 1g

Cheese Enchilada Casserole

NO DEFROSTING NEEDED!

INGREDIENTS | SERVES 4–6

1 cup ricotta cheese

2 cups shredded Cheddar cheese, divided

1 (10-ounce) can Ro-Tel tomatoes

¼ teaspoon salt

2 cloves garlic, minced

1 (10-ounce) can enchilada sauce

8 corn tortillas

Easy Enchiladas

This casserole is a breeze to put together and freeze. Serve it with chips and fresh guacamole or Garden Salsa (Chapter 13).

Freezing Day

In mixing bowl combine ricotta cheese, 1 cup Cheddar cheese, tomatoes (drained), salt, and garlic. Use either a disposable aluminum casserole dish, or prepare a casserole dish for freezing according to the casserole method in Chapter 1. Pour a small amount of enchilada sauce on the bottom of casserole dish. Fill each tortilla with cheese mixture and put in casserole dish, seam side down. Pour remaining enchilada sauce over tortillas, and top with remaining 1 cup of cheese.

Reheating Instructions

Bake defrosted casserole (covered) at 375°F for 30 minutes, or frozen casserole (covered) at 375°F for 1 hour 10 minutes–1 hour 20 minutes or until casserole is hot or cheese is melted.

PER SERVING
Calories: 357 | Fat: 20g | Protein: 21g | Sodium: 1123mg | Carbohydrates: 24g | Fiber: 2g

Eggplant Parmigiana

NO DEFROSTING NEEDED!

2 medium-sized eggplants

1½ cups Italian breadcrumbs

3 eggs

2 tablespoons milk

2 tablespoons olive oil

1 batch Basic Marinara Sauce (Chapter 14)

2 cups mozzarella cheese

½ cup freshly grated Parmesan cheese

How to Cook a Frozen Casserole

You can defrost casseroles first, or they can go straight from the freezer to the oven. To go the latter route, add 45 minutes–1 hour to the defrosted cooking time. Cover your casserole with aluminum foil while cooking to keep it from drying out.

Freezing Day

Cut the eggplant into ⅓" thick slices. Put the breadcrumbs in a shallow pan. Beat the eggs together in separate shallow pan. Add the milk to the eggs. Dip each piece of eggplant in the egg mixture and then in the breadcrumb mixture, coating all sides. In a skillet, lightly brown both sides of the eggplant in hot olive oil approximately 2 minutes per side. Prepare a casserole dish for freezing according to the casserole method in Chapter 1. Pour a small amount of Basic Marinara Sauce into the dish, enough to cover the bottom of the casserole. Place alternate layers of eggplant, sauce, and combination of cheeses, ending with cheese on the top. Wrap tightly according to the casserole method and freeze.

Reheating Instructions

Put frozen casserole into oven and cook at 350°F, covered, for 1 hour 30 minutes–1 hour 45 minutes, or until casserole is hot.

PER SERVING
Calories: 280 | Fat: 14g | Protein: 17g | Sodium: 474mg | Carbohydrates: 23g | Fiber: 4g

Spaghetti and Not-meatballs

Instead of marinara sauce, try the meatballs with
Marsala Mushroom Sauce (Chapter 14) served over linguine with crusty French bread.

INGREDIENTS | SERVES 4

1 batch Basic Marinara Sauce (Chapter 14)

¾ cup pine nuts, finely processed in food processor

4 eggs

⅔ packet onion soup mix

2 cups grated Asiago cheese

1 cup seasoned breadcrumbs

1 teaspoon Italian seasoning

2 cloves garlic, minced

Waste Not, Want Not

Make a habit of checking your refrigerator for perishables needing to be cooked. Think of how much money is wasted every year on food that has gone bad while sitting in the refrigerator. You may not be ready to eat a particular food, but surely you can find a freezer recipe that allows you to preserve it for another time.

Freezing Day

Prepare Basic Marinara Sauce. Mix together the pine nuts, eggs, onion soup mix, cheese, breadcrumbs, Italian seasoning, and garlic. Form into not-meatballs. Place balls on a lightly greased baking sheet and bake at 375°F for 30 minutes or until balls are browned. Turn meatballs every 10 minutes. Put meatballs in marinara sauce and simmer on low for 45 minutes–1 hour. Cool and freeze in Tupperware or freezer bag.

Reheating Instructions

Defrost in the refrigerator overnight and heat over medium-low heat until it reaches desired temperature. Serve over spaghetti.

PER SERVING
Calories: 605 | Fat: 41g | Protein: 33g | Sodium: 1211mg | Carbohydrates: 27g | Fiber: 3g

Vegetarian Vegetable Bean Soup

Keep a batch of this delicious soup on hand for those cold evenings when you want something warm and comforting to eat. It also makes the perfect meal to bring to a sick friend.

INGREDIENTS | SERVES 8–10

4 cups vegetable broth
1 (14-ounce) can diced tomatoes
3 cloves garlic, diced
3 large carrots, peeled, sliced
2 stalks celery, sliced
½ head cabbage, shredded
1 medium yellow onion, chopped
3 medium leeks, whites only, sliced
6–8 small red potatoes, cubed
Pinch of rosemary
1 (16-ounce) can white beans, drained
Salt and pepper to taste

Freezing Day

Combine vegetable broth, tomatoes, garlic, carrots, celery, cabbage, onion, leeks, potatoes, and rosemary in a slow-cooker. Cook on low for 8 hours. Add beans, salt, and pepper and cook for 30 minutes more. Freeze using freezer bags.

Reheating Instructions

Defrost soup in the refrigerator overnight and heat over medium heat for 15–20 minutes.

PER SERVING
Calories: 355 | Fat: 1g | Protein: 16g | Sodium: 275mg | Carbohydrates: 73g | Fiber: 17g

Zucchini Casserole

Zucchini is a type of summer squash and a popular vegetable to grow at home. You can freeze them in half-inch slices, but the vegetable must be water-blanched and quickly cooled first.

INGREDIENTS | SERVES 6–8

3 large zucchini
½ cup mushrooms, chopped
¼ cup onions, chopped
½ cup butter, melted
¼ teaspoon garlic powder
1¼ cups Saltine crackers, crushed
1 egg, beaten
¼ teaspoon pepper
½ teaspoon salt
1 cup Cheddar cheese, shredded (for use on reheating day)

Freezing Day

Grate zucchini and put in large mixing bowl. Add remaining ingredients (except cheese) and mix well. Put mixture in an aluminum casserole dish and partially cook at 350°F for 20 minutes. Cool and freeze.

Reheating Instructions

Defrost zucchini casserole in the refrigerator overnight. Cook at 350°F for 15 minutes. Remove from oven and sprinkle cheese over the top. Return to oven for 15 minutes.

PER SERVING
Calories: 244 | Fat: 21g | Protein: 8g | Sodium: 510mg | Carbohydrates: 6g | Fiber: 1g

Broccoli Strata

Strata is a casserole made from eggs and bread, and can also incorporate hash browns and, if desired, meat. Strata is also known as a breakfast casserole and is a great option to serve for brunch.

INGREDIENTS | SERVES 8–10

1 loaf Italian bread

1–2 cups grated Cheddar cheese, to taste

2 cups fresh broccoli, cooked

1 stick butter

8 eggs

2 cups milk

2 tablespoons minced onion

½ teaspoon salt

1 teaspoon yellow mustard

Dash red pepper

Dash paprika

Freezing Day

Prepare a 9" x 13" casserole dish for freezing according to the casserole method in Chapter 1. Slice Italian bread into 1" slices. Line the bottom of the dish with a layer of bread. Layer cheese, then broccoli on top of bread. In a saucepan, melt butter. Remove from heat. In a mixing bowl, whisk together the eggs and milk. Add egg mixture and remaining ingredients to butter and mix well. Slowly pour egg mixture over the top of the casserole. Wrap well according to casserole method and freeze.

Reheating Instructions

Following the casserole method, defrost casserole in the refrigerator overnight. Bake for 45 minutes–1 hour at 350°F, or until the eggs are cooked and a knife inserted into the middle of the dish comes out clean.

PER SERVING
Calories: 745 | Fat: 51g | Protein: 31g | Sodium: 1287mg | Carbohydrates: 42g | Fiber: 3g

Potato Patties

NO DEFROSTING NEEDED!

INGREDIENTS | SERVES 2–4

1 cup mashed potatoes
½ teaspoon minced onion
2–4 tablespoons flour
2 teaspoons butter

Make Leftovers New Again
This recipe is a great way to use up your leftover mashed potatoes. These patties can also be made from instant potatoes, or the Mashed Potatoes recipe on Chapter 11.

Freezing Day

Mix mashed potatoes with minced onion. Form mashed potatoes into 4–6 patties. Dip patties in flour. Heat butter in skillet over medium-high heat. Fry potato patties in butter for 3–5 minutes per side, turning once they become browned. Cool patties and flash freeze. Transfer to freezer bag.

Reheating Instructions

Put frozen patty in microwave and heat, or fry frozen patty in a skillet with butter until heated through.

PER SERVING
Calories: 75 | Fat: 2g | Protein: 1.5g | Sodium: 178mg | Carbohydrates: 12g | Fiber: 1g

Casseroles

Shepherd's Pie

*Shepherd's Pie is widely used today as a synonym for Cottage Pie,
although traditionally Shepherd's Pie was made with lamb instead of beef.*

INGREDIENTS | SERVES 6

2 pounds potatoes

2 pounds Basic Ground Beef Mixture
(Chapter 15)

1 serving Gravy for Any Occasion
(Chapter 15)

2 cups frozen corn

½ cup milk

3 tablespoons butter or margarine

Salt and pepper to taste

1 cup shredded Cheddar cheese

Salt-and-Pepper Shaker

Make your own customized salt-and-pepper
shaker and save time in the kitchen. Fill a
large shaker with five parts salt and one part
pepper. Adjust the salt and pepper ratio to
match your family's tastes.

Freezing Day

Peel potatoes and cut into quarters. Boil in water until
soft (about 20 minutes). Prepare a 9" x 13" casserole dish
for freezing. See instructions for the casserole method in
Chapter 1, or use an aluminum pan. In a large bowl, mix
Basic Ground Beef Mixture with Gravy for Any Occasion.
Add to the prepared casserole dish as bottom layer.
Layer the frozen corn on top of the meat. Once potatoes
are tender, drain and mash. Add milk, butter, salt, and
pepper. Mix well and layer on top of corn. Spread the
shredded Cheddar cheese over the mashed potato layer
and freeze the casserole.

Reheating Instructions

Following the casserole method, defrost casserole in the
refrigerator for 24 hours and cook in a 375°F oven for 30
minutes. To cook frozen, add 40 minutes–1 hour to
cooking time.

PER SERVING
Calories: 778 | Fat: 40g | Protein: 53g | Sodium: 373mg |
Carbohydrates: 51g | Fiber: 5g

South of the Border Lasagna

NO DEFROSTING NEEDED!

INGREDIENTS | SERVES 6–8

2 pounds ground beef

1 onion, diced

1 clove garlic, minced

Taco Seasoning Mix (Chapter 13)

1 cup water

2 (14.5-ounce) cans diced tomatoes, drained

1 (4-ounce) can green chili peppers, drained

3 cups Cheddar cheese, shredded

3 cups Monterey jack cheese, shredded

2 eggs

1 pint ricotta cheese

1 (10-ounce) can enchilada sauce

24 corn tortillas

Mexican Many Ways

This is a variation of a traditional lasagna recipe that has a Mexican flair. Try changing up the dish by adding a layer of black beans, corn, and cilantro; or a layer of salsa, jalapeño peppers, and Spicy Refried Beans (Chapter 15).

Freezing Day

In a skillet, brown ground beef and onion 7–10 minutes or until meat is fully cooked. Add garlic and cook an additional minute. Drain. Add the Taco Seasoning mix and 1 cup water. Bring to a gentle boil and cook 15 minutes over medium-low heat. Add the diced tomatoes and green chili peppers to the skillet. Mix well. In a bowl, mix the Cheddar cheese with the Monterey jack cheese. In a separate bowl, beat eggs and mix fully with ricotta cheese.

Prepare a 9" x 13" casserole dish for freezing. See instructions for the casserole method in Chapter 1, or use an aluminum pan. In the bottom of the dish, pour a thin layer of enchilada sauce followed by a layer of tortillas. Add a layer of meat, followed by a layer of shredded cheese mixture. Add another layer of tortillas, followed by all of the ricotta cheese mixture. Continue layering the lasagna and top with a layer of shredded cheese. Pour enough enchilada sauce to cover the top of the lasagna. Wrap well. Freeze according to the casserole method in Chapter 1.

Reheating Instructions

Unwrap frozen lasagna and put in original casserole dish. Cover loosely with aluminum foil. Bake frozen lasagna at 350°F for 1 hour 15 minutes–1 hour 45 minutes, or until it is fully heated. Remove foil during last 15–30 minutes. Bake defrosted lasagna at 350°F for 30–45 minutes.

PER SERVING
Calories: 862 | Fat: 49g | Protein: 61g | Sodium: 1695mg | Carbohydrates: 42g | Fiber: 4g

Ham and Pineapple Pizza Casserole

NO DEFROSTING NEEDED!

INGREDIENTS | SERVES 6–8

1½ cups Homemade Pizza Sauce
(Chapter 15)

16 ounces bowtie pasta, cooked

2 cups cooked ham, cubed

2 cups pineapple chunks

5 cups mozzarella cheese, shredded

How to Cut a Pineapple

To cut a pineapple you need a knife and a potato peeler. First cut off the stalk, and the bottom of the pineapple. Next, cut off the skin. If you miss any skin, use your potato peeler to remove it. Lay the pineapple on its side and cut slices. If the core of the slices is tough, remove it.

Freezing Day

Combine Homemade Pizza Sauce, pasta, ham, pineapple, and 2½ cups mozzarella cheese. Mix well and put into a casserole dish you have prepared for freezing according to the casserole method in Chapter 1. Top casserole with remaining mozzarella cheese, wrap well, and freeze.

Reheating Instructions

Defrost casserole in refrigerator overnight, or you may cook casserole frozen. If defrosted, heat casserole for 30 minutes at 350°F. If frozen, heat casserole for 1 hour 10 minutes–1 hour 30 minutes at 350°F.

PER SERVING
Calories: 500 | Fat: 19g | Protein: 33g | Sodium: 300mg | Carbohydrates: 49g | Fiber: 3g

Tater Tot Chili Bake Casserole

NO DEFROSTING NEEDED!

Beware of Frozen Cans

If a can of food is accidentally frozen, it may not be safe to eat. If the can is bulging, defrost it in the refrigerator. If it looks and smells good, it is probably safe. If the seams of the can burst or are rusted, wrap it in plastic and throw it away.

Freezing Day

In skillet, brown ground beef and onion. Drain. Stir in corn, chili, and chili seasoning mix. Prepare a 9" x 13" casserole dish for freezing. See instructions for the casserole method in Chapter 1, or use an aluminum pan. Lay the Tater Tots along the bottom of the pan. Top them with the meat mixture, and top that with shredded Cheddar. Wrap tightly and freeze.

Reheating Instructions

Frozen casserole can go straight into the oven. Cook the casserole in a 350°F oven for 1 hour 30 minutes–1 hour 45 minutes, or until it is heated all the way through.

PER SERVING
Calories: 509 | Fat: 25g | Protein: 34g | Sodium: 845mg | Carbohydrates: 39g | Fiber: 5g

Mom's Lasagna

NO DEFROSTING NEEDED!

Super for Sharing!

This is a traditional lasagna recipe, and makes a great meal to bring to a friend. Have this lasagna on hand, baked in a throw-away aluminum pan, to deliver at a moment's notice.

Freezing Day

Cook lasagna noodles according to the directions on the package. In skillet, brown the ground beef, onion, basil, Italian seasoning, salt, pepper, and garlic. In a bowl, mix the tomato paste with hot water. Add to skillet. Cook over medium heat for 15 minutes. In mixing bowl, combine the ricotta cheese and the eggs. Mix well. Prepare a 9" x 13" casserole dish for freezing. See instructions for the casserole method in Chapter 1, or use an aluminum pan.

Begin building the lasagna by putting a thin layer of meat sauce in the bottom of the casserole dish. Add a layer of noodles, then a layer of the ricotta cheese, then a layer of half the remaining meat sauce, then more noodles, half the mozzarella, the remaining meat sauce, the remaining noodles, and finally the remaining mozzarella. Sprinkle the top with freshly grated Parmesan cheese. Following the casserole method, wrap tightly for the freezer and flash freeze casserole.

Reheating Instructions

Cover the frozen lasagna with foil and bake at 375°F for 1 hour 30 minutes–1 hour 45 minutes, or until it is fully heated. Remove foil during the last 15 minutes of baking.

PER SERVING
Calories: 707 | Fat: 33g | Protein: 54g | Sodium: 550mg | Carbohydrates: 47g | Fiber: 4g

Baked Chicken with Broccoli

NO DEFROSTING NEEDED!

INGREDIENTS | SERVES 6–8

8 ounces bacon

3 tablespoons bacon drippings

3 tablespoons flour

2¾ cups chicken broth

1½ teaspoons tarragon

1½ teaspoons basil

¾ teaspoon salt

4 teaspoons minced onion

¾ teaspoon garlic powder

2½ teaspoons lime juice

2½ pounds chicken tender fillets

1 (24-ounce) bag frozen broccoli florets

2 cups Cheddar cheese

A Bit about Tarragon

Tarragon is an aromatic herb also commonly referred to as dragon herb or dragon's wort. It is one of the four "fine herbs" of French and Mediterranean cooking, along with parsley, chives, and chervil. It is commonly used in chicken, fish, and egg dishes.

Freezing Day

Chop bacon into bite-sized pieces and fry in skillet. Remove bacon from pan and set aside. Remove all but 3 tablespoons of bacon drippings from skillet. Add 3 tablespoons flour to bacon drippings and mix over heat to form a roux. Add chicken broth to the skillet and stir 4–5 minutes until sauce thickens. Add tarragon, basil, salt, minced onion, garlic powder, and lime juice to the sauce. Bring to a boil, and then reduce heat. Simmer for 10 minutes.

Prepare a 9" x 13" casserole dish for freezing. See instructions for the casserole method in Chapter 1, or use an aluminum pan. Layer the bottom of the dish with the chicken, and top with frozen broccoli. Pour sauce over the broccoli and chicken. Top with bacon, then cheese. Freeze using casserole freezing method.

Reheating Instructions

Following the casserole method, defrost casserole in the refrigerator overnight. Cover, and cook at 350°F for 1 hour–1 hour 15 minutes until chicken is fully cooked. To cook casserole frozen, cover and cook 2 hours–2 hours 15 minutes at 350°F.

PER SERVING

Calories: 496 | Fat: 29g | Protein: 53g | Sodium: 1058mg | Carbohydrates: 5g | Fiber: 0g

Cheese and Rice Enchiladas with Salsa Verde

For variety, add diced chicken to the dish. Add 1–2 cups cooked shredded chicken when you add the rice, and decrease the cheese in the filling to ¼–½ cup.

INGREDIENTS | SERVES 4–6

1 red bell pepper, chopped

1 onion, chopped

1 clove garlic, minced

2 tablespoons olive oil

1 (10-ounce) can Ro-Tel tomatoes

1 cup enchilada sauce, divided

2 cups rice, cooked

2 cups shredded Cheddar cheese, divided

¼ cup chopped fresh cilantro

Salsa Verde (Chapter 13)

Freezing Day

In a skillet, sauté the red pepper and onion in olive oil until vegetables are tender-crisp. The vegetables should just begin to get tender, but still retain a crisp texture. Add the garlic and sauté 1 minute more. Add Ro-Tel tomatoes, ½ cup enchilada sauce, rice, 1 cup Cheddar cheese, and cilantro. Mix well and heat 5–10 minutes until cheese melts.

Prepare a 9" x 13" casserole dish for freezing. See instructions for the casserole method in Chapter 1, or use an aluminum pan. Cover the bottom of the casserole dish with remaining enchilada sauce. Fill each flour tortilla with rice and cheese mixture. Roll it up, and place it seam side down in the casserole dish. Sprinkle each enchilada with cheese, then spoon Salsa Verde over each enchilada.

Reheating Instructions

Following the casserole method, defrost casserole in the refrigerator overnight. Cover the casserole with aluminum foil and bake at 350°F for 30–35 minutes. Remove cover during the last 10 minutes of cooking time.

PER SERVING
Calories: 303 | Fat: 17g | Protein: 14g | Sodium: 474mg | Carbohydrates: 24g | Fiber: 2g

Chile Rellenos Casserole

This dish could be considered a short-cut Chile Rellenos Casserole. For a more authentic flavor, use fresh Anaheim or Poblano chilies instead of canned green chilies.

INGREDIENTS | SERVES 4–6

Cooking spray

2 (5.75-ounce) cans whole green chilies, drained

½ cup shredded Cheddar cheese

1 (2.25-ounce) can black olives

6 eggs

1 cup milk

2 tablespoons flour

4 tablespoons fresh cilantro, chopped

¼ teaspoon paprika

1 cup shredded Cheddar cheese (used on reheating day)

1 (8-ounce) can enchilada sauce (used on reheating day)

Roasting Fresh Poblano Peppers for Chile Rellenos

You may roast them over an open gas flame, in an earthenware pan, or under a broiler. Roast the peppers until the skins are evenly charred. Place fresh roasted peppers in a plastic bag to "sweat" for 15 minutes to make them easier to peel. Peel off charred skin under running water.

Freezing Day

Prepare a 9" x 13" casserole dish for freezing. See instructions for the casserole method in Chapter 1, or use an aluminum pan. Spray the pan (or plastic wrap if you are flash freezing) with cooking spray. Place half the chilies on the bottom of the pan. Top with the cheese and olives. Place the other half of chilies on top. In separate bowl, whisk together the eggs, milk, flour, cilantro, and paprika. Pour over the top of the chilies. Following the casserole method, wrap the casserole well and freeze.

Reheating Instructions

Following the casserole method, defrost casserole in the refrigerator overnight. Bake at 350°F for 25 minutes. Remove from oven. Add 1 cup shredded Cheddar cheese to the top of the casserole, and pour the remaining enchilada sauce over the cheese. Return to oven for 15 minutes.

PER SERVING
Calories: 317 | Fat: 24g | Protein: 19g | Sodium: 667mg | Carbohydrates: 8g | Fiber: 0g

Chicken and Mashed Potato Pie

Flash freeze this dish before wrapping it. Place the pie on a baking sheet and put in freezer for 2–3 hours. Once frozen, wrap well with plastic wrap and remove plastic before defrosting. By following these tips, the potatoes will not stick to the plastic wrap.

INGREDIENTS | SERVES 6

Easy Pie Crust (Chapter 15)

Mashed Potatoes (Chapter 11)

2 pounds boneless chicken breast, cubed

Poultry seasoning to taste

1 (10.75-ounce) can condensed cream of chicken soup

¼ cup milk

1 (14.5-ounce) can mixed vegetables, drained

Salt and pepper to taste

½ cup freshly grated Parmesan cheese (used on reheating day)

Freezing Day

Prepare pie crust and mashed potatoes. Put chicken in a large saucepan and cover with water. Add poultry seasoning to the water. Simmer for 30–40 minutes until fully cooked. In bowl, mix cooked chicken, cream of chicken soup, milk, mixed vegetables, salt, and pepper. Add ¼ cup more milk if needed. Put chicken and vegetables in the pie crust. Spoon mashed potatoes over the chicken and vegetables, covering completely. Flash freeze, then wrap well.

Reheating Instructions

Defrost fully in the refrigerator overnight. Bake at 375°F for 30–35 minutes until fully heated through. Sprinkle Parmesan cheese over pie during last 10 minutes of cooking.

PER SERVING
Calories: 443 | Fat: 17g | Protein: 42g | Sodium: 906mg | Carbohydrates: 27g | Fiber: 1g

Breakfast Enchiladas

NO DEFROSTING NEEDED!

INGREDIENTS | SERVES 6–8

½ cup green onions, chopped

2 cups ham

2 tablespoons butter

10 flour tortillas

2½ cups shredded Cheddar cheese, divided

1 cup milk

1 tablespoon flour

1 cup half and half

6 eggs, beaten

¼ teaspoon yellow mustard

¼ teaspoon salt

⅛ teaspoon pepper

Company for Breakfast

Along with the Breakfast Enchiladas, you can give your guests a variety of foods and drinks to enjoy. Have available cut-up fruit such as oranges, apples, pineapple, or melons, as well as a selection of mini muffins. For beverages serve water, fresh squeezed orange juice, tea, and coffee.

Freezing Day

Prepare a 9" x 13" casserole dish for freezing. See instructions for the casserole method (Chapter 1), or use an aluminum pan. In a skillet, sauté green onions and ham in butter 5–6 minutes. Lay a tortilla flat on a plate, and spoon ham and onion mixture down the middle of the tortilla. Top with Cheddar cheese. Roll up the tortilla and place in casserole dish, seam side down. Repeat with all tortillas. In a measuring cup, mix milk with flour. Pour into a food processor with the half and half, eggs, mustard, salt, and pepper. Mix until smooth. Pour the egg mixture over the tortillas. Cover and refrigerate 6–8 hours. Bake covered at 350°F for 25 minutes. Remove from oven and cool. Sprinkle top of casserole with remaining Cheddar cheese. Freeze.

Reheating Instructions

Following the casserole method instructions, defrost casserole in the refrigerator overnight. Heat covered at 350°F for 30 minutes, or until casserole is fully cooked. To cook casserole frozen, add 40 minutes–1 hour to the defrosted cooking time.

PER SERVING

Calories: 490 | Fat: 32g | Protein: 24g | Sodium: 910mg | Carbohydrates: 27g | Fiber: 1g

Vegetable and Pork Chop Casserole

This one-dish meal is made with butter beans, which are closely related to lima beans. You may substitute these beans for cannellini beans.

INGREDIENTS | SERVES 2–4

1 (14-ounce) bag frozen green beans
1 (8-ounce) fresh mushrooms, sliced
1 (15-ounce) can diced tomatoes
1 (15-ounce) can butter beans, drained
4 1"-thick boneless pork chops
½ teaspoon salt
½ teaspoon black pepper
4 tablespoons olive oil
½ cup cooking sherry
2 teaspoons butter
1 (10.75-ounce) can cream of potato soup
3 tablespoons Dijon mustard
2 tablespoons tomato paste

Freezing Day

Prepare a 6-quart casserole dish for freezing. See instructions for the casserole method (Chapter 1). In a large bowl, combine green beans, mushrooms, tomatoes, and butter beans and put in bottom of casserole dish. Season pork chops with salt and pepper. Cook in skillet over medium-high heat in 4 tablespoons olive oil and brown for 3–4 minutes on each side. Place on top of vegetables in casserole dish. Deglaze pan with sherry and add butter to resulting mixture. Stir until butter dissolves. Add potato soup, Dijon mustard, and tomato paste. Immediately pour over pork chops. Following the casserole method, cover casserole tightly and freeze.

Reheating Instructions

Following the casserole method, defrost casserole in refrigerator 24 hours. Bake covered at 325°F for 1 hour 15 minutes.

PER SERVING
Calories: 615 | Fat: 33g | Protein: 31g | Sodium: 869mg | Carbohydrates: 43g | Fiber: 9g

Pork Chop and Rice Casserole

Consommé is a clarified stock, meaning all the fat has been removed, making it much clearer than broth or other stock. Campbell's Soup sells a beef consommé in the soup section of the grocery store.

INGREDIENTS | SERVES 4

4 pork chops
Salt and pepper to taste
2 tablespoons olive oil
2 cloves garlic, minced
1 (10.5-ounce) can beef consommé
½ cup rice, uncooked
1 onion, sliced
1 green pepper, sliced
1 tomato, sliced

Flavorful Pork Chops

Pork chops tend to dry out when cooking, as they have little marbled fat. For the juiciest and most flavorful pork chops, use thick cut chops with the bone in. Cook to an internal temperature of 170°F, being careful not to overcook.

Freezing Day

Prepare a 9" x 13" casserole dish for freezing. See instructions for the casserole method (Chapter 1), or use an aluminum pan. Season the pork chops on both sides with salt and pepper. In a skillet over medium-high heat, brown chops in olive oil for 3–4 minutes per side. Remove chops. Sauté garlic in same skillet until it is tender, 1–2 minutes. Remove from heat. Pour the beef consommé into skillet and scrape the bottom of the skillet mixing in all flavors with the consommé. Put the raw rice in the bottom of the casserole dish and lay the pork chops on top of the rice. Layer the vegetables on top of the pork chops. Pour consommé over everything. Wrap tightly according to the casserole method and freeze.

Reheating Instructions

Following the casserole method, defrost casserole in refrigerator 24 hours. Cover the dish tightly and bake at 350°F for 1 hour, 30 minutes.

PER SERVING
Calories: 416 | Fat: 28g | Protein: 20g | Sodium: 50mg | Carbohydrates: 19g | Fiber: 1g

Beef and Green Chilies Mexican Casserole

This casserole is served spooned over Sweet Cornbread (Chapter 12). Try it with picante sauce, sour cream, and extra Cheddar cheese on the side.

INGREDIENTS | SERVES 6–8

1½ pounds ground beef

1 onion, chopped

1 green pepper, chopped

1 clove garlic, minced

1 (15-ounce) can kidney beans, drained

1 (16-ounce) can chopped tomatoes, drained

1 (10-ounce) can Ro-Tel tomatoes

1 (4.5-ounce) can green chilies, drained

3 tablespoon chili sauce

½ cup shredded Cheddar cheese, divided

½ teaspoon salt, or to taste

1 cup shredded Cheddar cheese (used on reheating day)

1 batch Sweet Cornbread (Chapter 12) (used on reheating day)

Freezing Day

In skillet, brown the ground beef. After 4 minutes of browning, add the onion and green pepper. Cook an additional 3–6 minutes until meat is fully browned and vegetables are tender. Add garlic and cook 1 more minute. Drain pan. Stir in kidney beans, tomatoes, Ro-Tel tomatoes, green chilies, chili sauce, ½ cup Cheddar cheese, and salt. Mix well, and remove from heat to cool. Freeze in a freezer bag.

Reheating Instructions

Defrost meat mixture in the refrigerator overnight and spread it in the bottom of a casserole dish. Top with 1 cup Cheddar cheese and bake at 350°F for 30 minutes. Prepare Sweet Cornbread according to recipe. To serve, slice each piece of cornbread in half from side to side. Spoon the meat mixture on top of each half of cornbread. Top with additional cheese and sour cream, if desired.

PER SERVING
Calories: 693 | Fat: 29g | Protein: 45g | Sodium: 799mg | Carbohydrates: 62g | Fiber: 13g

Easy Mac and Meat Casserole

Whenever using pasta for a freezer meal, always undercook the pasta. If it is fully cooked before freezing and put with other food, it will absorb liquid and become mushy once defrosted.

INGREDIENTS | SERVES 6

1½ pounds ground beef

½ onion, chopped

½ green pepper, chopped

2 cloves garlic, minced

1 (28-ounce) can diced tomatoes

1½ teaspoons Italian seasoning

½ pound elbow macaroni

1 cup Cheddar cheese, shredded (used on reheating day)

¼ cup Parmesan cheese (used on reheating day)

Homemade Italian Seasoning

You can make a very fine homemade Italian seasoning by mixing equal parts thyme, oregano, savory, marjoram, basil, sage, rosemary, parsley, and garlic powder. Mix well and store in an airtight container. Salt is not added as most recipes will call for salt in addition to Italian seasoning.

Freezing Day

In skillet brown ground beef, onion, and green pepper 7–10 minutes until meat is fully cooked. Add garlic and cook an additional minute. Add tomatoes and Italian seasoning. Mix well. Remove from heat. Cook elbow macaroni in boiling water for 5 minutes. Drain. Stir macaroni into ground beef mixture and freeze in a freezer bag.

Reheating Instructions

Defrost macaroni and meat mixture in the refrigerator overnight. Put into a casserole dish and top with Cheddar cheese and Parmesan cheese. Bake at 350°F for 30–45 minutes until heated through and cheese is melted on top.

PER SERVING
Calories: 520 | Fat: 28g | Protein: 42g | Sodium: 637mg | Carbohydrates: 23g | Fiber: 3g

Bierock Casserole

A Bierock (pronounced beer-rock) is a baked pastry-sandwich traditionally stuffed with meat, cabbage, and onions. This casserole is a deconstructed Bierock— it has been rearranged into an easy and delicious casserole the whole family will love.

INGREDIENTS | SERVES 6

1 pound ground beef
1 pound ground pork sausage
1 onion, diced
1 clove garlic, minced
1 (16-ounce) package phyllo dough
1 head cabbage, shredded
8 slices Swiss cheese
Butter-flavored cooking spray

Freezing Day

In skillet, brown ground beef, ground pork sausage, and onion 10–15 minutes until meat is fully cooked. Add garlic and cook an additional minute. Drain. Place a layer of phyllo dough in the bottom of greased casserole dish that has been prepared for the freezer (or use a disposable aluminum pan). See instructions for the casserole method (Chapter 1). Spread shredded cabbage on top of dough, then meat mixture on top of cabbage. Top meat mixture with the slices of Swiss cheese. Top Swiss cheese with 4 layers of phyllo dough, spraying each layer with butter-flavored cooking spray. Cover tightly according to the casserole method instructions, and freeze.

Reheating Instructions

Following the casserole method, defrost casserole in refrigerator overnight and bring to room temperature. Bake at 425°F for 20–30 minutes until it is hot and phyllo dough is nicely browned.

PER SERVING
Calories: 716 | Fat: 38g | Protein: 46g | Sodium: 879mg | Carbohydrates: 43g | Fiber: 2g

Salisbury Steak Dinner Casserole

NO DEFROSTING NEEDED!

INGREDIENTS | SERVES 6

4 medium potatoes

⅔ cup half and half

2 tablespoons butter

3 tablespoons onion, chopped

¼ cup fresh mushrooms, chopped

2 tablespoons butter

1 pound ground beef

1 egg

3 tablespoons breadcrumbs

2 teaspoons Ground Beef Seasoning Mix (Chapter 13)

¼ cup flour

3 tablespoons vegetable oil

Gravy for Any Occasion made with beef broth (Chapter 15)

Freezer Breadcrumbs

Start a bag in the freezer for bread. Add the heels of bread no one wants to eat to the bag, and any crusts you cut off your children's sandwiches. Once you have gathered a lot of bread, let it defrost at room temperature for about an hour, then put it into a food processor and turn it into breadcrumbs. Return the breadcrumbs to the freezer until needed.

Freezing Day

Peel potatoes and cut into large chunks. Boil until potatoes are fork tender, about 15 minutes. Drain. Mash potatoes. Add half and half and butter to the potatoes and mix well. In skillet, sauté onion and mushrooms 5–10 minutes in butter until tender. Transfer onion and mushrooms to a bowl and mix with ground beef, egg, breadcrumbs, and Ground Beef Seasoning Mix. Mix well and form into 4 patties. Put flour onto a plate, and coat each side of patties with flour. In a skillet, cook the patties in oil 3–4 minutes per side over medium-high heat. Remove from skillet and set aside. Make the Gravy for Any Occasion. Prepare a 9" x 13" casserole dish for freezing. See instructions for the casserole method (Chapter 1), or use an aluminum pan. Put a layer of gravy on the bottom of the casserole dish. Add patties in a single layer on the bottom of the casserole dish. Pour gravy over the top. Put ¼ of the mashed potatoes on top of each steak. Wrap the casserole dish according to the casserole method and freeze.

Reheating Instructions

Following the casserole method, defrost casserole in the refrigerator for 24 hours and heat at 375°F for 30–45 minutes or until heated through. Or, bake frozen casserole at 375°F for 1 hour 10 minutes–1 hour 30 minutes or until desired temperature is reached.

PER SERVING
Calories: 664 | Fat: 40g | Protein: 29g | Sodium: 259mg | Carbohydrates: 48g | Fiber: 4g

Chicken and Stuffing Casserole

Cooking wine is often used by cooks who either do not drink wine or who don't use it frequently in cooking. If you substitute cooking wine for wine, the flavor of the dish will be more salty since preservatives are added to cooking wine to lengthen its shelf life.

INGREDIENTS | SERVES 6

6 small boneless, skinless chicken breasts

6 tomato slices

6 slices Swiss cheese

1 (14-ounce) can chicken broth

¼ cup wine

3 cups dry seasoned stuffing mix

¾ cup butter (used on reheating day)

Freezing Day

Prepare a 9" x 13" casserole dish for freezing. See instructions for the casserole method (Chapter 1), or use an aluminum pan. Place the 6 chicken breasts on the bottom of the casserole. Top each one with a slice of tomato, then a slice of cheese. In a large bowl, mix the chicken broth with the wine and pour over chicken. Top the dish with the stuffing mix. Wrap tightly following the casserole method and freeze.

Reheating Instructions

Following the casserole method, defrost the casserole in the refrigerator overnight. Melt butter and pour over the top of the stuffing. Bake at 350°F for 1 hour or until the chicken is fully cooked. Cover with foil after 45 minutes.

PER SERVING
Calories: 794 | Fat: 33g | Protein: 34g | Sodium: 2281mg | Carbohydrates: 89g | Fiber: 4g

Chicken Divan Casserole

NO DEFROSTING NEEDED!

INGREDIENTS | SERVES 6–8

2 cups Basic Seasoned Chicken (Chapter 15)

2½ cups cooked broccoli

2 (4½-ounce) cans sliced mushrooms

1 (8-ounce) can sliced water chestnuts

½ cup butter

6 tablespoons flour

1 cup chicken broth

½ cup cream

3 tablespoons white wine

Salt and pepper to taste

¼–½ cup toasted almonds, to taste

Wine for Cooking

Many cooks do not like using cooking wine because of its inferior quality and additives. To keep good wine on hand for cooking, make your own wine cubes. Pour a bottle of wine into ice cube trays and freeze, then transfer to a freezer bag. When a recipe calls for wine, add wine cubes to your dish.

Freezing Day

Prepare a 9" x 13" casserole dish for freezing. See instructions for the casserole method (Chapter 1), or use an aluminum pan. Combine chicken and broccoli and put on bottom of casserole dish. Add mushrooms and water chestnuts on top of chicken and broccoli. In a saucepan, melt butter over medium heat. Stir in flour and mix well. Add chicken broth, cream, and wine. Continue to stir about 5 minutes until sauce thickens. Add salt and pepper to taste. Pour sauce over chicken and broccoli. Top with toasted almonds. Wrap tightly according to the casserole method, and freeze.

Reheating Instructions

Following the casserole method, defrost casserole in the refrigerator overnight and bake at 350°F for 30–45 minutes until warm throughout. Or, bake frozen casserole at 350°F for 1 hour 10 minutes–1 hour 30 minutes until desired temperature is reached.

PER SERVING
Calories: 237 | Fat: 17g | Protein: 12g | Sodium: 219mg | Carbohydrates: 11g | Fiber: 2g

Scalloped Potatoes with Ham

Have you ever wondered how to cut thin slices of potatoes?
One option is a food processor with the slicing blade. A second option is a vegetable mandolin,
a handheld utensil that allows you to cut uniform slices more easily than with a knife.

INGREDIENTS | SERVES 6

4 large potatoes
6 tablespoons butter
1 small onion, chopped
3 tablespoons flour
1¼ cups milk
3 cups cooked ham
1 cup shredded Cheddar cheese

Freezing Day

Peel potatoes and slice into ⅛"–¼" slices. In skillet, melt butter and sauté onion 5–10 minutes until it is tender. Stir in flour and mix well. It should very quickly form a paste. In separate saucepan, heat milk on medium-low heat for 5 minutes. Stir hot milk into the skillet with the paste. Continue to whisk over medium heat 5–10 minutes until the sauce thickens. Prepare a 9" x 13" casserole dish for freezing. See instructions for the casserole method (Chapter 1), or use an aluminum pan. Put potatoes and ham in the casserole dish. Stir in prepared sauce and Cheddar cheese and mix well. Cover with foil and bake at 350°F for 35–40 minutes. Let cool, wrap tightly, and freeze.

Reheating Instructions

Following the casserole method, defrost casserole in the refrigerator overnight. Bake at 350°F for 40–45 minutes or until it is fully heated.

PER SERVING
Calories: 477 | Fat: 28g | Protein: 17g | Sodium: 857mg | Carbohydrates: 39g | Fiber: 4g

Hamburger Casserole

The Ground Beef Seasoning Mix (Chapter 13) has a bit of cayenne pepper in it, but just enough for a little zing rather than a lot of heat. This dish would taste delicious with a spicy twist so, if that is your pleasure, add more cayenne.

INGREDIENTS | SERVES 6–8

2 pounds ground beef

1 onion, chopped

2 green bell peppers, chopped

Ground Beef Seasoning Mix (Chapter 13)

4 eggs, beaten

4 cups whole kernel corn (canned or frozen)

4 tomatoes, sliced

2 cups crushed cornflakes (used on reheating day)

1 stick butter, melted (used on reheating day)

How to Freeze Whole Kernel Corn

When corn is in season, buy it cheap and freeze it for the whole year. Husk the corn and remove silk. Blanch in boiling water 4–6 minutes, then put in bowl of ice water 4–6 minutes. Drain, then cut the kernels off the cob. Put in a freezer bag, separate the kernels from each other, and freeze.

Freezing Day

In skillet, brown ground beef, onion, and green peppers 7–10 minutes until ground beef is fully cooked. Drain. Stir in Ground Beef Seasoning Mix. Add eggs and mix well. Remove from heat. Prepare a 9" x 13" casserole dish for freezing. See instructions for the casserole method (Chapter 1), or use an aluminum pan. Layer the bottom of the casserole dish with 2 cups of corn. Add half of the meat mixture on top of the corn, followed by a layer of sliced tomatoes. Repeat the layers. Wrap well according to the casserole method and freeze.

Reheating Instructions

Following the casserole method, defrost casserole in the refrigerator overnight. Top with crushed cornflakes, and pour melted butter over the top of the cornflakes. Bake at 350°F for 45 minutes.

PER SERVING
Calories: 541 | Fat: 35g | Protein: 37g | Sodium: 270mg | Carbohydrates: 26g | Fiber: 4g

Spicy Sausage Breakfast Casserole

This breakfast casserole can be tailor made to suit your tastes! For instance, substitute ground beef for the sausage, and add a layer of bacon or ham. Switch the Cheddar cheese for pepper jack, and add a tomato or broccoli layer. The possibilities are endless.

INGREDIENTS | SERVES 6–8

1 pound ground sausage, hot

1 small onion, chopped

½ green bell pepper, chopped

1 loaf Italian bread

1–2 cups shredded Cheddar cheese, to taste

1 (4-ounce) can chopped green chilies

6 eggs

3 cups milk

1 teaspoon yellow mustard

½ teaspoon salt

¼ teaspoon cayenne pepper, or to taste

Freezing Day

Prepare a 9" x 13" casserole dish for freezing. See instructions for the casserole method (Chapter 1), or use an aluminum pan. In a skillet, brown the sausage, onion, and bell pepper 8–10 minutes until the sausage is fully cooked. Drain and remove from heat. Cut the bread into 1" slices and layer on the bottom of the casserole dish. Layer the meat on top of the bread, followed by the cheese, then the green chilies. In a large mixing bowl, add the eggs, milk, mustard, salt, and cayenne pepper and mix to combine. Pour the egg mixture over the casserole layers. Wrap tightly according to the casserole method and freeze.

Reheating Instructions

Following the casserole method, defrost casserole in the refrigerator overnight. Bake at 350°F for 45 minutes–1 hour until the egg is fully cooked and a knife inserted in the dish's middle comes out clean.

PER SERVING

Calories: 454 | Fat: 30g | Protein: 24g | Sodium: 888mg | Carbohydrates: 21g | Fiber: 1g

CHAPTER 9

Lunches

Spicy Taco Roll-ups

NO DEFROSTING NEEDED!

INGREDIENTS | SERVES 6–8

1 pound ground beef

1 cup water

Taco Seasoning Mix (Chapter 13)

¾ cup shredded Cheddar cheese

1 (16-ounce) can refried beans

1 (14.5-ounce) can diced tomatoes with green chilies, drained

3 packages refrigerator crescent rolls

Hold the Heat

It is easy to make these Spicy Taco Roll-ups without the hot spices. First, substitute plain diced tomatoes for the diced tomatoes with green chilies. Don't add cayenne pepper when you make the Taco Seasoning Mix. Also, instead of 1 tablespoon of chili powder, substitute 1½ teaspoons cumin (in addition to cumin already listed in recipe), and 1½ teaspoons oregano.

Freezing Day

In skillet over medium heat, brown ground beef. Add water and Taco Seasoning. Bring to a gentle boil, and cook additional 15 minutes. Mix in the refried beans, cheddar cheese, and tomatoes with green chilies. Immediately remove from heat. Open the crescent rolls, and divide package into 4 rectangles. Smooth together the perforation that runs diagonally across each of the rectangles. Roll or press out with your fingers each rectangle so it measures approximately 4" x 4". Cut in half and make two 2" x 4" rectangles. In the center of each rectangle, spread 2 tablespoons of meat mixture. Roll the rectangle the long way (so it looks like a fat pencil) and flash freeze.

Reheating Instructions

Defrost rolls in the refrigerator. Bake at 375°F for 11–13 minutes, or until golden brown. Bake frozen rolls at 375°F for 20–25 minutes, or until golden brown.

PER SERVING
Calories: 380 | Fat: 17g | Protein: 26g | Sodium: 759mg | Carbohydrates: 30g | Fiber: 5g

Chicken Verde Quesadillas

NO DEFROSTING NEEDED!

INGREDIENTS | SERVES 2–4

3 cups cubed chicken, uncooked

1 tablespoon vegetable oil

1 onion, coarsely diced

1½ cups green tomatillo (jarred)

3 tablespoons olive oil

Salt and pepper to taste

1 (8-count) package flour tortillas

1 cup Monterey jack cheese, shredded

2–3 tablespoons vegetable oil (used on reheating day)

Chicken Verde Two Ways

Prepare a large batch of Chicken Verde and make it into two different meals: Quesadillas and Chicken Verde Wraps (Chapter 4).

Freezing Day

In a large skillet over medium-high heat, sauté the chicken 4–5 minutes in oil until white in color. Add the onion and sauté 8–10 minutes until most of the juices have disappeared. Drain any remaining juices. Add the tomatillo and cook over low heat until the mixture thickens, 20–30 minutes. Season the mixture with salt and pepper. Place spoonfuls of Chicken Verde on one half of a flour tortilla, and sprinkle with cheese. Fold the tortilla in half-covering the filling. In a large skillet, cook quesadillas in oil over medium heat for 2 minutes on each side. Let cool and flash freeze. Once frozen, transfer to a freezer bag.

Reheating Instructions

Defrost each frozen quesadilla in a microwave for 1 minute. In a skillet over medium heat, add 1 teaspoon vegetable oil. Add quesadilla to skillet and cook on each side 2 minutes or until quesadilla is browned.

PER SERVING
Calories: 437 | Fat: 28g | Protein: 26g | Sodium: 394mg | Carbohydrates: 18g | Fiber: 1g

Mini French Bread Pizza

NO DEFROSTING NEEDED!

INGREDIENTS | SERVES 4

1 loaf fresh French bread
Homemade Pizza Sauce (Chapter 15)
Mozzarella cheese
Desired pizza toppings

Freezing Day

Cut French bread into 1"–2" slices. Toast bread and top with Homemade Pizza Sauce, cheese, and pizza toppings. Flash freeze and transfer to freezer bag.

Reheating Instructions

Put frozen pizza on a cookie sheet and bake at 375°F for 10–15 minutes, or until cheese has melted.

PER SERVING
Calories: 492 | Fat: 23g | Protein: 21g | Sodium: 790mg | Carbohydrates: 54g | Fiber: 5g

Salmon Patties with Dill Sauce

You can vary this recipe by adding 2 tablespoons of capers and a tablespoon of Dijon mustard. Use more or less according to taste. Mix the capers and mustard directly into the salmon patties. Try the salmon with Dill Sauce (Chapter 14).

INGREDIENTS | SERVES 4

1 (14.75-ounce) can pink salmon, flaked
½ cup breadcrumbs
1 egg
1 small onion, chopped
1 teaspoon dill
1 tablespoon olive oil (used on reheating day)
Dill Sauce (Chapter 14) (used on reheating day)

Freezing Day

Mix salmon, breadcrumbs, egg, onion, and dill. Form into patties and flash freeze. Transfer to a freezer bag.

Reheating Instructions

Defrost patties in the refrigerator overnight. In skillet over medium heat, heat the oil and cook the patties until they are well browned, about 5 minutes on each side. Top patties with Dill Sauce and serve.

PER SERVING
Calories: 240 | Fat: 12g | Protein: 20g | Sodium: 586mg | Carbohydrates: 10g | Fiber: 1g

Chicken and Bean Enchiladas

Feta cheese is a white cheese with a salty and tangy flavor.
It is a delicious alternative to the cheeses typically found in enchiladas.

INGREDIENTS | SERVES 4

1 pound boneless chicken

½ teaspoon cumin

½ teaspoon salt

¼ teaspoon pepper

1½ tablespoons vegetable oil

1 (15-ounce) can black beans, drained

½ cup enchilada sauce

½ cup fresh cilantro, chopped

8 flour tortillas (used on reheating day)

8 ounces feta cheese (used on reheating day)

Freezing Day

Cut chicken into bite-sized slices, and season with cumin, salt. and pepper. Stir-fry chicken 4–5 minutes in vegetable oil until the chicken is no longer pink in the center. Set aside to cool. Transfer to quart-sized freezer bag. In food processor, mix the beans and enchilada sauce until smooth. Stir in cilantro. Transfer to a separate quart-sized freezer bag. Place both quart-sized freezer bags into a one gallon freezer bag. Freeze.

Reheating Instructions

Defrost in the refrigerator overnight. Individually heat the beans and chicken in the microwave for 1 minute. Stir, then heat an additional 2–3 minutes until desired temperature is reached. Wrap the flour tortillas in moist paper towels and heat in microwave for 1 minute. Spread the bean mixture on each tortilla and top with chicken. Roll up tortilla, and sprinkle with feta cheese.

PER SERVING
Calories: 555 | Fat: 25g | Protein: 41g | Sodium: 1491mg | Carbohydrates: 40g | Fiber: 2g

Chicken Fajitas

Have toppings like shredded Cheddar cheese, sour cream, and jalapeño peppers available for the fajitas. They also taste great with Garden Salsa (Chapter 13).

INGREDIENTS | SERVES 6

2 pounds boneless chicken, sliced thin

2 tablespoons cilantro, chopped

¼ cup olive oil

¼ balsamic vinegar

¼ cup Worcestershire sauce

4 tablespoons lime juice

1 clove garlic, minced

1 teaspoon Mrs. Dash

6 drops hot sauce

3 tablespoons olive oil (used on reheating day)

1 onion, cut into rings (used on reheating day)

1 green bell pepper, thinly sliced (used on reheating day)

10–12 flour tortillas (used on reheating day)

Save the Citrus!

After you have squeezed your oranges, lemons, and limes, save the peels to make zest. Wash the peels well and dry them. Put them into a freezer bag and freeze for up to 3 months. The next time a recipe calls for zest, you can go right to your frozen rind and grate the amount needed.

Freezing Day

Put sliced chicken and cilantro in the bottom of a freezer bag. In a food processor, combine olive oil, balsamic vinegar, Worcestershire sauce, lime juice, garlic, Mrs. Dash, and hot sauce. Pour marinade over the chicken. Freeze.

Reheating Instructions

Defrost chicken in the refrigerator overnight and discard marinade. Heat skillet over high heat, then add oil and chicken. Stir-fry chicken, onions, and green peppers 5–10 minutes until chicken is fully cooked and vegetables are to desired tenderness. Wrap the flour tortillas in moist paper towels and heat in microwave for 1 minute. To serve, fill each tortilla with chicken, vegetables, and any other desired toppings and wrap burrito style.

PER SERVING
Calories: 474 | Fat: 19g | Protein: 41g | Sodium: 453mg | Carbohydrates: 34g | Fiber: 2g

Ham and Pesto Burritos

NO DEFROSTING NEEDED!

INGREDIENTS | SERVES 6–8

½ cup Basil and Pine Nut Pesto (Chapter 13)
12 flour tortillas
1 cup Homemade Pizza Sauce (Chapter 15)
8 ounces sliced deli ham
2 cups shredded mozzarella cheese

Get Creative

These burritos are delicious made with ham, but you can use other ingredients as well. Try filling the tortilla with roasted chicken and tomatoes or leftover roasted pork. Skip the pizza sauce and go vegetarian by filling it with green vegetables like broccoli or asparagus.

Freezing Day

Spread Basil and Pine Nut Pesto on flour tortilla, and top with Homemade Pizza Sauce, ham, and cheese. Roll up tortilla like a burrito and wrap with plastic wrap. Freeze.

Reheating Instructions

Microwave frozen burrito 30 seconds, turn, and heat an additional 30 seconds. In oven, heat frozen burrito 30–35 minutes at 375°F. Heat defrosted burrito 15–20 minutes at 375°F.

PER SERVING
Calories: 330 | Fat: 14g | Protein: 19g | Sodium: 749mg | Carbohydrates: 32g | Fiber: 3g

Mini Bagel Pizzas

NO DEFROSTING NEEDED!

INGREDIENTS | YIELDS 40

20 mini bagels
1 cup Homemade Pizza Sauce (Chapter 15)
2 cups shredded mozzarella cheese
Desired pizza toppings

Freezing Day

Split apart the mini bagels. Lay each half on a cookie sheet, flat side up. Spread Homemade Pizza Sauce on each bagel, followed by cheese, and desired toppings. Flash freeze then transfer to a freezer bag.

Reheating Instructions

Bake frozen pizza bagels at 375°F for 20 minutes, or until cheese is melted on top.

PER SERVING
Calories: 58 | Fat: 1.5g | Protein: 3.5g | Sodium: 99mg | Carbohydrates: 8g | Fiber: 0.5g

Beef Taquitos

NO DEFROSTING NEEDED!

INGREDIENTS | SERVES 12

6–8 tablespoons vegetable oil, divided

48 corn tortillas

1 batch Italian Beef, shredded (Chapter 6)

2–3 cups Cheddar cheese, to taste

Working with Corn Tortillas

Dipping the tortillas in hot oil before you roll them not only softens the tortillas, but also brings out the corn flavor. If you'd like to cut down on calories, you can soften them in the microwave or in a tortilla warmer. To cut down on the oil, you can also spray the tortillas with cooking oil on both sides, then heat in the skillet.

Freezing Day

Heat enough vegetable oil to coat the bottom of the skillet. Using tongs, dip a corn tortilla in the hot oil for just a few seconds, and then turn it over. Hold it above the skillet so it can drain, then lay it on your work surface. Spoon the shredded beef onto half the tortilla and top with Cheddar cheese. Roll the tortilla up and place, seam side down, on a baking sheet. Flash freeze taquitos, then transfer to a freezer bag.

Reheating Instructions

Put frozen taquitos in the oven at 375°F for 10–15 minutes until they are fully heated. To microwave frozen taquitos, cook for 1 minute 30 seconds.

PER SERVING

Calories: 420 | Fat: 14g | Protein: 27g | Sodium: 913mg | Carbohydrates: 48g | Fiber: 4g

Chicken Tenders

NO DEFROSTING NEEDED!

INGREDIENTS | SERVES 4–6

2 pounds boneless, skinless chicken
  breasts
1 egg
¼ cup Dijon mustard
½ cup Italian-seasoned breadcrumbs
½ cup Parmesan cheese

An Effortless Lunch

These chicken tenders make a fast and
easy lunch. Try dicing them up once
cooked and serving them on top of a salad.

Freezing Day

Cut the chicken breasts in strips and pat dry with a
paper towel. In a shallow bowl, beat the egg then mix in
Dijon mustard. In another shallow bowl, mix
breadcrumbs and Parmesan cheese. Dip the chicken in
the egg mixture, then coat with breadcrumbs. Lay
breaded chicken on a lightly greased baking sheet. Bake
at 375°F for 15–20 minutes. Cool and flash freeze.
Transfer to freezer bag.

Reheating Instructions

Put frozen chicken tenders on a baking sheet. Cook
chicken at 400°F for 5–10 minutes or until heated
through.

PER SERVING
Calories: 423 | Fat: 12g | Protein: 62g | Sodium: 583mg |
Carbohydrates: 11g | Fiber: 0.5g

Meatball Sub

These individually wrapped subs make a hearty lunch, and are a great solution for a quick dinner. Keep extra sauce on hand for dipping.

INGREDIENTS | SERVES 4

4 hoagie rolls

2 cups mozzarella cheese

12 Basic Meatballs (Chapter 15)

2 cups Basic Marinara Sauce (Chapter 14)

All Plastic Bags Are Not Created Equal

When buying zip-top bags for freezing, don't skimp on quality. Quality applies in two areas: thickness of the bag and quality of the closure device. If the manufacturer does not specify thickness, you will have to go by feel. Don't use bags with the slider closure as they can more easily leak air, leading to freezer burn.

Freezing Day

Slice hoagie rolls in half lengthwise, about ⅓ of the way down from the top of the roll. Hollow out the bottom of the roll, leaving about ½" of bread. Put a layer of cheese in the bottom roll, followed by 3 meatballs, and cover with sauce. Top with more cheese. Put the top of the roll on, and wrap each sub in aluminum foil and freeze.

Reheating Instructions

Defrost the meatball sub in the refrigerator overnight. Bake sub on a baking sheet at 375°F for 15 minutes, or until desired temperature is reached.

PER SERVING

Calories: 667 | Fat: 31g | Protein: 49g | Sodium: 992mg | Carbohydrates: 46g | Fiber: 2g

Peanut Butter and Jelly Sandwich

These sandwiches can be packed frozen in a lunch box and taken on a picnic, or even a trip to the beach! Make them ahead of time and simplify your mornings.

INGREDIENTS | SERVES APPROXIMATELY 10

1 loaf sourdough bread
1 jar peanut butter
1 jar of your favorite jam

Freezing Day

Spread peanut butter all the way to the edge of one slice of bread. Spread jam on the other slice of bread, stopping ½" from the edge of bread. Make into a sandwich, wrap with foil, and freeze.

Reheating Instructions

Defrost in the refrigerator for several hours, or even in a lunchbox, and serve at room temperature.

PER SERVING
Calories: 327 | Fat: 10g | Protein: 10g | Sodium: 478mg | Carbohydrates: 51g | Fiber: 3g

South of the Border Chicken Sandwich

Serve these chicken sandwiches on a kaiser roll with sliced tomatoes, sliced red onions, avocados, and Dijon mustard for a lunch you are sure to enjoy.

INGREDIENTS | SERVES 4

⅔ cup vegetable oil
½ cup lime juice
4 tablespoons green chilies
2 tablespoons fresh cilantro
1 clove garlic, minced
½ teaspoon salt
¼ teaspoon pepper
4 boneless, skinless, chicken breasts

Freezing Day

In a bowl, combine oil, lime juice, green chilies, cilantro, garlic, salt, and pepper. Put chicken breasts in the bottom of a freezer bag. Pour marinade over chicken and freeze.

Reheating Instructions

Defrost chicken in the refrigerator overnight and discard marinade. Grill chicken over medium heat 12–15 minutes or until no longer pink. Slice chicken and place on buns.

PER SERVING
Calories: 448 | Fat: 30g | Protein: 20g | Sodium: 339mg | Carbohydrates: 2g | Fiber: 0g

Linguine with Ham

Not only is this meal delicious, it is a very inexpensive dish to make.
You can use it as either a main dish or as a side dish.

INGREDIENTS | SERVES 4–6

2 tablespoons olive oil

2 cloves garlic, minced

1 cup ham, sliced into thin strips

1 cup heavy cream

½ teaspoon black pepper

⅓ cup Parmesan cheese

1 (10-ounce) box linguine

1 cup frozen peas

Time-Saving Tip

Instead of preparing ham for just one recipe, such as Linguine with Ham, consider cooking an entire spiral-cut ham. The typical spiral-cut ham will provide not only ham for the linguine dish, but it will give you sliced ham for sandwiches, a hambone for soup, and both sliced and chunked ham for other recipes.

Freezing Day

In skillet over medium heat, heat olive oil and sauté garlic and ham for 5–6 minutes. Add cream and pepper and cook for 5 minutes. Stir in Parmesan cheese, and immediately remove from heat to cool. In a large pot, cook linguine al dente. Mix together sauce with linguine. Stir in frozen peas and immediately freeze in a freezer bag or plastic container.

Reheating Instructions

Defrost linguine and sauce in the refrigerator overnight. Heat in a saucepan over medium heat 15–20 minutes until dish reaches desired temperature.

PER SERVING
Calories: 420 | Fat: 23g | Protein: 16g | Sodium: 481mg | Carbohydrates: 40g | Fiber: 3g

Black Bean and Corn Wraps

If you prefer corn tortillas to flour tortillas, you have a couple of options. You can bake corn taco shells in the oven and fill with the bean mixture, or heat corn tortillas in a skillet with a bit of oil to soften, then wrap.

INGREDIENTS | SERVES 4

1 (15.5-ounce) can black beans, drained

1 (15.5-ounce) can whole kernel corn, drained

1 (14-ounce) can tomatoes, diced

2 tablespoons tomato paste

3 tablespoons water

2 tablespoons fresh basil, chopped

Salt to taste

1 (8-count) package flour tortillas (used on reheating day)

Freezing Day

Mix all ingredients together, except the tortillas, and freeze in a freezer bag.

Reheating Instructions

Defrost bean mixture in the refrigerator overnight. Heat in a saucepan over medium heat 15–20 minutes or until it is desired temperature. Wrap the flour tortillas in moist paper towels and heat in microwave for 1 minute. Spoon bean mixture down the center of the tortillas. Fold up bottom and roll in sides to make a burrito.

PER SERVING
Calories: 531 | Fat: 5g | Protein: 26g | Sodium: 430mg | Carbohydrates: 101g | Fiber: 19g

Open-Faced Italian Sandwiches

NO DEFROSTING NEEDED!

INGREDIENTS | SERVES 2–4

1 pound ground beef

2 tablespoons onion, chopped

2 cloves garlic, minced

2 teaspoons Italian seasoning

2 tablespoons tomato paste

3–5 tablespoons water

1 loaf Italian bread

8 ounces cream cheese

1–2 cups mozzarella cheese, to taste

Substitute the Ground Beef

You can also make these sandwiches using the mouth-watering Italian Beef recipe found in Chapter 6, the slow cooker chapter.

Freezing Day

In skillet, brown ground beef and onion 7–10 minutes or until meat is thoroughly cooked. Add garlic and cook an additional minute. Drain. Stir in Italian seasoning, tomato paste, and water. Set aside to cool. Cut Italian bread into 1" slices. Spread cream cheese on each slice of bread. On each piece of bread, spread meat mixture over cream cheese, and top with mozzarella cheese. Flash freeze then transfer to freezer bag.

Reheating Instructions

Arrange frozen slices of bread on a baking sheet. Bake at 450°F for 8–12 minutes.

PER SERVING

Calories: 766 | Fat: 47g | Protein: 50g | Sodium: 634mg | Carbohydrates: 34g | Fiber: 2g

Cheeseburger Cups

NO DEFROSTING NEEDED!

INGREDIENTS | SERVES 8

3 (8-count) cans refrigerator biscuits

2 pounds ground beef

2 cloves garlic, minced

6 tablespoons ketchup

1 teaspoon mustard

24 dill pickle slices

2 cups Cheddar cheese

Fun to Make and Eat!

These fun little cups are a perfect after-school snack the kids can pop right into the microwave. They also make a fast and easy lunch on the go.

Freezing Day

Lightly grease 2 muffin tins. Put a biscuit in the bottom of each muffin cup and push the sides up to form the shape of a cup. In skillet, brown the ground beef 7–10 minutes or until meat is thoroughly cooked. Add garlic and cook an additional minute. Drain. Add ketchup and mustard, mix well, and remove from heat. Put a pickle on the bottom of each biscuit, and spoon meat mixture on top of the pickle. Top with cheese. Bake at 400°F for 10–12 minutes. Remove from oven and let cool in muffin tin. Once cool, put the muffin pans in freezer to flash freeze and then transfer to freezer bag.

Reheating Instructions

Bake frozen cups at 450°F for 8–10 minutes until hot. Or, microwave a single frozen cup for 1 minute–1 minute 15 seconds.

PER SERVING
Calories: 834 | Fat: 48g | Protein: 45g | Sodium: 1643mg | Carbohydrates: 55g | Fiber: 1g

Beef Croquettes

To cook the croquettes in a skillet instead of a deep fryer, shape the croquettes into patties.
Fry in about ½ cup of oil until they are well browned on both sides.

INGREDIENTS | SERVES 4–6

1½ pounds ground beef

Ground Beef Seasoning Mix (Chapter 13)

1 tablespoon butter

4 tablespoons flour

1 cup milk

1 tablespoon minced onion

1 cup flour

2 eggs

¼ cup milk

1 cup plain breadcrumbs

1 cup grated Parmesan cheese

1 quart oil for frying, or as needed

Freezing Day

In a skillet over medium heat, brown ground beef with seasoning mixed in. Set aside. In a large saucepan, melt butter. Add 4 tablespoons flour and mix. Add 1 cup milk and cook over medium heat, stirring constantly, until sauce thickens, 5–10 minutes. Add cooked meat and onion to the saucepan and mix well with the sauce. Chill in refrigerator for 1 hour. Put 1 cup flour on a shallow plate. In a small bowl, mix together 2 eggs and ¼ cup milk. On a second shallow plate, mix the breadcrumbs with the Parmesan cheese. Once meat mixture has chilled, form into pyramid shapes. Dip first into flour, then into egg mixture, then dredge with breadcrumb mixture. Put on a baking sheet lined with wax paper and flash freeze. Once frozen, transfer to freezer bag.

Reheating Instructions

Defrost croquettes in the refrigerator overnight and keep cold. Heat the oil in a deep-fryer to 385°F. Deep fry the croquettes 3–4 minutes until golden brown, and let drain on a paper towel.

PER SERVING
Calories: 614 | Fat: 40g | Protein: 45g | Sodium: 550mg | Carbohydrates: 36g | Fiber: 2g

Lemon Basil Grilled Chicken

*Have a supply of these marinated chicken breasts on hand for quick and easy meals.
Throw one on the grill for a fresh, delicious lunch. Enjoy it on a kaiser roll,
or slice it up and lay the chicken on top of a garden salad.*

INGREDIENTS | SERVES 6

6 boneless, skinless chicken breasts

2 tablespoons olive oil

¼ cup white wine

3 tablespoons fresh basil, chopped

¼ teaspoon salt

½ cup lemon juice

Lemon pepper to taste (used on reheating day)

Freezing Day

Put chicken in a freezer bag. In a bowl, combine the oil, wine, basil, salt, and lemon juice. Pour over chicken and freeze.

Reheating Instructions

Defrost chicken in the refrigerator overnight. Season with lemon pepper, then grill chicken over medium heat 12–15 minutes or until no longer pink.

PER SERVING
Calories: 150 | Fat: 7g | Protein: 20g | Sodium: 145mg | Carbohydrates: 0 | Fiber: 0g

Crab Quiche

NO DEFROSTING NEEDED!

INGREDIENTS | SERVES 4–6

1 9" unbaked pastry shell

1 tablespoon butter, softened

4 eggs

2 cups heavy cream

½ teaspoon salt

1 teaspoon Old Bay seasoning

1 cup Swiss cheese, shredded

¼ cup chopped green onion

1 cup crab meat

Freezing Day

Spread the pastry shell with the softened butter, and put in the refrigerator. Whisk eggs, cream, salt, and Old Bay. Stir in cheese and onion. Remove shell from refrigerator and line the bottom with crab meat. Pour egg mixture over the top. Bake quiche for 20 minutes at 375°F. Cool and wrap tightly with plastic wrap and freeze.

Reheating Instructions

Bake frozen quiche at 350°F for 50 minutes.

PER SERVING
Calories: 667 | Fat: 57g | Protein: 17g | Sodium: 776mg | Carbohydrates: 23g | Fiber: 1g

Burgers

Blue Cheese Burgers

NO DEFROSTING NEEDED!

INGREDIENTS | SERVES 4

2 pounds ground beef

Ground Beef Seasoning Mix (Chapter 13)

Salt and pepper to taste

½ cup blue cheese, crumbled

5 ounces cream cheese, softened

¼ cup roasted pine nuts

1 teaspoon Worcestershire sauce

How to Store Seeds and Nuts

The best way to store seeds and nuts is in the freezer, and there is no need to remove the shells! When the nuts are frozen in the shell, they crack much easier. Not only will your nuts and seeds stay fresher longer, but you don't need to defrost them—use them directly from the freezer.

Freezing Day

Mix the ground beef with the Ground Beef Seasoning Mix. Divide the ground beef into 8 parts and shape into patties. Salt and pepper each patty. In separate bowl combine the blue cheese, cream cheese, pine nuts, and Worcestershire sauce. Spread cheese mixture on 4 patties. Top the 4 patties with 4 plain patties and seal the edges. Flash freeze and transfer to freezer bag, or wrap each individually in plastic wrap.

Reheating Instructions

Cook frozen or defrosted burgers in a skillet over medium heat until they reach desired level of doneness.

PER SERVING

Calories: 891 | Fat: 63g | Protein: 72g | Sodium: 725mg | Carbohydrates: 3g | Fiber: 0.5g

Avocado Chicken Burgers

NO DEFROSTING NEEDED!

INGREDIENTS | SERVES 4

1 pound ground chicken

½ teaspoon paprika

1 egg

¼ cup Italian-seasoned breadcrumbs

1 tablespoon Worcestershire sauce

1 ripe avocado (used on reheating day)

1 tablespoon lemon juice (used on reheating day)

2 tablespoons sour cream (used on reheating day)

Salt and pepper to taste (used on reheating day)

Desired burger toppings such as lettuce, tomato, red onion (used on reheating day)

4 whole wheat buns (used on reheating day)

The Perfect Avocado

Use the following tips to select the perfect avocado. If the avocado is bright green or hard it is not yet ripe. Look for one that is a dark green or black. Gently press the avocado with your thumb. It should be soft, but not so soft that you'll pierce the skin. When you slice the avocado open there should be no dark spots.

Freezing Day

In bowl, mix chicken, paprika, egg, breadcrumbs, and Worcestershire sauce. Form mixture into 4 patties. Flash freeze, and transfer to freezer bag.

Reheating Instructions

Cook frozen patties in a small amount of oil over medium-high heat 6–8 minutes per side. Cover and cook an additional 2–3 minutes until burgers are fully cooked, and no longer pink in the center. To make the sauce, combine avocado, lemon juice, sour cream, salt, and pepper in a small bowl. Spread sauce on buns and top with burgers and desired toppings.

PER SERVING
Calories: 342 | Fat: 14g | Protein: 33g | Sodium: 342mg | Carbohydrates: 23g | Fiber: 4g

Black Bean "Burgers"

NO DEFROSTING NEEDED!

INGREDIENTS | SERVES 4

2 (16-ounce) cans black beans, fully drained

½ green bell pepper, finely diced

2 tablespoons fresh cilantro, finely diced

3 tablespoons teriyaki sauce

1 tablespoon minced onion

1 egg

1 teaspoon sesame oil

½ cup breadcrumbs, or more if needed

3 tablespoons vegetable oil (used on reheating day)

Freezing Day

In a bowl, mash the black beans. Add peppers, cilantro, teriyaki sauce, onion, egg, and sesame oil and mix well. Add breadcrumbs a little at a time until the mixture holds together. Form into patties. Flash freeze on a baking sheet lined with wax paper. Transfer to freezer bag once frozen.

Reheating Instructions

Cook patties in oil over medium heat until heated through.

PER SERVING
Calories: 845 | Fat: 15g | Protein: 47g | Sodium: 637mg | Carbohydrates: 134g | Fiber: 30

Blackened Burgers

** NO DEFROSTING NEEDED **

INGREDIENTS | SERVES 6

2 pounds ground beef

1 egg, slightly beaten

½ cup breadcrumbs

Blackened Seasoning Mix (Chapter 13)

Hamburger buns (used on reheating day)

Desired hamburger toppings (used on reheating day)

Freezing Day

Mix ground beef, egg, and breadcrumbs. Form into patties. Rub desired amount of Blackened Seasoning Mix on burgers. Flash freeze burgers then transfer to freezer bag.

Reheating Instructions

Cook frozen burgers over high on a lightly oiled grill until desired doneness. Place on hamburger buns and add desired toppings.

PER SERVING
Calories: 659 | Fat: 29g | Protein: 50g | Sodium: 594mg | Carbohydrates: 46g | Fiber: 2.5g

Gourmet Onion Mushroom Burgers

Dijon mustard originated in Dijon, France, and was originally made from brown or black mustard seeds and verjuice, a juice made from unripe grapes. Dijon mustard has a more pungent flavor than yellow mustard, and shouldn't be substituted.

INGREDIENTS | SERVES 4

1 pound ground beef

Ground Beef Seasoning Mix (Chapter 13)

1 tablespoon Worcestershire sauce

3–5 tablespoons butter (used on reheating day)

1 onion, sliced into rings (used on reheating day)

½ pound mushrooms, sliced (used on reheating day)

4 tablespoons Dijon mustard (used on reheating day)

¾ cup dry sherry (used on reheating day)

Onion Storage

Onions should be stored in a cool, dry place with good air flow. They shouldn't be stored in the refrigerator or in plastic bags, but onions can also be frozen. To freeze the onions, chop them and flash freeze on a baking sheet. Transfer to a freezer bag. When a recipe calls for chopped onion, you can measure right from the freezer bag.

Freezing Day

Mix ground beef with seasoning mix and Worcestershire sauce. Form into 4 patties, flash freeze, and transfer to freezer bag.

Reheating Instructions

Defrost hamburger patties in the refrigerator overnight. In skillet, melt 3 tablespoons butter over medium-high heat. Brown patties 2–3 minutes per side and remove from skillet. Add additional butter to skillet (if needed) and sauté onions and mushrooms 5–7 minutes. Leave in skillet, but push to side to make room for burgers. Spread 1 tablespoon Dijon mustard on each hamburger, and return to skillet, Dijon side down. Pour sherry over the top of the hamburgers. Cook until desired doneness. Serve burgers with sautéed onions and mushrooms on toasted rolls.

PER SERVING

Calories: 439 | Fat: 28g | Protein: 32g | Sodium: 253mg | Carbohydrates: 6g | Fiber: 1g

Broccoli and Swiss Cheese "Burgers"

NO DEFROSTING NEEDED!

INGREDIENTS | SERVES 4

4 eggs

2 cups cooked broccoli, chopped

1 cup toasted almonds, chopped

½ cup red onion, chopped

2 cups Italian-seasoned breadcrumbs

½ cup Swiss cheese, shredded

Salt and pepper to taste

½–¾ cup water

Veggie Burgers

These meatless broccoli "burgers" are easy to make and cook up in minutes, making them a great solution for those nights when you need a quick dinner.

Freezing Day

In a large mixing bowl, combine all ingredients except water. Mix ingredients with your hands. Add water until the mixture is the right consistency for forming into patties. Form into 4 burgers and flash freeze. Transfer to freezer bag.

Reheating Instructions

Defrost patties in the refrigerator overnight and bake at 375°F for 25 minutes. Burgers can also be cooked frozen 3–5 minutes per side in a skillet, or in the microwave for 1 minute on high.

PER SERVING
Calories: 504 | Fat: 25g | Protein: 25g | Sodium: 1050mg | Carbohydrates: 50g | Fiber: 6g

Mini Burgers

NO DEFROSTING NEEDED!

INGREDIENTS | SERVES 2–4

1 pound lean ground beef

½ onion, finely diced

¼ cup mayonnaise

1 cup Cheddar cheese

¼ teaspoon salt

¼ teaspoon pepper

1 package dinner rolls in aluminum tray, 12 count

12–24 dill pickle slices

Sweet Rolls

These burgers taste fantastic when made with King's Hawaiian Sweet rolls which are located in the deli section of many grocery stores.

Freezing Day

In skillet, brown ground beef for 4 minutes then add onion to skillet. Cook an additional 4–6 minutes until ground beef is fully cooked. Drain. Remove from heat and let cool. Stir in mayonnaise, cheese, salt, and pepper. Without separating rolls, slice the dinner rolls in half side to side. Remove top half and set aside. Spread the meat mixture across the bottom half of rolls. Top each roll with 1–2 dill pickles. Replace the top of rolls. Mini Burgers can either be wrapped in foil and frozen as a whole, or separated into 12 burgers, and wrapped individually.

Reheating Instructions

Microwave frozen burgers, two at a time, for 60 seconds.

PER SERVING
Calories: 380 | Fat: 19g | Protein: 32g | Sodium: 417mg | Carbohydrates: 30g | Fiber: 3g

Apple Turkey Burgers

NO DEFROSTING NEEDED!

INGREDIENTS | SERVES 6–8

2 eggs

½ cup applesauce

2 pounds ground turkey

1 green onion, finely chopped

½–¾ cup breadcrumbs

1 teaspoon dried sage

1 clove garlic, minced

1 teaspoon salt

1 teaspoon pepper

1 tablespoon vegetable oil (used on reheating day)

Freezing Day

In a bowl, beat eggs and stir in applesauce. Mix well. Add ground turkey, onion, ½ cup breadcrumbs, sage, garlic, salt, and pepper. If mixture is sticky, add additional breadcrumbs a tablespoon at a time. Form into patties and flash freeze on a baking sheet lined with wax paper. Once patties are frozen, transfer to a freezer bag.

Reheating Instructions

Cook patties in oil approximately 4–6 minutes per side until turkey reaches an internal temperature of 165°F.

PER SERVING
Calories: 164 | Fat: 7g | Protein: 19g | Sodium: 416mg | Carbohydrates: 7g | Fiber: 0.5g

Greek Burgers

NO DEFROSTING NEEDED!

INGREDIENTS | SERVES 4–6

2 pounds ground beef

½ cup crushed garlic croutons

1 egg

2 tablespoons red onion, diced

2 teaspoons dried oregano

1 cup feta cheese

Freezing Day

Mix ground beef with crushed garlic croutons, egg, onion, and oregano. Divide the ground beef into 8 parts, and shape into patties. Spread feta cheese on 4 patties. Top the 4 patties with 4 plain patties and seal the edges. Flash freeze and transfer to freezer bag.

Reheating Instructions

Cook frozen or defrosted burgers in a skillet over medium heat until they reach desired level of doneness.

PER SERVING
Calories: 500 | Fat: 32g | Protein: 45g | Sodium: 445mg | Carbohydrates: 3g | Fiber: 0g

Ranch Burgers

NO DEFROSTING NEEDED!

INGREDIENTS | SERVES 4–6

2 pounds ground beef

1 egg, beaten

½ cup Italian seasoned breadcrumbs

1 tablespoon minced onion

1 (1-ounce) package ranch dressing mix

Freezing Day

Combine the ground beef with the egg, breadcrumbs, onion, and ranch dressing mix. Shape into patties and flash freeze. Transfer to a freezer bag once frozen.

Reheating Instructions

Cook frozen or defrosted burgers in a skillet over medium heat until they reach desired level of doneness.

PER SERVING
Calories: 543 | Fat: 29g | Protein: 44g | Sodium: 445mg | Carbohydrates: 5g | Fiber: 1g

Teriyaki Ginger Burgers

NO DEFROSTING NEEDED!

INGREDIENTS | SERVES 4–6

2 pounds ground beef

⅓ cup bottled teriyaki sauce

1 tablespoon fresh ginger, grated

1 tablespoon onion, grated

¼ teaspoon fresh garlic, minced

Freezing Day

Combine the ground beef with the teriyaki sauce, ginger, onion, and garlic. Mix well. Shape into patties and flash freeze. Transfer to a freezer bag once frozen.

Reheating Instructions

Cook frozen or defrosted burgers in a skillet over medium heat until they reach desired level of doneness.

PER SERVING
Calories: 500 | Fat: 31g | Protein: 45g | Sodium: 944mg | Carbohydrates: 6g | Fiber: 0g

Barbecue Onion Burgers

NO DEFROSTING NEEDED!

INGREDIENTS | SERVES 4–6

2 pounds ground beef

½ cup barbecue sauce

1 (6-ounce) can French-fried onions

Freezing Day

Combine the ground beef with the barbecue sauce and onions. Mix well. Shape into patties and flash freeze. Transfer to a freezer bag once frozen.

Reheating Instructions

Cook frozen or defrosted burgers in a skillet over medium heat until they reach desired level of doneness.

PER SERVING
Calories: 788 | Fat: 47g | Protein: 45g | Sodium: 173mg | Carbohydrates: 7g | Fiber: 1g

Taco Burgers

NO DEFROSTING NEEDED!

INGREDIENTS | SERVES 4–6

2 pounds ground beef

1 (1.25-ounce) package taco seasoning mix

½ cup picante sauce

1 egg

¼ cup breadcrumbs, plain

Freezing Day

Combine the ground beef with the taco seasoning mix, picante sauce, egg, and breadcrumbs. Mix well. Shape into patties and flash freeze. Transfer to a freezer bag once frozen.

Reheating Instructions

Cook frozen or defrosted burgers in a skillet over medium heat until they reach desired level of doneness.

PER SERVING
Calories: 455 | Fat: 27g | Protein: 42g | Sodium: 608mg | Carbohydrates: 6g | Fiber: 0g

Mozzarella Basil Burgers

NO DEFROSTING NEEDED!

INGREDIENTS | SERVES 4–6

2 pounds ground beef

Ground Beef Seasoning Mix (Chapter 13)

1 egg

½ cup breadcrumbs

2 tablespoons Worcestershire sauce

1 cup mozzarella cheese, grated

6 ounces cream cheese, softened

¼ cup fresh basil, chopped

Get Out of the Bun!

Part of a great hamburger is the bread you serve it on. For something new, try serving your burger on flat bread, pita bread, yeast rolls, an English muffin, onion rolls, Hawaiian bread, or even your own homemade hamburger buns. Toasting the buns or bread can also give the old burger a new presentation.

Freezing Day

Mix ground beef with Ground Beef Seasoning Mix, egg, breadcrumbs, and Worcestershire sauce. Divide the ground beef into 8 parts and shape into patties. In separate bowl combine the mozzarella cheese, cream cheese, and basil. Spread cheese mixture on 4 patties. Top the 4 patties with the 4 plain patties and seal the edges. Flash freeze and transfer to freezer bag, or wrap each individually in plastic wrap.

Reheating Instructions

Cook frozen or defrosted burgers in a skillet over medium heat until they reach desired level of doneness.

PER SERVING

Calories: 712 | Fat: 41g | Protein: 51g | Sodium: 358mg | Carbohydrates: 9g | Fiber: 0.5g

Chili Burgers

NO DEFROSTING NEEDED!

INGREDIENTS | SERVES 4–6

1½ pounds ground beef

½ pound ground sausage

Ground Beef Seasoning Mix (Chapter 13)

1 egg

½ cup breadcrumbs

⅓ cup chili sauce

1 cup pepper jack cheese, shredded

6 ounces cream cheese

Build a Better Burger

Love cheese with your chili? Melt a slice of sharp Cheddar cheese over each burger, and top it with a sliced onion. And to make it a little hotter, add sliced jalapeño peppers.

Freezing Day

Mix ground beef, ground sausage, seasoning mix, egg, breadcrumbs, and chili sauce. Divide the ground beef into 8 parts and shape into patties. In a separate bowl, mix the pepper jack cheese with the cream cheese. Spread cheese mixture on 4 patties. Top the 4 patties with 4 plain patties and seal the edges. Flash freeze and transfer to freezer bag, or wrap each individually in plastic wrap.

Reheating Instructions

Cook frozen or defrosted burgers in a skillet over medium heat until they reach desired level of doneness.

PER SERVING

Calories: 1004 | Fat: 72g | Protein: 71g | Sodium: 969mg | Carbohydrates: 12g | Fiber: 1g

Sweet and Sour Burgers

NO DEFROSTING NEEDED!

INGREDIENTS | SERVES 4–6

2 pounds ground beef

Ground Beef Seasoning Mix (Chapter 13)

1 egg

½ cup breadcrumbs, plain

½ cup Sweet and Sour Sauce (Chapter 14)

1 (8-ounce) can crushed pineapple, well drained

Freezing Day

Combine the ground beef with the Seasoning Mix, egg, breadcrumbs, Sweet and Sour Sauce, and pineapple. Mix well. Shape into patties and flash freeze. Transfer to a freezer bag once frozen.

Reheating Instructions

Cook frozen or defrosted burgers in a skillet over medium heat until they reach desired level of doneness.

PER SERVING
Calories: 475 | Fat: 27g | Protein: 43g | Sodium: 257mg | Carbohydrates: 11g | Fiber: 1g

Turkey Pesto Burgers

NO DEFROSTING NEEDED!

INGREDIENTS | SERVES 4–6

2 pounds ground turkey

Ground Beef Seasoning Mix (Chapter 13)

2 tablespoons Basil and Pine Nut Pesto (Chapter 13)

1 tablespoon red onion, finely diced

½ cup breadcrumbs, plain

1 egg

Freezing Day

Combine turkey with Ground Beef Seasoning Mix, Basil and Pine Nut Pesto, onion, breadcrumbs, and egg. Mix well. Shape into patties and flash freeze. Transfer to a freezer bag once frozen.

Reheating Instructions

Cook frozen or defrosted burgers in a skillet over medium heat until they are fully cooked.

PER SERVING
Calories: 217 | Fat: 10g | Protein: 25g | Sodium: 189mg | Carbohydrates: 7g | Fiber: 0.5g

Reuben Burgers

NO DEFROSTING NEEDED!

INGREDIENTS | SERVES 4–6

2 pounds ground beef

Ground Beef Seasoning Mix (Chapter 13)

1 egg

½ cup breadcrumbs

1 cup Swiss cheese, shredded

Reinventing the Reuben

Serve this twist on a Reuben sandwich on toasted rye bread with Thousand Island salad dressing and topped with sauerkraut. And for a truly authentic taste, add a couple of slices of corned beef to your burger.

Freezing Day

Mix ground beef with seasoning mix, egg, and breadcrumbs. Divide the ground beef into 8 parts and shape into patties. Spread cheese on 4 patties. Top the 4 patties with 4 plain patties and seal the edges. Flash freeze and transfer to freezer bag, or wrap each individually in plastic wrap.

Reheating Instructions

Cook frozen or defrosted burgers in a skillet over medium heat until they reach desired level of doneness.

PER SERVING

Calories: 542 | Fat: 33g | Protein: 49g | Sodium: 256mg | Carbohydrates: 8g | Fiber: 0.5g

Jalapeño Burgers

NO DEFROSTING NEEDED!

INGREDIENTS | SERVES 4–6

2 jalapeño peppers
2 pounds ground beef
Ground Beef Seasoning Mix (Chapter 13)
1 egg
½ cup breadcrumbs
½ cup jarred picante sauce

Freezing Day

Remove seeds from jalapeño peppers, and dice. In bowl, mix diced peppers, ground beef, Ground Beef Seasoning Mix, egg, breadcrumbs, and picante sauce. Shape into patties and flash freeze. Transfer to freezer bag once frozen.

Reheating Instructions

Cook frozen or defrosted burgers in a skillet over medium heat until they are fully cooked.

PER SERVING
Calories: 461 | Fat: 27g | Protein: 43g | Sodium: 127mg | Carbohydrates: 7g | Fiber: 0.5g

Bacon Cheeseburger Pockets

NO DEFROSTING NEEDED!

INGREDIENTS | SERVES 4

2 pounds ground beef
Ground Beef Seasoning Mix (Chapter 13)
1 egg
½ cup breadcrumbs
1 cup Cheddar cheese
8 cooked slices bacon, crumbled

Freezing Day

Mix ground beef with Ground Beef Seasoning Mix, egg, and breadcrumbs. Divide the ground beef into 8 parts and shape into patties. Place the bacon and the cheese on top of 4 patties. Top those 4 patties with the remaining 4 patties and seal the edges, forming pockets. Flash freeze and transfer to freezer bag.

Reheating Instructions

Cook burgers in a skillet over medium heat until they reach desired level of doneness.

PER SERVING
Calories: 966 | Fat: 64g | Protein: 81g | Sodium: 919mg | Carbohydrates: 11g | Fiber: 1g

Pepperoni Pizza Burgers

NO DEFROSTING NEEDED!

INGREDIENTS | SERVES 4

2 pounds ground beef

Ground Beef Seasoning Mix (Chapter 13)

1 egg

¼ cup breadcrumbs

¼ cup grated Parmesan cheese

3 ounces tomato paste

1 cup mozzarella cheese

12 slices pepperoni

Don't Waste the Paste

If a recipe calls for a small amount of tomato paste, there is no reason to waste an entire can. Use a measuring spoon and make 1 tablespoon scoops of leftover paste. Place the scoops on a baking sheet lined with wax paper, and flash freeze. Transfer the tomato paste to a freezer bag.

Freezing Day

Mix ground beef with Ground Beef Seasoning Mix, egg, breadcrumbs, Parmesan cheese, and tomato paste. Divide the ground beef into 8 parts and shape into patties. Put mozzarella cheese and 3 pepperoni slices on 4 of the patties. Top the 4 patties with 4 plain patties and seal the edges. Flash freeze and transfer to freezer bag, or wrap each individually in plastic wrap.

Reheating Instructions

Cook frozen or defrosted burgers in a skillet over medium heat until they reach desired level of doneness.

PER SERVING

Calories: 800 | Fat: 48g | Protein: 75g | Sodium: 401mg | Carbohydrates: 11g | Fiber: 1.5g

Burgers Florentine

NO DEFROSTING NEEDED!

INGREDIENTS | SERVES 4

2 pounds ground beef

1 egg

½ cup breadcrumbs

Ground Beef Seasoning Mix (Chapter 13)

1 (10-ounce) package frozen chopped
spinach, squeezed of excess water

1 cup grated mozzarella cheese

6 ounces cream cheese

For More Pizzazz

You can sauté onion, garlic, sliced mush-rooms, and fresh spinach in butter to jazz up these burgers even more. Top the burger with this delicious sauté mix.

Freezing Day

Mix ground beef with egg, breadcrumbs, Ground Beef Seasoning Mix, and spinach. Divide the ground beef into 8 parts and shape into patties. In a small bowl, mix the mozzarella cheese with the cream cheese. Put the cheese mixture on top of 4 patties. Top the 4 patties with 4 plain patties and seal the edges. Flash freeze and transfer to freezer bag, or wrap each individually in plastic wrap.

Reheating Instructions

Cook frozen or defrosted burgers in a skillet over medium heat until they reach desired level of doneness.

PER SERVING
Calories: 957 | Fat: 61g | Protein: 79g | Sodium: 557mg | Carbohydrates: 15g | Fiber: 2g

Soups and Sides

Flavored White Rice

This rice is lightly flavored with onion and garlic. It is delicious enough to stand on its own as a side dish, yet mild enough to go with a sauce or gravy.

INGREDIENTS | SERVES 4–6

1 small onion, chopped

1 clove garlic, minced

1 tablespoon olive oil

1 cup white rice

2 cups water

Portion Control

You can freeze rice by the serving. Fill a large ice cream scoop with rice, and place it onto a wax-covered baking sheet. Flash freeze the scoop of rice, then transfer to a freezer bag. When you are ready to reheat the rice, simply choose the number of scoops you will need and heat it!

Freezing Day

In large saucepan, sauté onion in the olive oil 5–10 minutes until onions are soft and translucent. Add the garlic and sauté 1–2 minutes until garlic is golden brown. Add rice and cook for 3–5 minutes, stirring constantly. Add 2 cups water and bring to a boil. Reduce heat to low, cover tightly, and cook for 20 minutes. Let stand additional 5 minutes off the heat, with lid still on tight. Freeze in a freezer bag.

Reheating Instructions

Defrost in the refrigerator overnight. Heat rice in the microwave for 1–5 minutes (depending upon portion size), and serve.

PER SERVING
Calories: 135 | Fat: 2g | Protein: 2.5g | Sodium: 1mg | Carbohydrates: 25g | Fiber: 1g

Cornbread Stuffing

This stuffing is a real crowd pleaser! You can make this side dish into a main dish by adding cubed cooked chicken into the stuffing.

INGREDIENTS | SERVES 6

1 (6-ounce) package of cornbread mix (Recipe tastes better if you do not use a sweet cornbread mix)

½ cup butter or margarine

½ cup onion, chopped

½ cup celery, chopped

1 (10.75-ounce) can cream of chicken soup

1 (10.75-ounce) can chicken and rice soup

1 cup chicken broth

1–2 teaspoons sage, to taste

Salt and pepper to taste

Freezing Day

Bake cornbread according to package directions and cool. Crumble into pieces. In large skillet, melt butter. Sauté chopped onion and celery over medium heat 5–10 minutes until vegetables are tender. Remove skillet from heat and add the soups, broth, and crumbled cornbread. Add sage, salt, and pepper to taste. Mix well and freeze in freezer bag.

Reheating Instructions

Defrost mixture in the refrigerator overnight and pour into a greased casserole dish. Bake at 350°F for 45 minutes or until firm.

PER SERVING
Calories: 408 | Fat: 25g | Protein: 8.5g | Sodium: 1309mg | Carbohydrates: 37g | Fiber: 3g

Cheesy Double Baked Potatoes

NO DEFROSTING NEEDED!

INGREDIENTS | SERVES 8–10

8 medium baking potatoes

1 cup shredded Cheddar cheese

¼ cup milk

¼ cup butter

1 cup sour cream

Salt and pepper to taste

Beautiful Double Baked Potatoes

When filling double baked potatoes, use a wide tipped pastry bag to create swirls and patterns on the top of the potato for an artistic touch. For a creamier potato filling, overcook the potato the first time in order to render it much softer and easier to mix.

Freezing Day

Lay potatoes directly on oven rack and bake at 350°F for 1 hour. Do not wrap potatoes in foil when baking. Let cool 10 minutes, and then slice in half lengthwise. Scoop out the potatoes from each half, leaving about ¼" of potato next to the skin. Put the scooped out potato filling in a large mixing bowl. In the mixing bowl add remaining ingredients to potatoes and mash. Spoon mashed potatoes back into the skins and flash freeze. Transfer to freezer bag.

Reheating Instructions

Put frozen potatoes on a baking sheet. Heat potatoes in the oven at 350°F until potatoes are heated through, approximately 45 minutes–1 hour. Potatoes can also be heated in the microwave for approximately 3 minutes per potato. Cooking times will vary depending on potato sizes.

PER SERVING
Calories: 323 | Fat: 14g | Protein: 8g | Sodium: 157mg | Carbohydrates: 42g | Fiber: 4g

German Potato Salad

A roux is a mixture of flour and fat that is used to thicken sauces. The ratio is 1:1; one part fat to one part flour. Be careful not to cook your roux too long; you need to start over if it burns or has black specks in it.

INGREDIENTS | SERVES 20

8–10 pound bag of new red potatoes

1½ cups sweet pickle juice (like the juice from a jar of bread and butter pickles)

5½ cups cold water

1½ cups apple cider vinegar

1 cup sugar

¼ teaspoon salt

1½ pounds bacon, chopped

1 large onion, chopped

Flour (enough to form roux)

Freezing Day

Boil potatoes until a fork easily pierces them. Drain and cool immediately in cold water, changing water as needed until it stays cool. Drain and peel potatoes. Cut into bite-size pieces. Set aside.

In a mixing bowl, combine the sweet pickle juice, water, apple cider vinegar, sugar, and salt. Set aside. Cook bacon until almost crisp, then add onion. Cook onion until translucent 8–10 minutes. You should have at least 4–5 tablespoons grease in skillet. If you don't, add olive oil until amount is achieved. Whisk in an equal amount of flour to make roux. It should have a slightly glossy look. Cook roux for 4–5 minutes, stirring constantly. Slowly add the pickle juice mixture until a thin sauce is formed. Pour over potatoes, stir. Freeze.

Reheating Instructions

Defrost potato salad in refrigerator for 24 hours. It may be served warm or cold.

PER SERVING
Calories: 358 | Fat: 15g | Protein: 13g | Sodium: 584mg | Carbohydrates: 43g | Fiber: 3g

Spicy Corn Casserole

This corn casserole is an easy side dish. Serve it with Blue Cheese Burgers (Chapter 10), Sweet Ginger Sloppy Joes (Chapter 3), or Avocado Chicken Burgers (Chapter 10).

INGREDIENTS | SERVES 6–8

3½ cups frozen corn

8 ounces cream cheese, softened

1 stick butter, softened

¼ cup milk

1 (4-ounce) can green chili peppers, drained

½ pound cooked bacon, crumbled

Freezing Day

In large bowl, mix all ingredients. Freeze in a freezer bag.

Reheating Instructions

Defrost corn casserole in the refrigerator overnight and heat at 350°F for 25–30 minutes, or until fully heated.

PER SERVING
Calories: 412 | Fat: 35g | Protein: 13g | Sodium: 602mg | Carbohydrates: 16g | Fiber: 2g

Hamburger Soup

This thick hearty beef and vegetable soup is great to have on hand. Serve it with crusty French bread for a delicious meal.

INGREDIENTS | SERVES 8

1 pound ground beef, lean

1 cup carrots, chopped

1 cup onion, chopped

1 (16-ounce) package frozen corn

4 cups beef broth

1 (28-ounce) can Italian-seasoned tomatoes with juice

1 (14-ounce) can tomato sauce

¼ cup ketchup

1½ teaspoons Italian seasoning

Salt and pepper to taste

Freezing Day

Brown the ground beef and drain. Add beef to a stockpot with all remaining ingredients. Simmer, uncovered for 1 hour, 30 minutes. Stir often. Cool and freeze in a freezer bag.

Reheating Instructions

Defrost soup in the refrigerator overnight and heat in a stockpot over medium heat for 15–20 minutes or until desired temperature is reached.

PER SERVING
Calories: 268 | Fat: 10g | Protein: 20g | Sodium: 768mg | Carbohydrates: 25g | Fiber: 4g

Creamy Leek Soup

Goes great with the Open-Faced Italian Sandwiches found in Chapter 9, or served with a side of toasted sliced Italian bread topped with melted mozzarella or Swiss cheese.

INGREDIENTS | SERVES 6

3 tablespoons butter

4 leeks, thinly sliced

2 large potatoes, peeled and cubed

2 (14-ounce) cans chicken broth

½ teaspoon salt

¼ teaspoon pepper

2 cups half and half

¼ cup sherry

Freezing Day

In skillet, melt butter and sauté leeks until tender. In large saucepan, add potatoes, chicken broth, salt, and pepper. Bring to a boil and immediately reduce heat. Simmer until potatoes are tender. Remove from heat and cool. Pour into blender and mix until smooth. Pour back into saucepan and add leeks with butter and half and half. Simmer for 20 minutes. Remove from heat and stir in sherry. Cool and freeze in a freezer bag or plastic container.

Reheating Instructions

Defrost soup in refrigerator for 24 hours. Warm in saucepan over medium-low heat for 25–30 minutes or until desired temperature is reached.

PER SERVING
Calories: 314 | Fat: 18g | Protein: 7g | Sodium: 991mg | Carbohydrates: 35g | Fiber: 3g

Hush Puppies

NO DEFROSTING NEEDED!

INGREDIENTS | SERVES 20

1 cup yellow cornmeal

1 cup flour

3 teaspoons baking soda

½ teaspoon salt

1½ teaspoons sugar

1 small onion, grated

1 (15-ounce) can creamed corn

2 eggs

1 quart peanut oil for frying

What's in a Name?

There are a lot of stories about how hush puppies got their name. One interesting story tells of Confederate soldiers sitting around a campfire at night cooking their dinner. They tossed their dogs hush puppies to stop them from barking when Yankee soldiers were approaching.

Freezing Day

In a mixing bowl combine the cornmeal, flour, baking soda, salt, and sugar. In a separate mixing bowl combine onion, corn, and eggs. Combine together. If the batter is too runny, add more cornmeal until it can hold its shape. Heat 2 inches of oil to 365°F. Drop batter into the oil by the spoonful and cook on both sides until browned. Remove from oil and place on paper towels to drain. Cool. Flash freeze and transfer to freezer bag.

Reheating Instructions

Place frozen hush puppies on baking sheet and cook at 425°F for 14–16 minutes. Turn once after 7 minutes.

PER SERVING

Calories: 78 | Fat: 1g | Protein: 2.5g | Sodium: 245mg | Carbohydrates: 16g | Fiber: 1g

Monica's Drunken Sweet Potatoes

NO DEFROSTING NEEDED!

INGREDIENTS | SERVES 6–8

5 medium sweet potatoes (orange variety)

½ cup butter or margarine

2 tablespoons brown sugar

½ cup light cream

2 tablespoons bourbon

½ cup flour (for topping)

½ cup brown sugar (for topping)

¼ cup butter or margarine (for topping)

1 cup chopped pecans (for topping)

Teetotaler Version

Bourbon adds a delicious vanilla and caramel flavor to the dish. If you want to avoid adding alcohol to the sweet potatoes, substitute 1½–2 teaspoons vanilla extract for the bourbon.

Freezing Day

Peel potatoes and cut into chunks. Boil in water until a fork inserts easily into the potatoes. Drain and whip potatoes in large mixing bowl. Prepare a casserole dish for freezing or use an aluminum pan. To potatoes add ½ cup butter, 2 tablespoons brown sugar, light cream, and bourbon. Mix well and add to casserole dish. In separate bowl prepare topping: Mix the flour and brown sugar. Cut in the butter until crumbly. Mix in chopped pecans. Add topping to the casserole dish, wrap tightly, and freeze.

Reheating Instructions

For defrosted casserole, bake at 350°F for 25 minutes. For frozen casserole, add 45 minutes to an hour to defrosted casserole baking time.

PER SERVING
Calories: 453 | Fat: 32g | Protein: 4g | Sodium: 232mg | Carbohydrates: 41g | Fiber: 4g

Mashed Potatoes

Try adding 1 bulb of Roasted Garlic (Chapter 15) to mashed potatoes. Serve mashed potatoes with Homestyle Beef Stew (Chapter 6), or Steak and Tomatoes (Chapter 3).

INGREDIENTS | SERVES 15

5 pounds (about 15) potatoes, peeled

2½ cups half and half

½ cup butter, softened

1 egg

Portion Control

Rather than freezing 5 pounds of mashed potatoes, divide them into smaller portions. To make single-serving portions, freeze potatoes in muffin tins. Once potatoes have frozen, remove them from the muffin tins and put them into a freezer bag. Heat frozen potatoes in the oven according to the reheating instructions in this recipe.

Freezing Day

Cut potatoes into large chunks, put in large pot, cover with water, and bring to a boil. Cook over medium heat 15–20 minutes until potatoes are tender. Drain. Mash potatoes. Add half and half, butter, and egg to the potatoes and mix well. Freeze in a freezer bag, casserole dish, or Tupperware container.

Reheating Instructions

Defrost potatoes in the refrigerator for 24 hours and heat at 350°F until potatoes are heated through, 30–45 minutes. Microwaving is not recommended for heating.

PER SERVING
Calories: 253 | Fat: 11g | Protein: 4.5g | Sodium: 91mg | Carbohydrates: 35g | Fiber: 1.5g

Sweet Italian Sausage and Tortellini Soup

*This soup is the perfect dinner to enjoy on a cold winter night in front of a roaring fire.
Try topping your soup with freshly grated Parmesan cheese.*

INGREDIENTS | SERVES 6

1 pound sweet Italian sausage

1 onion, chopped

1 clove garlic, chopped

2 (9-ounce) bags of three cheese stuffed tortellini

1 bag frozen Italian vegetables

2 (14-ounce) cans chicken broth

1 (14.5-ounce) can diced tomatoes

1 cup water

1 teaspoon oregano

1 teaspoon basil

Freezing Day

Cut sausage into bite-sized pieces. In stockpot, brown sausage and onion for 10 minutes. Add garlic and cook an additional minute. Drain. Add remaining ingredients and bring to a boil. Reduce heat and simmer for 5 minutes. Remove from heat and cool. Freeze in a freezer bag.

Reheating Instructions

Defrost soup in the refrigerator for 24 hours. Bring to a boil and simmer for 5–10 minutes.

PER SERVING
Calories: 391 | Fat: 13g | Protein: 24g | Sodium: 738mg | Carbohydrates: 45g | Fiber: 3g

Mashed Potato Bombs

*These bombs are great to serve at parties. Make them a bit bigger when serving
them as a side dish—the kids will love them! This is a great solution for your leftover
mashed potatoes, or you can make a batch just for fun.*

INGREDIENTS | SERVES 15

Mashed Potatoes (this chapter)

½ cup flour

3 eggs, beaten

½ cup breadcrumbs

1 quart peanut oil for frying (used on reheating day)

Freezing Day

Prepare mashed potatoes and cool in refrigerator. Form into balls the size of a golf ball. Applying breading by rolling them in flour, then in beaten egg, then in breadcrumbs. Flash freeze, then transfer to freezer bag.

Reheating Instructions

Defrost for 30 minutes, then deep fry the bombs at 325°F until they turn gold in color, approximately 3 minutes.

PER SERVING
Calories: 152 | Fat: 3g | Protein: 3.5g | Sodium: 249mg | Carbohydrates: 18g | Fiber: 2g

Cheesy Bacon and Potato Soup

This thick and hearty soup makes a delicious dinner when served with a loaf of crunchy French bread and a salad.

INGREDIENTS | SERVES 10–12

6 slices bacon

5 medium potatoes, cooked

6 tablespoons butter

⅔ cups flour

6 cups milk

1 cup sour cream

2 cups Cheddar cheese

Salt and pepper, to taste (used on reheating day)

3–5 tablespoons chopped green onions, to taste (used as topping on reheating day)

3–5 tablespoons crumbled cooked bacon, to taste (used as topping on reheating day)

Cool Down Soup

Soup must be cool before it can be put into the freezer. To quickly cool down your soup, fill your kitchen sink with cold water and ice cubes. Place your soup pot into the cold water and stir the soup. The surrounding ice water will help it to cool quickly.

Freezing Day

Cook bacon and cut into small pieces. Cut cooked potatoes into cubes. In a large stockpot, melt butter. Add flour and whisk. Slowly pour in milk. Continue to stir 5–10 minutes until milk thickens slightly. Add potatoes, bacon, sour cream, and Cheddar cheese. Heat until cheese is melted, about 5 minutes. Remove from heat and cool. Divide into serving portions and freeze in a freezer bag.

Reheating Instructions

Defrost soup in the refrigerator for 24 hours and heat. Add salt and pepper to taste. Top each serving with chopped green onions and crumbled bacon.

PER SERVING
Calories: 326 | Fat: 19g | Protein: 12g | Sodium: 311mg | Carbohydrates: 27g | Fiber: 2g

Chicken Tortilla Soup

To serve, put corn tortilla chips in the bottom of each bowl and ladle the soup over them. Top with a dollop of sour cream and fresh cilantro leaves. Season with Tabasco to taste.

INGREDIENTS | SERVES 8

6 skinless, boneless chicken thighs

½ teaspoon olive oil

¼ teaspoon ground cumin

1 (32-ounce) carton chicken broth

1 (15-ounce) can whole corn, drained

1 (15-ounce) can black beans

1 (15-ounce) can kidney beans, drained

1 cup onion, chopped

1 clove garlic, minced

½ teaspoon chili powder

3 teaspoons lime juice

1 (10-ounce) can Ro-Tel tomatoes with liquid

1 teaspoon salt

Freezing Day

In a large pot over medium heat, cook the chicken in oil until lightly browned, about 3–5 minutes per side. Add all remaining ingredients except cilantro and corn tortilla chips. Cover, reduce heat to low, and simmer for 60 minutes. Cool and freeze in a freezer bag.

Reheating Instructions

Defrost soup in the refrigerator for 24 hours, and warm on the stove top over medium heat for 15–20 minutes, or until desired temperature is reached.

PER SERVING
Calories: 453 | Fat: 4g | Protein: 39g | Sodium: 741mg | Carbohydrates: 69g | Fiber: 19g

Cold Carrot Soup

This is the perfect choice to serve at a light luncheon on a hot summer day as well as an ideal complement to cool cucumber sandwiches.

INGREDIENTS | SERVES 4

1 tablespoon butter

½ shallot, diced

2 large carrots

1 large potato

1 (14-ounce) can chicken broth

1 tablespoon lemon juice

Pinch salt

Pinch dried marjoram

Pinch dried thyme

Pinch dried parsley

Pinch ground nutmeg

⅛ teaspoon pepper

1 cup half and half

Buy Whole Spices Whenever Possible

Spices such as nutmeg, cinnamon, and allspice will last years longer when bought whole than when bought ground because the essential oils are still contained within the spice. They will also have a much stronger flavor. Purchase a spice grinder or file grader and store your whole spices in a small freezer bag in the freezer.

Freezing Day

In large saucepan, melt butter and sauté shallots for 5–8 minutes. Meanwhile peel and chop carrots and potato. Once shallots are tender, add chicken broth, carrots, potatoes, lemon juice, and spices. Add enough water so potatoes and carrots are covered. Bring to a boil, then reduce heat to medium-low and simmer until carrots and potatoes are tender, about 30–40 minutes. Pour into blender and mix until smooth. Let cool. Add half and half and freeze.

Reheating Instructions

Defrost soup in the refrigerator for 24 hours and serve chilled.

PER SERVING

Calories: 207 | Fat: 10g | Protein: 6g | Sodium: 348mg | Carbohydrates: 25g | Fiber: 3.5g

Chicken Fried Rice

*Jasmine or Basmati rice is a good choice for this dish because
they both tend to be less sticky than other white rice.*

INGREDIENTS | SERVES 4–6

2 cups rice

4 cups chicken broth

1 shallot, chopped

¼ teaspoon ginger

3 tablespoons vegetable oil

2 eggs, beaten

1 cup chicken, cooked

½ cup frozen peas

¼–½ cup oyster sauce, to taste

⅓ cup soy sauce, or to taste

Sesame oil, to taste (used on reheating day)

Freezing Day

In a large saucepan, bring rice and chicken broth to a
boil over medium heat. Turn the heat down to low and
cover the pan. Cook for 20 minutes. Put rice in
refrigerator until it is cold. In skillet (or wok), sauté shallot
with ginger in vegetable oil for 6–8 minutes. Add eggs
and stir until scrambled, about 5 minutes. Remove from
heat. Stir in rice, chicken, peas, oyster sauce, and soy
sauce. Cool. Freeze in a freezer bag.

Reheating Instructions

Defrost in the refrigerator overnight and heat in skillet
over medium heat for 15–20 minutes until it reaches
desired temperature. Toss with sesame oil.

PER SERVING
Calories: 294 | Fat: 9g | Protein: 10g | Sodium: 1540mg |
Carbohydrates: 42g | Fiber: 1.5g

Corn Chowder

Serve Corn Chowder with Cheddar Garlic Biscuits (Chapter 12).
To add variety to the chowder, add cooked ham or cooked chicken.

INGREDIENTS | SERVES 10

1 pound bacon, diced

1 medium onion, chopped

2 tablespoons shredded carrot

1 clove garlic, minced

5 cups chicken broth

½ cup sherry

3 (15-ounce) cans white corn

4 (15-ounce) cans cream-style corn, drained

4 teaspoons chopped fresh oregano

2 teaspoons salt

2 cups half and half

2 (14-ounce) cans sweetened condensed milk

¼ teaspoon ground nutmeg

Ground black pepper, to taste

Homemade Chicken Broth When You're Ready

Anytime you roast a whole chicken, the leftover carcass is great for making chicken broth. Simply freeze the carcass until you are ready. To make broth, put the carcass in water with celery, onion, carrots, ½ teaspoon dried thyme, ½ teaspoon dried rosemary, 1 bay leaf, and 8 whole peppercorns. Bring it to a boil, skim the foam, lower the heat, and cook for 2 hours covered. Strain and you have broth.

Freezing Day

Cook bacon until crisp. Cool and crumble. In about 3 tablespoons of bacon drippings, sauté onion and carrot until onion is translucent, about 5–10 minutes. Add garlic and sauté 1–2 minutes. In large pot, add chicken broth and sherry. Bring to boil, add white corn, cover, reduce heat, and maintain low boil for 15 minutes. Add sautéed vegetables to corn stock. Add remaining ingredients except bacon, and season with ground black pepper to taste. Simmer for 15 minutes. Add bacon and simmer 15 more minutes. Cool and freeze in a freezer bag, or a plastic container.

Reheating Instructions

Defrost corn chowder in the refrigerator overnight and heat in a saucepan over medium heat for 15–20 minutes or until it reaches desired temperature.

PER SERVING
Calories: 744 | Fat: 34g | Protein: 27g | Sodium: 1516mg | Carbohydrates: 90g | Fiber: 2g

Calico Bean Soup

This soup is a cinch to make using the Dried Bean Mix recipe (Chapter 13), and is delicious served with Sweet Cornbread. (Chapter 12).

INGREDIENTS | SERVES 8–10

2 cups Dried Bean Mix (Chapter 13)

2 pounds smoked ham hocks

8 cups water

2 carrots, chopped

1 large onion, chopped

1 (28-ounce) can chopped tomatoes

1 (4.5-ounce) can chopped green chilies (optional)

2 tablespoons fresh lemon juice

What Are Ham Hocks?

Ham hocks are the lower portion of the leg of a pig, typically around the ankle. What makes the ham hock so good for cooking is, while not very meaty, they are quite flavorful. This makes them a great item with which to season a slow-cooked dish. Fresh or smoked, ham hocks freeze well.

Freezing Day

Put beans in a stockpot and cover them with water. Bring beans to a boil, cover, remove from heat, and let sit covered for 1 hour. Drain water and return beans to stockpot. Add the Dried Bean Mix, ham hocks, water, carrots, onion, tomatoes, green chilies if desired, and lemon juice. Bring to a boil, reduce heat, cover, and simmer for 2 hours or until beans are tender. Remove ham hocks, cut meat off, and it to the beans. Let cool and freeze.

Reheating Instructions

Defrost soup in the refrigerator overnight and warm in a saucepan over medium heat for 15–20 minutes or until desired temperature is reached.

PER SERVING
Calories: 293 | Fat: 6g | Protein: 28g | Sodium: 1075mg | Carbohydrates: 34g | Fiber: 9g

Baby Carrot Herb Medley

In a hurry? Steam baby carrots in the microwave with ½ cup of water and a tablespoon of butter. Cover and cook 4–5 minutes or until desired tenderness.

INGREDIENTS | SERVES 4

1 tablespoon lemon juice

25 baby carrots

2 tablespoons butter

1 tablespoon chopped fresh sage

1 teaspoon chopped fresh dill

¼ teaspoon salt

¼ teaspoon pepper

Rosemary Herb Butter

Here is an all-purpose herb butter suitable for topping almost any vegetable. Mix: ¼ cup softened butter, ½ teaspoon dried and crumbled rosemary, ¼ teaspoon dried and crushed marjoram, and ½ teaspoon dried parsley flakes. Cream or whip butter until fluffy. Stir in rosemary, marjoram, and parsley until evenly mixed. Yields ¼ cup.

Freezing Day

Place ½ inch water and 1 tablespoon lemon juice in bottom of a saucepan. Put carrots in a steamer basket and hang over water. The basket should not touch the water. Cover the saucepan and heat to boiling. Reduce heat and steam carrots for 7 minutes until they are tender-crisp. The carrots should just begin to get tender, but still retain a crisp texture.

In a skillet, melt butter over medium heat. Add sage, dill, salt, and pepper. Add carrots and mix well. Allow to cool, and freeze in a freezer bag or plastic container.

Reheating Instructions

Defrost carrots in the refrigerator overnight. Sauté uncovered 2–3 minutes, stirring gently until hot.

PER SERVING
Calories: 73 | Fat: 6g | Protein: 0.5g | Sodium: 253mg | Carbohydrates: 5g | Fiber: 1.5g

Greg's Gourmet Potatoes

Prosciutto is a dry-cured ham that is sliced very thin.
Try stirring Greek yogurt into your potatoes with the milk!

INGREDIENTS | SERVES 12

4 pounds Idaho potatoes

1 cube chicken bouillon

2 tablespoons butter

2 cups chopped wild mushrooms

2 tablespoons dried shallots

Milk, as needed for desired texture

5 slices prosciutto, finely chopped

2 cups freshly grated Gouda cheese

2 tablespoons dried chives

Pepper to taste

Freezing Day

Peel potatoes and place in boiling water with a cube of chicken bouillon. In a large skillet, melt the butter and lightly sauté the mushrooms, approximately 5 minutes. Add shallots and cook 1 more minute. When potatoes are done (a fork inserts easily into them), drain and put back in pan and mash. Add milk to potatoes until they are creamy. Mix in the prosciutto, cheese, chives, cooked mushroom mixture, and mix well. Add pepper to taste. Freeze in a freezer bag or Tupperware.

Reheating Instructions

Defrost potatoes in the refrigerator 24 hours and put in a greased casserole dish. Stir well. Bake, covered, at 350°F for 30 minutes.

PER SERVING

Calories: 249 | Fat: 5g | Protein: 12g | Sodium: 407mg | Carbohydrates: 39g | Fiber: 4g

Roasted Peppers and Tomatoes

Green, yellow, and red peppers are all the same pepper, but they are harvested at different stages of ripening. Red peppers are sweeter and fruitier in taste and have higher nutritional value.

INGREDIENTS | SERVES 4

2 red, yellow, or green bell peppers
2 Roma tomatoes
1 garlic clove
Olive oil to taste (used on reheating day)
Salt to taste (used on reheating day)

The Benefits of Red Bell Peppers

Red bell peppers are very nutrient-rich and are an excellent source of vitamins A, B6, and C. Red bell peppers also provide a good source of fiber and the antioxidant vitamin E. This diet-friendly vegetable has no fat, cholesterol, or sodium and very few carbohydrates.

Freezing Day

Cut each pepper in half lengthwise. Remove stems and seeds. Place peppers skin side up on a plate and cook on high in microwave for 3 minutes. Transfer the peppers to a foil-lined cookie sheet (skin side up). Cut tomatoes in half lengthwise. Squeeze out most of the seeds. Place tomatoes on the cookie sheet. Turn oven on broil. Place cookie sheet on top shelf of oven. Watching carefully, broil approximately 8–10 minutes until the skins turn partially black and loose.

Remove from oven and place peppers and tomatoes in a bowl; cover with foil. When they are cool to the touch, peel skin off. Slice or chop peppers and tomatoes. Slice garlic clove and add to the peppers. Freeze the peppers, tomatoes, and garlic in a freezer bag or plastic container.

Reheating Instructions

Defrost vegetables in refrigerator overnight and put on baking sheet. Drizzle olive oil over peppers and tomatoes and salt to taste. Heat at 425°F for 5 minutes or until vegetables are desired temperature. As an alternative heating method, you can heat in microwave for 2–3 minutes on high.

PER SERVING
Calories: 32 | Fat: 0g | Protein: 1.5g | Sodium: 6mg | Carbohydrates: 8g | Fiber: 2g

Spanish-Style Lentil Stew

Spanish chorizo comes both dry-cured and fresh. Fresh chorizo needs to be fully cooked, but dry chorizo can be eaten as is.

Freezing Day

Purée garlic, onion, and tomato and set aside. Peel chorizo, chop into very small pieces, and place in boiling water. When the red grease from chorizo has gone to the surface after about 3–4 minutes, strain and set aside. Add olive oil to the large pot, over medium heat. Cook onion, tomato, and garlic purée in the pot with cumin and Tabasco for about 5 minutes. Add red wine, potatoes, and carrots and cook for another 5 minutes. Add lentils, ham bone, lard, prosciutto, and the chorizo and mix. Cover with chicken broth and water if needed. Cook over low-medium heat, stirring occasionally, for about 1 hour–1 hour, thirty minutes until lentils are tender and stew has a creamy texture. If desired, add the cup of cooking cream when nearly finished. Let cool, separate into desired portions, and freeze in a freezer bag.

Reheating Instructions

Defrost stew in refrigerator 24 hours. Heat over medium heat for 15–20 minutes or until desired temperature is reached.

PER SERVING
Calories: 806 | Fat: 41g | Protein: 41g | Sodium: 1133mg | Carbohydrates: 68g | Fiber: 29g

Tomatoes and Okra

Fresh-cut okra releases a sticky substance that works well in thickening soups and stews. To freeze fresh okra, first blanch for 2 minutes, cool in ice water, drain, and package for the freezer.

INGREDIENTS | SERVES 6–8

1½ pounds fresh okra

4–5 Roma tomatoes

3 tablespoons butter

1 onion, chopped

½ teaspoon salt

¼–½ teaspoon red pepper flakes, to taste

1 cup tomato sauce

3 tablespoons chopped parsley (used on reheating day)

An Alternative to Canned Tomatoes

You can freeze fresh tomatoes with either the skin on or off. Thawed tomatoes will become mushy, and so they should be used in recipes calling for cooked tomatoes. Clean tomatoes, cut away stem scar, and place on cookie sheets in freezer. To freeze skinless, dip in boiling water for 60 seconds, peel when cool, and freeze on cookie sheet. Bag when frozen solid.

Freezing Day

Cut off stems of okra and slice into ½" pieces. Cut tomatoes into pieces and set aside. In skillet, melt butter. Sauté okra and onion for about 3 minutes. Add tomatoes and sauté additional 2–3 minutes. Stir in salt, red pepper flakes, and tomato sauce. Remove from heat and cool. Pour into freezer bag and freeze.

Reheating Instructions

Defrost okra and tomatoes in the refrigerator overnight. Pour into lightly greased baking dish and top with parsley. Bake at 350°F for 30 minutes.

PER SERVING

Calories: 81 | Fat: 4.5g | Protein: 3g | Sodium: 201mg | Carbohydrates: 10g | Fiber: 4g

Black Bean Soup

After you ladle soup in each bowl, top it with a dollop of sour cream and fresh cilantro.
Soup is delicious served with Sweet Cornbread (Chapter 12).

INGREDIENTS | SERVES 4

1 sweet onion, chopped

2 cloves garlic, minced

2 tablespoons olive oil

¼ cup sherry

1 teaspoon cumin

1 teaspoon oregano

¼ teaspoon thyme

¼ teaspoon cayenne pepper

2 (15.2-ounce) cans black beans

2 (14-ounce) cans chicken broth

Freezing Day

In stockpot over medium-high heat, sauté the onion in olive oil for 5–10 minutes. Add garlic and sauté 1 additional minute. Add the sherry, cumin, oregano, thyme, and cayenne pepper. Mix well and remove from heat. Drain and rinse the black beans. Put half the beans in a blender and purée. Add the whole beans and puréed beans to the stockpot. Pour the broth into the stockpot. Mix well. Put soup into a freezer bag or plastic container and freeze.

Reheating Instructions

Defrost soup in the refrigerator for 12–24 hours. Put into pan and heat on medium for 15–20 minutes or until soup reaches desired temperature.

PER SERVING
Calories: 710 | Fat: 9g | Protein: 43g | Sodium: 495mg |
Carbohydrates: 116g | Fiber: 28g

CHAPTER 12

Breads

Cereal Bread

Try this trick for letting your dough rise. Heat a large mug filled with water in the microwave for 3 minutes on high. When finished heating, place the bowl of dough in the microwave. Close the door for 1 hour until the dough has risen.

INGREDIENTS | YIELDS 2 LOAVES

½ cup Bob's Red Mill Mighty Tasty Hot Cereal

2 cups water

1 teaspoon salt

1 tablespoon butter

¼ cup brown sugar

2 (2.5-ounce) packages dry active yeast

¾ cup warm water

1 teaspoon sugar

5 cups flour

4 teaspoons wheat gluten

Bread Machine Recipe

Bread machines are wonderful for baking bread. They automatically let the dough rise, and do the kneading for you. To make the Cereal Bread in a bread maker, cut the ingredient amounts in half. Do steps 1 and 2, then finish with bread maker. Follow your instruction manual for the order of ingredients.

Freezing Day

In large saucepan, stir cereal into water and salt. Mix well and bring to a boil, stirring constantly. Remove from heat. Add butter and brown sugar to cereal mixture, mix well, and cool in refrigerator about 30 minutes. Dissolve yeast in ¾ cup warm water and sugar. Let sit for 10 minutes until the mixture has a foam on top. Add yeast to the cereal mixture. In a separate bowl, mix flour and wheat gluten. Gradually add flour to the cereal mixture to form the dough. Knead dough for 10–15 minutes on a lightly floured surface. Place the kneaded dough in a greased bowl. Roll dough around in the bowl to cover dough with oil. Cover bowl with a towel and let rise for about 1 hour until it is double in size. Knead dough a second time for 10–15 minutes, then divide in two and put in two loaf pans. Cover loaves, set in warm place, and let them rise about 40 minutes until double in size. Use a knife to cut 3 diagonal stripes across the top of each dough. Bake at 400°F for 15 minutes. Lower temperature to 350°F and bake 35–40 minutes until bread is golden brown. Cool. Wrap well with plastic wrap and freeze.

Reheating Instructions

Defrost bread wrapped in plastic wrap at room temperature for 2–3 hours. To heat, wrap in aluminum foil and warm in a 350°F oven for 20–30 minutes, or serve at room temperature or cut into slices and toast.

PER LOAF
Calories: 1610 | Fat: 13g | Protein: 67g | Sodium: 1331mg | Carbohydrates: 309g | Fiber: 24g

Chocolate Banana Nut Bread

Heat up a slice of bread and spread on a little butter for a delicious treat. Try substituting the chocolate chips with chopped strawberries or apples.

INGREDIENTS | YIELDS 1 LOAF

1¾ cups flour
2 teaspoons baking powder
¼ teaspoon baking soda
½ teaspoon salt
½ cup butter, softened
⅔ cup sugar
2 eggs, beaten
1½ cups bananas, mashed
½ cup chocolate chips
¼ cup walnuts, chopped

Freezing Day

In a small mixing bowl, mix flour, baking powder, baking soda, and salt. In large mixing bowl, mix the butter, sugar, and eggs. Alternate adding the flour mixture and bananas to the large mixing bowl, a little at a time. Mix just enough to combine—do not over mix. Fold in chocolate chips and walnuts. Pour into greased loaf pan and bake at 350°F for 1 hour–1 hour 10 minutes. A knife inserted into the center should come out clean.

Reheating Instructions

To defrost bread, wrap the loaf in plastic wrap and defrost at room temperature for 2–3 hours and serve.

PER LOAF
Calories: 3456 | Fat: 57g | Protein: 46g | Sodium: 3198mg | Carbohydrates: 483g | Fiber: 20g

Tomato, Basil, and Asiago Focaccia

Focaccia is an Italian flatbread that is similar to a pizza without all the toppings. You may experiment and try different herbs and vegetables on top of your Focaccia.

INGREDIENTS | YIELDS 1 LARGE FLATBREAD

3 (.25-ounce) packets yeast

1½ cups warm water

1 teaspoon sugar

7 tablespoons olive oil, divided

5 cups flour

2 teaspoons salt

2 cloves garlic, minced

2 tomatoes, sliced

¼–½ cup fresh basil, according to taste

¼ cup grated Asiago cheese

Freeze Dough Before Baking

To freeze the dough before baking, let the dough rise once in the bowl (step 4), and then freeze it. Defrost it fully at room temperature for several hours, and continue with step 5. When the dough rises after being frozen, it will not rise and be puffy, but will still taste delicious.

Freezing Day

Mix yeast with water and sugar. Let sit for 10 minutes until foam forms on top. Add 3 tablespoons olive oil. In large bowl, mix flour and salt. Add the yeast mixture and form into dough. Knead the dough for 10 minutes until it is smooth. Form into a ball. Oil the inside of a bowl, and roll the dough to coat it. Cover with a damp cloth and set in warm place for 1 hour or until the dough has doubled in size.

Punch down the dough and spread on a large baking sheet. With your fingers or the end of a wooden spoon, make slight indentations along the top of the bread. Cover and let rise 30 minutes or until it has doubled in size. Brush with olive oil and top with garlic, sliced tomatoes, basil, and cheese. Bake at 400°F for 20–25 minutes, or until focaccia has turned golden brown. Remove from baking sheet and cool on a wire rack. Cut into slices, wrap with plastic wrap, and freeze.

Reheating Instructions

To defrost bread, wrap it in plastic wrap and defrost at room temperature for about an hour. Heat in the oven and serve, or serve at room temperature.

PER LOAF
Calories: 3270 | Fat: 109g | Protein: 77g | Sodium: 5054mg | Carbohydrates: 485g | Fiber: 21g

Pancake Donuts

NO DEFROSTING NEEDED!

INGREDIENTS | SERVES 6

2 cups flour

4 teaspoons baking powder

¼ teaspoon salt

⅛ teaspoon cinnamon

⅛ teaspoon nutmeg

2 eggs

1 cup sugar

1 cup milk

½ cup oil

Sweet Treat

Try pancake donuts with butter and confectioners' sugar for a sweet treat. These also make a great way to grab a quick breakfast in the mornings when you are short on time.

Freezing Day

In a medium bowl, combine flour, baking powder, salt, cinnamon, and nutmeg and whisk together. In a mixing bowl, beat eggs slightly, add sugar, and beat at medium speed until mixture is lemon colored and well blended (about 2 minutes). Add milk, oil, and dry ingredients alternately to egg mixture. Beat well after each addition.

Preheat griddle to medium-low. Ladle batter on hot griddle, spreading slightly with back of ladle as batter is thick. Turn only once, after approximately 1–5 minutes, when edges look done. Use your spatula to lift the edge of the donut and peek underneath. They should be light brown in color when ready. Flash freeze, and wrap in bundles of 3 or use sandwich-sized freezer bags.

Reheating Instructions

Pancake Donuts can be warmed in the microwave for 30 seconds–1 minute or heated in the toaster.

PER SERVING
Calories: 499 | Fat: 22g | Protein: 7.5g | Sodium: 460mg | Carbohydrates: 68g | Fiber: 1.5g

Healthy Apple Muffins

Make several batches of muffins to freeze, and you have a ready supply of healthy after-school snacks!

INGREDIENTS | YIELDS 12 MUFFINS

2½ cups whole wheat flour

2 cups honey

1 tablespoon pumpkin pie spice

1 teaspoon baking soda

½ teaspoon salt

2 eggs

1 cup puréed pumpkin

½ cup applesauce

2 cups apples, peeled and diced

Freezing Day

In a large bowl, combine all ingredients except apples. Mix well. Fold in apples. Pour into paper-lined muffin tins. Bake at 350°F for 35 minutes. Cool, flash freeze, and transfer to freezer bag.

Reheating Instructions

Defrost muffins at room temperature for about 1 hour. Serve at room temperature.

PER SERVING
Calories: 290 | Fat: 1.5g | Protein: 4.5g | Sodium: 215mg | Carbohydrates: 70g | Fiber: 4g

Pumpkin Nut Bread

To make fresh pumpkin purée, cut your pumpkin into large chunks, cover with water, and bring to a boil. Cook the pumpkin until tender. Once it has cooled, use a food processor to purée it.

INGREDIENTS | YIELDS 2 LOAVES

1 cup vegetable oil

3 cups sugar

2 cups pumpkin purée

1½ teaspoons salt

1 teaspoon cinnamon

1 teaspoon nutmeg

½ teaspoon cloves or ginger

½ teaspoon black walnut flavoring

1 teaspoon burnt sugar flavoring

3½ cups flour

2 teaspoons baking soda

⅔ cup water

1 cup chopped nuts

4 eggs

Freezing Day

In large mixing bowl, combine all ingredients. Spray a 9" x 5" baking pan with cooking oil and pour batter into pan. Bake at 350°F for 1 hour or until a knife inserted comes out clean.

Reheating Instructions

To defrost bread, wrap the loaf in plastic wrap and defrost at room temperature for 2–3 hours and serve.

PER LOAF
Calories: 3526 | Fat: 164g | Protein: 44g | Sodium: 3120mg | Carbohydrates: 484g | Fiber: 11g

Zucchini Bread

Zucchini bread is a wonderful way to get your kids to eat zucchini!
It tastes delicious heated and served with butter and cream cheese.

INGREDIENTS | YIELDS 2 LOAVES

3 eggs

1 cup vegetable oil

2 cups sugar

2 cups white sugar

½ cup brown sugar

2 teaspoons vanilla extract

¼ teaspoon almond extract

3 cups flour

1¼ teaspoons baking powder

1 teaspoon baking soda

1 tablespoon cinnamon

1 teaspoon salt

3 cups zucchini, peeled and grated

Growing Zucchini

Zucchini is one of the easiest vegetables to grow in your garden. The plants need lots of sunlight and steady watering. If you are limited on space, try growing your zucchini upward on a fence or lattice. Zucchini can grow quite fast, and you may not be able to eat it fast enough. If that's the case, slice and flash freeze it for later use.

Freezing Day

In large mixing bowl, mix eggs, vegetable oil, sugar, brown sugar, vanilla extract, and almond extract. In second bowl, mix flour, baking powder, baking soda, cinnamon, and salt. Alternate adding zucchini and dry ingredients to the large bowl containing eggs and sugar. Mix just enough to combine—do not over mix. Grease 2 loaf pans and pour in batter. Bake at 350°F for 40 minutes–1 hour until a knife inserted into center comes out clean. Cool on wire rack, wrap well, and freeze.

Reheating Instructions

To defrost the bread, wrap the loaf in plastic wrap and defrost at room temperature for 2–3 hours and serve.

PER LOAF

Calories: 2891 | Fat: 121g | Protein: 11g | Sodium: 4304mg | Carbohydrates: 460g | Fiber: 2g

Pita Bread Crackers

The red pepper flakes give these Pita Crackers a bit of heat, and you can add more or less pepper flakes according to your taste. Try these crackers with the Hummus (Chapter 13).

INGREDIENTS | YIELDS APPROXIMATELY 32 CRACKERS

4 round pieces of pita bread

Olive oil to taste

¼ cup Parmesan cheese, freshly grated

½ teaspoon Italian seasoning

¼–½ teaspoon red pepper flakes, to taste

¼ teaspoon garlic salt

Freezing Day

Separate the two sides of pita bread from each other, and tear each side into 4 crackers. With the rough side up, brush each piece with olive oil and sprinkle with Parmesan cheese, Italian seasoning, red pepper flakes, and garlic salt. Bake on a baking sheet at 350°F for about 8 minutes, or until browned. Cool completely. Flash freeze and transfer to freezer bag.

Reheating Instructions

Defrost pita crackers at room temperature for about an hour. Eat at room temperature, or bake at 350°F for 5–10 minutes to heat through.

PER SERVING
Calories: 24 | Fat: 0.5g | Protein: 1g | Sodium: 61mg | Carbohydrates: 4g | Fiber: 0g

Garlic Toast

NO DEFROSTING NEEDED!

INGREDIENTS | SERVES 4

1 loaf Italian or French bread
1 stick butter, softened
½ teaspoon garlic powder
⅓ cup grated Parmesan cheese
1 teaspoon dried parsley

Garlic Equivalents

Would you rather use fresh garlic instead of garlic powder? 1 clove of garlic yields approximately 1 teaspoon chopped garlic, which equals approximately ½ teaspoon minced garlic, which equals approximately ⅛ teaspoon garlic powder. If you'd like to use garlic salt instead of garlic powder, ½ teaspoon garlic salt is equal to 1 clove of garlic.

Freezing Day

Cut bread into 1-inch slices. Mix butter, garlic powder, Parmesan cheese, and parsley in a medium mixing bowl. Spread garlic butter on each slice of bread and flash freeze. Transfer to a freezer bag once frozen.

Reheating Instructions

Place frozen slices of garlic bread on a baking sheet. Bake on middle rack at 425°F for 5–7 minutes.

PER SERVING
Calories: 321 | Fat: 20g | Protein: 3g | Sodium: 539mg | Carbohydrates: 36g | Fiber: 1g

Cinnamon Raisin Monkey Bread

*This bread is easy for kids to make as well as fun to eat—just pull off pieces!
Try adding diced apple or pears to the bread instead of raisins.*

INGREDIENTS | SERVES 14

¾ cup white sugar

3 tablespoons cinnamon

3 tubes refrigerator buttermilk biscuits

½ cup pecans, chopped and divided

½ cup raisins

½ cup unsalted butter

1 cup brown sugar

1 teaspoon vanilla extract

Freezing Day

Mix sugar and cinnamon together in a plastic bag. Cut biscuit dough into quarters, and put in bag with cinnamon sugar. Shake to coat pieces. Grease bottom and sides of a Bundt pan. Place ¼ cup pecans in bottom of pan. Put a layer of biscuit pieces on top of pecans. Continue to add biscuit pieces to pan. Intersperse raisins and remaining pecans among the biscuit pieces.

In a saucepan, melt butter. Add brown sugar and vanilla. Heat until brown sugar is dissolved in butter. Pour melted butter and sugar over top of biscuits. Bake at 350°F for 35–40 minutes. Remove from oven and turn out on a plate. Let cook, wrap tightly, and freeze.

Reheating Instructions

Defrost bread at room temperature for 2–3 hours. Bread can be served at room temperature or heated in oven at 350°F for 10–15 minutes.

PER SERVING
Calories: 532 | Fat: 26g | Protein: 8g | Sodium: 594mg | Carbohydrates: 69g | Fiber: 2g

Sweet Cornbread

This bread tastes great with butter and is a delicious accompaniment to Blue Ribbon Chili (Chapter 3) and Sweet Italian Sausage and Tortellini Soup (Chapter 11).

INGREDIENTS | SERVES 4–6

1 cup yellow cornmeal

1 cup flour

¼ cup sugar

½ teaspoon salt

2½ teaspoons baking powder

1 cup heavy cream

¼ cup applesauce

¼ cup honey

2 eggs

Cornbread Muffins

This recipe can also be used to make cornbread muffins! Line each cup of your muffin tin with muffin (cupcake) papers and use a ladle to pour in the batter. Bake the muffins at 400°F for 15–20 minutes, or until a toothpick inserted into them comes out clean.

Freezing Day

Sift together cornmeal, flour, sugar, salt, and baking powder. In separate bowl, mix together heavy cream, applesauce, honey, and eggs. Combine wet and dry ingredients, and stir just enough to mix them. Pour batter into a greased 9" x 9" pan. Bake at 400°F for 20–25 minutes until a knife inserted in the center comes out clean. Cool, wrap well with plastic wrap, and freeze.

Reheating Instructions

Defrost cornbread at room temperature for 1–2 hours and serve at room temperature. To warm bread, place in oven at 350°F for 10 minutes.

PER SERVING
Calories: 370 | Fat: 17g | Protein: 7g | Sodium: 432mg | Carbohydrates: 49g | Fiber: 2g

Cheddar Garlic Biscuits

These biscuits are easy to make and a delicious addition to many meals. Serve them with Vegetarian Vegetable Bean Soup (Chapter 7) or Grilled Citrus Chicken (Chapter 4).

INGREDIENTS | YIELDS 12 BISCUITS

2 cups all-purpose baking mix such as Bisquick

⅔ cup buttermilk

1 cup Cheddar cheese

¾ teaspoon garlic powder, divided

¼ cup butter

¼ teaspoon parsley flakes

Freezing Day

Mix together baking mix, buttermilk, Cheddar cheese, and ¼ teaspoon garlic powder. Mix well. Using a teaspoon, drop batter onto lightly greased baking sheet to form 12 biscuits. Bake at 400°F for 18–20 minutes until tops begin to brown. In a saucepan melt butter and mix with ½ teaspoon garlic powder and parsley flakes. Brush butter mixture over the top of biscuits and let cool. Flash freeze then transfer to freezer bag.

Reheating Instructions

Defrost biscuits at room temperature for 1–2 hours. Biscuits can either be served at room temperature or heated in a 350°F oven 6–10 minutes or until they reach the desired temperature.

PER SERVING
Calories: 238 | Fat: 9g | Protein: 8g | Sodium: 669mg | Carbohydrates: 32g | Fiber: 0g

Lemon Poppy Seed Bread

To get the most juice out of your lemon, microwave it for 15 seconds.
Afterwards, roll it with your palm on a flat surface, then juice.

INGREDIENTS | YIELDS 1 LOAF

½ cup butter

¾ cup sugar

2 eggs

4 tablespoons fresh lemon juice

Zest of 1 lemon

1½ cups flour

1 teaspoon baking powder

⅛ teaspoon salt

½ cup milk

1 teaspoon poppy seeds

Lemon Glaze

Once your bread has been baked and is still warm, you can add a glaze to the top. Mix together 2 tablespoons lemon juice with ½ cup confectioners' sugar. Add additional tablespoons of confectioners' sugar until glaze is thick. With a toothpick, make small holes in the top of the bread and pour the glaze over the entire loaf.

Freezing Day

In a mixing bowl, cream butter and sugar, then add eggs one at a time. Mix in lemon juice and lemon zest. In separate bowl, sift together flour, baking powder, and salt. Alternate adding the dry ingredients and milk to the egg mixture. Stir in poppy seeds. Pour batter into a greased loaf pan. Bake at 350°F for 45 minutes or until a knife inserted in the center comes out clean. Cool, wrap with plastic wrap, and freeze.

Reheating Instructions

Defrost bread at room temperature for 2–3 hours, and serve at room temperature.

PER LOAF
Calories: 1624 | Fat: 107g | Protein: 17g | Sodium: 1907mg | Carbohydrates: 159g | Fiber: 0g

Coffee Cake

Coffee cake seldom contains coffee, but was originally made to eat with your coffee as a snack or dessert. This light and fluffy coffee cake will certainly complement your morning coffee or afternoon tea.

INGREDIENTS | SERVES 6

½ cup vegetable oil

¾ cup sugar

1 egg

½ cup milk

1½ cups flour

1½ teaspoons baking powder

¼ teaspoon salt

1 teaspoon vanilla extract

2 tablespoons butter

¼ cup brown sugar

1 teaspoon flour

1 teaspoon cinnamon

½ cup chopped pecans

Freezing Day

Mix together oil and sugar. Add egg and milk, and mix. In a separate bowl, sift together flour, baking powder, and salt. Add flour mixture to egg mixture a little at a time and mix well. In separate bowl prepare topping by mixing the vanilla extract, butter, brown sugar, teaspoon of flour, cinnamon, and nuts. Pour coffee cake batter into a greased 9" x 9" pan. Add topping. Bake at 350°F for 35 minutes or until edges are browned and a knife inserted in the center comes out clean. Cool, wrap with plastic wrap, and freeze.

Reheating Instructions

Defrost coffee cake at room temperature for 1–2 hours and serve at room temperature.

PER SERVING
Calories: 458 | Fat: 31g | Protein: 3.5g | Sodium: 184mg | Carbohydrates: 44g | Fiber: 2g

Garlic Parmesan Rolls with Marinara Sauce

Try coating these savory treats with cheeses or herbs.
After dipping the rolls in butter, sprinkle them with rosemary or basil.

INGREDIENTS | SERVES 8–12

½ cup butter

3 tablespoons minced garlic

2 cans (13.8-ounce) refrigerated pizza crust

¼–½ cup Parmesan cheese, to taste

1 jar chunky marinara sauce for dipping (used on reheating day)

Freezing Parmesan Cheese

Canned Parmesan cheese just cannot hold a candle to the taste of real fresh-ground cheese. Unfortunately, fresh block parmesan has a shelf life of only a few weeks in the refrigerator and therefore does not store well. Grated Parmesan cheese, however, does freeze well. Finely grate and seal in an airtight container (preferably in small, single-use amounts) and freeze.

Freezing Day

In saucepan, melt 1 tablespoon butter and sauté garlic for 1–2 minutes. Add remaining butter and mix. Remove from heat. Remove the pizza dough from the cans and roll it out a bit. Cut dough into strips, and tie strips into knots. Place knots on greased baking sheet and bake at 400°F for 15–20 minutes until knots begin to turn light golden brown. While still hot, dip each knot into garlic butter, sprinkle with Parmesan cheese, and cool. Flash freeze on a baking sheet. Transfer to freezer bag.

Reheating Instructions

Defrost knots at room temperature for 1 hour. Put on greased baking sheet and bake at 400°F until knots are golden brown, 3–5 minutes. Heat marinara sauce in the microwave for 30 seconds–1 minute and serve with garlic knots for dipping.

PER SERVING
Calories: 210 | Fat: 13g | Protein: 4g | Sodium: 207mg | Carbohydrates: 21g | Fiber: 2g

Cranberry Quick Bread

The secret to keeping quick bread moist is in the mixing. When combining wet and dry ingredients, take care to just combine—do not over mix. Over mixing will cause your quick bread to crumble when sliced.

INGREDIENTS | YIELDS 1 LOAF

2 cups flour
1½ teaspoons baking powder
½ teaspoon baking soda
¾ teaspoon salt
1 cup sugar
1 egg
2 tablespoons vegetable oil
¾ cup orange juice
Zest 1 orange
1 cup chopped cranberries
Small dash grated nutmeg

Freezing Day

Sift together flour, baking powder, baking soda, and salt. In a separate bowl, combine sugar, egg, vegetable oil, orange juice, and orange zest. Lightly stir in cranberries and nutmeg. Combine wet and dry ingredients together, stirring just enough to combine. Pour batter into a greased 9" x 5" loaf pan. Bake at 350°F for 50 minutes–1 hour until a knife inserted into center comes out clean. Once fully cooled, wrap well with plastic wrap, and freeze.

Reheating Instructions

Defrost bread at room temperature for 2–3 hours and serve at room temperature.

PER LOAF
Calories: 2147 | Fat: 36g | Protein: 33g | Sodium: 3160mg | Carbohydrates: 425g | Fiber: 13g

Sweet Potato Biscuits

These biscuits make a delicious dessert item when glazed with any white, vanilla, or orange-flavored frosting. Warm frosting in microwave and drizzle over biscuits.

INGREDIENTS | YIELDS 25 BISCUITS

1½ cups flour

2 tablespoons baking powder

1 tablespoon brown sugar

1 teaspoon cinnamon

Small pinch grated nutmeg

¾ teaspoon salt

½ cup shortening

1 cup milk

1½ cups sweet potatoes, mashed

Cinnamon Honey Butter

For a delicious treat, serve these biscuits hot out of the oven and topped with Cinnamon Honey Butter. To make the butter, beat together ½ cup softened butter, ½ cup honey, ¼ cup confectioners' sugar, and 1 teaspoon cinnamon. You'll also love it spread on homemade bread and pancakes!

Freezing Day

Sift together the flour, baking powder, brown sugar, cinnamon, nutmeg, and salt. Use a pastry blender (or 2 knives), and cut in shortening. In a separate bowl, mix milk and sweet potatoes. Combine the sweet potato mixture with the flour mixture. Knead for about 30 seconds, then roll out onto a lightly floured board. Roll to ½" thickness, then cut with a biscuit cutter. If you don't have a biscuit cutter, use the rim of a drinking glass to cut biscuits. Place biscuits on lightly greased baking sheet. Bake for 12–15 minutes at 425°F. Cool and flash freeze. Once frozen, transfer to a freezer bag.

Reheating Instructions

Defrost biscuits at room temperature for 1–2 hours and warm in a 425°F oven for 3–5 minutes or until desired temperature is reached.

PER SERVING
Calories: 81 | Fat: 4.5g | Protein: 1.5g | Sodium: 195mg | Carbohydrates: 9g | Fiber: 0.5g

Carrot Bread

Although carrot bread is often served with a meal, this recipe's carrot bread is more of a dessert since it is a bit too sweet to accompany a meal.

INGREDIENTS | YIELDS 1 LOAF

1 cup butter

½ cup white sugar

½ cup brown sugar

3 eggs

1 teaspoon vanilla extract

2 cups flour

1 teaspoon baking soda

1 teaspoon baking powder

½ teaspoon salt

2 teaspoons cinnamon

½ teaspoon nutmeg

2 cups carrots, grated

1 cup walnuts

½ cup raisins

Freezing Day

In a bowl, cream butter, white sugar, and brown sugar until light and fluffy. Add eggs and vanilla and mix. In separate bowl, sift together the flour, baking soda, baking powder, salt, cinnamon, and nutmeg. Add the dry ingredients to the butter mixture, and mix just enough to combine. Do not over mix. Stir in the carrots, walnuts, and raisins. Pour batter into a greased 9" x 5" loaf pan. Bake at 350°F for 1 hour or until a knife inserted into the center comes out clean. Cool the bread, wrap well with plastic wrap, and freeze.

Reheating Instructions

Defrost the bread at room temperature for 2–3 hours and serve at room temperature. You can also heat the bread in the oven at 350°F for about 5–10 minutes.

PER LOAF
Calories: 4695 | Fat: 280g | Protein: 68g | Sodium: 5186mg | Carbohydrates: 506g | Fiber: 26g

Dinner Rolls

To quickly warm, place these rolls in a paper bag and heat in the microwave for 20–30 seconds (until warm, but not hot) and serve with honey butter.

INGREDIENTS | SERVES 12

2 (.25-ounce) packages yeast

2 cups warm water

Pinch sugar

½ cup butter

3 eggs

½ cup sugar

1 teaspoon salt

6 cups flour

Honey Butter

This butter is delicious on almost any roll. Mix ½ pound butter (softened), ⅓ cup honey, ¼ teaspoon cinnamon, ¼ teaspoon vanilla extract, and a dash of salt. Use a melon baller to form scoops of butter, and flash freeze on a baking sheet covered with wax paper. Once frozen, transfer to a freezer bag.

Freezing Day

In a large bowl, mix together the yeast, warm water, and pinch of sugar. Let mixture sit for about 10 minutes until it starts to froth on top. Add butter and eggs to yeast and mix. Add sugar, salt, and 3 cups flour and mix. Continue to add flour until the dough is easy to handle. Knead the dough on a lightly floured surface until it becomes elastic. Put the dough in a lightly greased bowl, cover it with a towel, and set the bowl in a warm place for about 1 hour until the dough has doubled in size. Shape into rolls and put in a greased baking pan. Cover the rolls with a towel and let rise for 30 minutes. Bake rolls at 400°F for 15–20 minutes. Let rolls cool, then flash freeze on a baking sheet. Once frozen, transfer to a freezer bag.

Reheating Instructions

Let rolls defrost at room temperature for 1 hour, and serve. If you want to warm the rolls, heat in a 350°F oven for 5–10 minutes.

PER SERVING
Calories: 383 | Fat: 10g | Protein: 12g | Sodium: 295mg | Carbohydrates: 61g | Fiber: 4g

Mixes, Dips, and Spreads

Taco Seasoning Mix

Taco seasoning mix can be used with ground beef, turkey, or pork to make a variety of Mexican dishes such as Spicy Taco Roll-ups (Chapter 9).

INGREDIENTS | YIELDS 2.6 TABLESPOONS DRY MIX

1 tablespoon chili powder

2 teaspoons dried minced onion

1 teaspoon cumin

1 teaspoon garlic powder

1 teaspoon paprika

Dash cayenne, or more according to taste

Freezing Day

Mix all ingredients together and freeze in a freezer bag. To make with meat before freezing, add to browned meat with 1 cup water. Bring to a boil, reduce heat, and simmer 10–15 minutes. Freeze in a freezer bag.

Reheating Instructions

Use spices according to recipe.

PER SERVING
Calories: 20 | Fat: 0g | Protein: 0g | Sodium: 40mg | Carbohydrates: 4g | Fiber: 1g

Pico de Gallo

The secret to making delicious Pico de Gallo is fresh ingredients. Using high-quality ingredients—from beautiful ripe tomatoes to garden-fresh cilantro— is a surefire way to make your Pico de Gallo a wonderful accompaniment to your food.

INGREDIENTS | SERVES 4

2 large ripe tomatoes, diced

1 red onion, diced

3 tablespoons fresh cilantro, chopped

1 jalapeño pepper, diced

½ clove minced garlic

Juice 1–2 limes, or to taste

Salt to taste

Freezing Day

Mix tomatoes, onions, cilantro, jalapeño, and garlic. Add lime juice and salt to taste. Freeze in a freezer bag or Tupperware.

Reheating Instructions

Defrost in the refrigerator overnight and serve.

PER SERVING
Calories: 34 | Fat: 0g | Protein: 1.5g | Sodium: 6mg | Carbohydrates: 8g | Fiber: 2g

Basil and Pine Nut Pesto

Pesto, a sauce that originated in Italy, is traditionally made using a mortar and pestle. It is most commonly served over pasta, but can be used in a wide variety of ways such as over baked potatoes, on top of a steak, or even with steamed vegetables.

INGREDIENTS | YIELDS APPROXIMATELY 3½ CUPS

½ cup pine nuts

2 cups fresh basil

4 cloves garlic, peeled

¾ cup fresh Parmesan cheese, grated

1 tablespoon salt

1½ cups olive oil

Freezing Day

In food processor, mix the pine nuts, basil, garlic, cheese, and salt. Gradually add olive oil until pesto reaches desired consistency. Transfer to a freezer bag and freeze.

Reheating Instructions

Defrost pesto in the refrigerator overnight and use as desired.

PER TABLESPOON
Calories: 64 | Fat: 7g | Protein: 1g | Sodium: 145mg | Carbohydrates: 0g | Fiber: 0g

Salsa Verde

This Salsa Verde is made primarily from tomatillos. Try making your own recipe of salsa verde using fresh herbs by combining fresh thyme, a little sage, parsley, cilantro, garlic, shallot, basil, salt, pepper, and olive oil in a blender. Taste as you go to come up with the perfect recipe!

INGREDIENTS | SERVES 6–8

1 pound fresh tomatillos

1 shallot, peeled

1 clove garlic

2 Poblano chilies

½ cup fresh cilantro

3 tablespoons fresh oregano

½ teaspoon cumin

3 tablespoons lime juice

Olive oil as needed

Salt to taste

Freezing Day

Remove husks from tomatillos and put in saucepan with water. Bring to a boil. Reduce heat and simmer about 10 minutes. Add all ingredients to a food processor and purée. Add olive oil to reach desired consistency, and salt to taste. Freeze in a freezer bag.

Reheating Instructions

Defrost sauce in refrigerator overnight and use as desired.

PER SERVING
Calories: 31 | Fat: 0g | Protein: 1.5g | Sodium: 8mg | Carbohydrates: 7g | Fiber: 2g

Garden Salsa

Jalapeño peppers are delicious to eat, but handling them can cause skin irritation, like redness and burning, that can last for several days. To avoid this, wear gloves when cutting the peppers. If you don't have gloves, put your hands inside a freezer bag or plastic grocery bag.

INGREDIENTS | SERVES 15

3 (28-ounce) cans diced tomatoes (you may substitute with vine-ripened tomatoes)

1 onion, chopped

2 green bell peppers, diced

1 red bell pepper, diced

½ cup chopped fresh cilantro

2–3 teaspoons salt, according to taste

2–4 jalapeño peppers, seeded and diced

Juice of 2 limes

Freezing Day

Combine all ingredients and mix well. Add additional salt as needed. Freeze in a plastic container.

Reheating Instructions

Defrost salsa in refrigerator overnight and serve.

PER SERVING
Calories: 36 | Fat: 0g | Protein: 2g | Sodium: 587mg | Carbohydrates: 10g | Fiber: 3g

Orange Butter

Try Orange Butter on your next steak; the combination of citrus with the richness of butter will add mouth-watering flavor. It also tastes delicious when paired with fish, or melted over vegetables.

INGREDIENTS | YIELDS 9 TABLESPOONS

1 stick butter, softened

¼ cup orange juice

1 teaspoon lemon juice

1 tablespoon chopped parsley

Freezing Day

Mix all ingredients together well. This butter can be frozen in freezer bags, or you can spread servings in plastic ice cube trays, freeze, and then transfer cubes to a freezer bag.

Reheating Instructions

Defrost butter at room temperature and use as desired.

PER SERVING
Calories: 93 | Fat: 10g | Protein: 0g | Sodium: 104mg | Carbohydrates: 1g | Fiber: 0g

Ground Beef Seasoning Mix

Add this seasoning to make delicious hamburgers, or add it to your meatloaf, or even meatballs. This recipe is enough to season 2 pounds of ground beef.

INGREDIENTS | YIELDS 4 TEASPOONS

½ teaspoon salt

½ teaspoon black pepper

½ teaspoon brown sugar

1½ teaspoons paprika

¼ teaspoon garlic powder

¼ teaspoon onion powder

¼ teaspoon cumin

⅛ teaspoon cayenne pepper

Freezing Day

Mix all ingredients together and store in an airtight container. Either freeze on its own or add to food before freezing (as called for in the recipe).

Reheating Instructions

Use according to chosen recipe.

PER SERVING
Calories: 5 | Fat: 0g | Protein: 0g | Sodium: 291mg | Carbohydrates: 1.5g | Fiber: 0.5g

Uncle Frank's Hot Stuff

Serve this zesty condiment with Spicy Taco Roll-ups (Chapter 9), Skillet Beef with Black Beans (Chapter 3), or Chicken and Bean Enchiladas (Chapter 9).

INGREDIENTS | SERVES 6–8

2 jalapeño peppers, sliced

3 tomatoes, diced

¾ cup purple onion, finely diced

¼ cup diced fresh cilantro

1 avocado, diced (used on reheating day)

Garlic salt to taste (used on reheating day)

Lime juice to taste (used on reheating day)

Freezing Day

In mixing bowl combine jalapeño peppers, tomatoes, onion, and cilantro. Mix well, put in freezer bag and freeze.

Reheating Instructions

Defrost mixture in the refrigerator overnight. Add avocado, garlic salt, and lime juice to taste.

PER SERVING
Calories: 49 | Fat: 3g | Protein: 1g | Sodium: 105mg | Carbohydrates: 6g | Fiber: 2g

Lemon Butter

Try lemon butter on fish, shellfish, or vegetables.
You can also use it as a rub on steak or chicken before grilling.

INGREDIENTS | YIELDS ½ CUP

1 stick butter, softened
2 tablespoons lemon juice
1 teaspoon lemon zest
2 tablespoons chopped fresh parsley

Freezing Day

Combine all ingredients in a food processor. Freeze in Tupperware or a freezer bag.

Reheating Instructions

Defrost butter at room temperature for 1 hour and use as desired.

PER TABLESPOON
Calories: 103 | Fat: 12g | Protein: 0g | Sodium: 117mg | Carbohydrates: 0g | Fiber: 0g

Greek Olive Spread

Fill a beautiful bowl with Greek Olive Spread and set it in the center of a plate. Arrange a variety of crackers or toasted baguette slices around the bowl on the plate.

INGREDIENTS | SERVES 24

1¼ cups black olives, pitted
1¼ cups green olives, pitted
½ cup feta cheese
4 tablespoons red wine vinegar
3 tablespoons olive oil
½ teaspoon garlic powder
½ teaspoon basil
½ teaspoon oregano
¼ teaspoon salt
¼ teaspoon Dijon mustard
¼ teaspoon minced onion

Freezing Day

In a food processor, mix olives and feta cheese. Add remaining ingredients and mix until smooth. Freeze spread in a freezer bag.

Reheating Instructions

Defrost spread in the refrigerator and serve at room temperature.

PER SERVING
Calories: 38 | Fat: 4g | Protein: 0.5g | Sodium: 150mg | Carbohydrates: 1g | Fiber: 0g

Barbecue Rub

Keep a container of this rub in your freezer so it'll be ready to go for your next cookout.
Rub oil over meat followed by this rub before putting it in the freezer.
When you are ready to cook, you'll have a deliciously seasoned meat.

INGREDIENTS | YIELDS 6 TABLESPOONS

3 tablespoons paprika

1 tablespoons salt

2 teaspoons onion powder

2 teaspoons garlic powder

2 teaspoons pepper

Dash cayenne, or to taste

Freezing Day

Combine all ingredients and freeze in a freezer bag or plastic container.

Reheating Instructions

Use straight from freezer.

PER SERVING
Calories: 13 | Fat: 0g | Protein: 0.5g | Sodium: 1164mg | Carbohydrates: 3g | Fiber: 1.5g

Queso Dip

This cheesy dip is delicious served with tortilla chips or as a topping on tacos or burritos. Spice up the dip with chopped jalapeños or green chili peppers.

INGREDIENTS | SERVES 6–8

¼ pound ground beef

1 small onion

1 (16-ounce) block Velveeta

1 cup jarred salsa

Freezing Day

In skillet, brown ground beef with chopped onion for about 8–10 minutes. Drain. In a large saucepan, melt Velveeta. Add salsa and ground beef mixture to melted cheese. Mix well. Let mixture cool and freeze in freezer bag.

Reheating Instructions

Defrost in the refrigerator overnight. Heat defrosted Queso Dip in saucepan over medium heat for 5–10 minutes.

PER SERVING
Calories: 222 | Fat: 15g | Protein: 13g | Sodium: 914mg | Carbohydrates: 9g | Fiber: 0.5g

Roasted Eggplant Dip

By adding salt to the eggplant before roasting, you help draw out the eggplant's natural bitter juices during the cooking process.

INGREDIENTS | SERVES 4

1 large eggplant

3 tablespoons olive oil, plus 2 teaspoons used for roasting eggplant

½ teaspoon salt

2 cloves garlic, minced

⅓ cup pecans

½ cup fresh chopped basil leaves

½ cup cream cheese, softened

Salt and pepper to taste

Freezing Day

To roast the eggplant, preheat oven to 450°F. Slice the eggplant in half lengthwise, and put small cuts across the flesh of the eggplant, being careful not to cut the skin. Rub olive oil and salt over the flesh of the eggplant, and place face down on a foil-lined baking sheet. Bake for 20–30 minutes until it is soft and looks like it will collapse. Let cool, discarding any juice. While eggplant is cooling, combine remaining ingredients in a mixing bowl. Slide the skin off the eggplant and add the flesh to the bowl. Mix. Freeze using a freezer bag.

Reheating Instructions

Defrost in the refrigerator overnight and serve at room temperature.

PER SERVING
Calories: 281 | Fat: 27 g | Protein: 4g | Sodium: 89mg | Carbohydrates: 9g | Fiber: 4g

Garden Fiesta Dip

Tortilla chips taste great with this dip, but it goes especially well with vegetables. It is also a hit with the kids, and is a great way to get them to eat their veggies!

INGREDIENTS | SERVES 6

12 ounces cottage cheese

2 (8-ounce) packages cream cheese, softened

1 (1.25-ounce) envelope taco seasoning mix

Orange Salsa

Serve this salsa with tortilla chips. Mix the following: 1 orange cut into small pieces, 3 slices jalapeño pepper chopped, 2 tablespoons brown sugar, 2 tablespoons cilantro, 1 tablespoon chopped green onion, and the juice from 1 orange.

Freezing Day

Mix together cottage cheese, cream cheese, and taco seasoning mix. Put into freezer bag and freeze.

Reheating Instructions

Defrost dip in refrigerator overnight and spread on a plate. Cover dip with desired toppings (shredded lettuce, diced tomatoes, Cheddar cheese, sliced olives, diced onions, or sliced jalapeño peppers.)

PER SERVING
Calories: 320 | Fat: 29g | Protein: 12g | Sodium: 506mg | Carbohydrates: 4g | Fiber: 0g

Blackened Seasoning Mix

Make a batch of this mix and keep it on hand for use on steaks, chicken, and hamburgers. Just rub over your favorite meat and grill.

INGREDIENTS | YIELDS 5 TABLESPOONS

2 tablespoons paprika

1 teaspoon white pepper

1 teaspoon ground red pepper (or less to taste)

1 teaspoon ground black pepper

2 teaspoons onion powder

2 teaspoons garlic powder

1 teaspoon dried oregano

1 teaspoon dried thyme

Freezing Day

Mix all spices together and freeze in a freezer bag, or plastic container.

Reheating Instructions

Use straight from the freezer as desired.

PER SERVING
Calories: 19 | Fat: 0g | Protein: 0.5g | Sodium: 3mg | Carbohydrates: 4g | Fiber: 1.5g

Spicy Black Bean Dip

This dip tastes great served with tortilla chips, toasted bread, or bagel chips.
It also makes a great filling for tacos and burritos!

INGREDIENTS | YIELDS 1 CUP

1 (15-ounce) can black beans, drained (reserve liquid)

¼ cup fresh cilantro, chopped

1 teaspoon chili powder

1 teaspoon cilantro

1 teaspoon salt

1 (4-ounce) can green chilies, drained

Freezing Day

Combine all ingredients in food processor and process until smooth. Use reserved liquid from black beans to bring the dip to the desired consistency. Freeze dip in a freezer bag.

Reheating Instructions

Defrost dip in the refrigerator overnight and serve either hot or cold.

PER TABLESPOON
Calories: 85 | Fat: .5g | Protein: 5.5g | Sodium: 179mg | Carbohydrates: 16g | Fiber: 4g

Hummus

If you like your hummus spicy, add cayenne pepper and sliced jalapeño peppers.
Serve the hummus with Pita Bread Crackers (Chapter 12).

INGREDIENTS | SERVES 8

1 (15-ounce) can garbanzo beans, drained, liquid reserved

2 tablespoons lemon juice

1 tablespoon sesame oil

2 tablespoons sesame seeds

2 tablespoons onion, minced

2 cloves garlic, minced

Freezing Day

Combine garbanzo beans, lemon juice, sesame oil, sesame seeds, onion, and garlic in food processor. Mix until blended. Add reserve garbanzo bean liquid a tablespoon at a time until the hummus reaches a creamy consistency. Freeze in freezer bag or Tupperware.

Reheating Instructions

Defrost in the refrigerator overnight and serve at room temperature.

PER SERVING
Calories: 68 | Fat: 3g | Protein: 4g | Sodium: 230mg | Carbohydrates: 10g | Fiber: 3g

Dried Bean Mix

This mix makes a large batch of beans and seasoning that is enough for approximately 6 batches of Calico Bean Soup (Chapter 11).

INGREDIENTS | YIELDS 6 BATCHES SOUP

2 cups great northern beans

2 cups kidney beans

2 cups lima beans

2 cups pinto beans

1 cup black eyed peas

1 cup navy beans

½ cup split peas

½ cup black beans

2 tablespoons chili powder

1½ teaspoons garlic powder

6 tablespoons dried onion

1 tablespoons oregano

1½ teaspoons black pepper

Divide Beans into Portions

If you would like to divide this mix into portions for making Calico Bean Soup (Chapter 11) or giving as gifts, separate into batches containing 2 cups beans and 3 tablespoons spices. Freeze the spices in a separate freezer bag, and put that freezer bag inside the freezer bag containing the beans. This will keep them together in your freezer.

Freezing Day

Mix all dried beans together and freeze in a freezer bag. Mix the spices together and freeze in a separate smaller freezer bag. Store the seasoning freezer bag inside the bean freezer bag.

Reheating Instructions

Remove from freezer (no need to defrost!) and use as desired.

PER SERVING

Calories: 1035 | Fat: 3.5g | Protein: 67g | Sodium: 43mg | Carbohydrates: 190g | Fiber: 62g

CHAPTER 14

Marinades and Sauces

Sweet and Sour Sauce

This versatile sauce will carry you through many meals.
Try it with Basic Meatballs (Chapter 15), shredded pork, chicken, or as a dipping sauce.

(Chapter 15)

INGREDIENTS | SERVES 6

1 (15-ounce) can pineapple chunks with juice

½ cup white vinegar

¼ cup ketchup

¾ cup brown sugar

1 tablespoon Worcestershire sauce

Dash hot sauce

3 tablespoons cornstarch (optional)

¼ cup cold water (optional)

Freezing Day

Pour the pineapple juice into a measuring cup. Add enough water to make 1 cup. Save the pineapples to serve with dinner, or for use in another recipe. Combine all ingredients in a saucepan and bring to a boil. Simmer 5 minutes. Freeze in a freezer bag or in Tupperware. If you prefer your sweet and sour sauce thick, mix 3 tablespoons cornstarch with ¼ cup cold water. Mix until the cornstarch is completely dissolved. Pour the cornstarch mixture into the saucepan and stir continually until the sauce thickens.

Reheating Instructions

Defrost sauce in the refrigerator overnight and serve at room temperature.

PER SERVING
Calories: 144 | Fat: 0g | Protein: 0g | Sodium: 150mg |
Carbohydrates: 36g | Fiber: 1g

Three Ingredient Hollandaise Sauce

Making hollandaise sauce can sound intimidating, but it is really quite easy. The trick is using a double boiler because it keeps the saucepan the perfect temperature to cook the hollandaise without scrambling the eggs.

INGREDIENTS | YIELDS 1 CUP

4 egg yolks
1 tablespoon lemon juice
½ cup butter, softened

Sauce Cubes

Use plastic ice cube trays to freeze your different sauces. Simply spray the tray with a light layer of nonstick cooking spray to keep the flavors from seeping into the plastic, and pour in the sauce. Once cubes are formed, pop them out of the ice cube tray and put in a freezer bag. Defrost as many cubes as needed.

Freezing Day

In a double boiler over gently boiling water, add egg yolks and lemon juice. Mix together using a whisk. Gradually add butter, spoonful by spoonful, whisking the entire time. Continue to cook, stirring continually about 3–5 minutes, until sauce thickens. Freeze in a Tupperware container or freezer bag.

Reheating Instructions

Defrost hollandaise sauce in the refrigerator overnight and heat over a low heat for 5–10 minutes, or until desired temperature is reached. If sauce is too thick, add warm water.

PER TABELSPOON
Calories: 100 | Fat: 10g | Protein: 2.5g | Sodium: 69mg | Carbohydrates: 5g | Fiber: 0g

Alfredo Sauce

Alfredo sauce is very versatile. You can serve it with grilled chicken and fettuccine noodles, as a topping for vegetables, or with seafood.

INGREDIENTS | SERVES 6

⅓ cup butter

1 small clove garlic, minced

2 cups heavy cream

1½ cups fresh Parmesan cheese, grated

¼ cup fresh parsley, chopped

1 (8-ounce) can sliced mushrooms

⅛ teaspoon black pepper, or more to taste

Freezing Day

In saucepan over medium-low heat, melt butter. Add garlic and heavy cream. Little by little add the Parmesan cheese. Stir constantly. Stir in parsley, mushrooms, and pepper to taste. Freezer in freezer bag.

Reheating Instructions

Defrost sauce in refrigerator overnight and heat in saucepan over medium heat for 8–12 minutes. If sauce is too thick, thin out by adding milk or more butter.

PER SERVING
Calories: 473 | Fat: 47g | Protein: 12g | Sodium: 516mg | Carbohydrates: 3.5g | Fiber: 0g

Stir-fry Sauce

This sauce is easy to whip up, tastes fantastic on both beef and chicken, and is a great option to keep on hand in the freezer to prepare for a quick dinner.

INGREDIENTS | YIELDS 1¼ CUPS

¼ cup soy sauce

¼ cup honey

¾ cup olive oil

2 tablespoons balsamic vinegar

2 cloves garlic, minced

1 tablespoon onion, minced

¼ teaspoon fresh ginger

Freezing Day

In a food processor, mix all ingredients. Freeze in a freezer bag.

Reheating Instructions

Defrost sauce in the refrigerator overnight and use as desired.

PER RECIPE
Calories: 1771 | Fat: 162g | Protein: 8g | Sodium: 3689mg | Carbohydrates: 80g | Fiber: 0g

Lemon Tarragon Sauce

This light and tangy sauce tastes delicious over vegetables, fish, or even grilled chicken breasts. If you are a sauce lover, double the recipe to be sure you have enough!

INGREDIENTS | SERVES 4

3 tablespoons lemon juice

3 tablespoons fresh tarragon

½ teaspoon Dijon mustard

1 teaspoon red onion, minced

3 tablespoons chicken broth

¾ cup olive oil

Salt and pepper to taste

Freezing Day

Add lemon juice, tarragon, Dijon mustard, onion, and chicken broth to a food processor. Mix well. With the food processor running, pour in the olive oil. Add salt and pepper to taste. Freeze the sauce in a freezer bag.

Reheating Instructions

Defrost sauce in the refrigerator overnight. Heat over medium-low heat for 5–10 minutes and use as desired.

PER SERVING
Calories: 363 | Fat: 41g | Protein: 0g | Sodium: 28mg | Carbohydrates: 1g | Fiber: 0g

Cucumber Dipping Sauce

This sauce is wonderful served with Spicy Beef Kabobs (Chapter 2), or a variety of cut-up vegetables such as red and green bell peppers, carrots, and celery.

INGREDIENTS | SERVES 8

1 medium cucumber

2 cups plain yogurt

1 tablespoon fresh dill

2 teaspoons lemon juice

Salt and pepper to taste

1 clove garlic, minced (used on reheating day)

2 tablespoons red onion, finely chopped (used on reheating day)

Freezing Day

Peel, seed, and chop the cucumber. In mixing bowl, mix cucumber, yogurt, dill, lemon juice, salt, and pepper. Freeze in freezer bag or Tupperware.

Reheating Instructions

Defrost dip in the refrigerator overnight. Stir in garlic and red onion, and serve chilled.

PER SERVING
Calories: 45 | Fat: 1.5g | Protein: 3.5g | Sodium: 43mg | Carbohydrates: 6g | Fiber: 0.5g

Basic Marinara Sauce

This sauce can be paired with a variety of dishes such as Basic Meatballs (Chapter 15), or with Eggplant Parmigiana (Chapter 7). Dress up the sauce by adding sautéed bell peppers, zucchini, and mushrooms.

INGREDIENTS | SERVES 4–6

½ cup chopped onion

2 cloves garlic, minced

2 tablespoons olive oil

2 (14.5-ounce) cans diced tomatoes

1 (6-ounce) can tomato paste

1½ teaspoons basil

1½ teaspoons oregano

1 whole bay leaf

Freezing Day

In a skillet, sauté onion in olive oil for 8–10 minutes. Add garlic and sauté an additional 1–2 minutes. Add diced tomatoes with liquid, tomato paste, and spices. Bring to a boil, then reduce heat and simmer 1–2 hours. Remove bay leaf. Freeze in Tupperware or freezer bag.

Reheating Instructions

Defrost sauce in refrigerator overnight and use as desired.

PER SERVING
Calories: 128 | Fat: 5g | Protein: 4g | Sodium: 424mg | Carbohydrates: 20g | Fiber: 4g

Cajun Marinade

Use this marinade on pork or chicken. You can marinate the meat for several hours in the refrigerator, or you can freeze the meat with the marinade to cook at a later time.

INGREDIENTS | YIELDS 1 CUP

1 cup chicken broth

½ teaspoon cayenne pepper, or more to taste

½ teaspoon black pepper

1 clove garlic, minced

½ teaspoon onion powder

½ teaspoon salt

1 teaspoon brown sugar

2 teaspoons sweet paprika

Freezing Day

In food processor, combine all ingredients. Freeze in freezer bag.

Reheating Instructions

Defrost marinade in the refrigerator overnight and use as desired.

PER SERVING
Calories: 56 | Fat: 0.5g | Protein: 4g | Sodium: 1721mg | Carbohydrates: 10g | Fiber: 2g

Teriyaki Marinade

Cayenne is a hot spice used to flavor dishes. Adjust the cayenne to suit your tastes, and be sure to add extra cayenne slowly—the heat can sneak up on you!

INGREDIENTS | YIELDS ½ CUP

½ cup teriyaki sauce

2 tablespoons orange juice concentrate

1 clove garlic, minced

¼ teaspoon ground ginger

⅛ teaspoon cayenne pepper

Freezing Day

In food processor, combine all ingredients and mix. Freeze in a freezer bag or plastic container.

Reheating Instructions

Defrost marinade in the refrigerator overnight and use as desired.

PER SERVING
Calories: 138 | Fat: 0g | Protein: 9g | Sodium: 5477mg | Carbohydrates: 27g | Fiber: 0g

Red Wine Marinade

Use this marinade on a steak such as London broil. Score steak on both sides and freeze in a freezer bag with the marinade. Roll the steak around so it is coated in the marinade. The steak will absorb the delicious flavors during the freezing and defrosting time.

INGREDIENTS | YIELDS 1 CUP

⅔ cup red wine

⅓ cup soy sauce

2 tablespoons olive oil

2 cloves garlic, chopped

1¼ teaspoons ginger

1 tablespoon minced onion

To Marinate Without Freezing

Marinate 6–24 hours to tenderize meat. For most cuts that need tenderizing, marinating for 12–16 hours is enough time to tenderize without risking making the meat mushy. For safety, always marinate in the refrigerator and never at room temperature.

Freezing Day

In a food processor, combine all ingredients. Mix well and freeze.

Reheating Instructions

Defrost marinade in the refrigerator overnight and use as desired.

PER SERVING
Calories: 319 | Fat: 27g | Protein: 11g | Sodium: 4858mg | Carbohydrates: 2.5g | Fiber: 0g

Sweet Barbecue Sauce

This is a sauce that kids love. Put a batch of chicken legs in a freezer bag, pour the barbecue sauce over them, and freeze. When you are ready to cook, defrost the chicken and throw the legs on the grill.

INGREDIENTS | YIELDS 3 CUPS

2 cups ketchup

1 cup brown sugar

2 teaspoons liquid smoke

1 teaspoon garlic powder

½ teaspoon Worcestershire sauce

Freezing Day

Combine all ingredients and mix well. Freeze in a freezer bag.

Reheating Instructions

Defrost sauce in the refrigerator overnight and use as desired.

PER RECIPE
Calories: 1307 | Fat: 2g | Protein: 10g | Sodium: 5400mg | Carbohydrates: 337g | Fiber: 5g

Dill Sauce

Dill seeds have a stronger flavor than dill weed and add a crunch to your dip. You can also use ¼ cup fresh dill in place of the dried dill weed.

INGREDIENTS | YIELDS ½ CUP

½ cup plain yogurt

1 teaspoon dried dill weed

½ teaspoon sugar

1 teaspoon lemon zest

2 teaspoons lemon juice

Salt to taste

Freezing Day

Combine all ingredients and freeze in freezer bag.

Reheating Instructions

Defrost sauce in the refrigerator overnight and serve chilled.

PER SERVING
Calories: 311 | Fat: 4g | Protein: 4g | Sodium: 65mg | Carbohydrates: 90g | Fiber: 0g

Eastern NC BBQ Sauce

Eastern NC BBQ Sauce is a vinegar-based sauce that tastes quite different than traditional barbecue sauce. It is delicious on pork—try it as a condiment with Pulled Pork (Chapter 6).

INGREDIENTS | YIELDS 2 CUPS

2 cups apple cider vinegar
1½ tablespoons brown sugar
1½ teaspoons red pepper flakes
1½ teaspoons hot sauce (or to taste)
1 teaspoon salt
½ teaspoon white pepper

Freezing Day

Add all ingredients into a food processor and mix well. Freeze using a freezer bag or Tupperware.

Reheating Instructions

Defrost sauce in the refrigerator overnight and use as desired.

PER SERVING
Calories: 129 | Fat: 0g | Protein: 0g | Sodium: 2414mg | Carbohydrates: 12g | Fiber: 0.5g

Sesame Ginger Dipping Sauce/Marinade

Dip homemade Pot Stickers (Chapter 5) in this sauce, or use it as a marinade for chicken, fish, or beef. It also tastes delicious mixed with vegetables and stir-fried.

INGREDIENTS | YIELDS 1 CUP

⅓ cup sesame oil
⅓ cup soy sauce
2½ tablespoons grated fresh ginger
2 cloves garlic, minced
2½ tablespoons brown sugar
1 teaspoon red pepper flakes

Freezing Day

Combine all ingredients in a food processor. Freeze in freezer bag.

Reheating Instructions

Defrost marinade in the refrigerator overnight and use as desired.

PER SERVING
Calories: 827 | Fat: 72g | Protein: 11g | Sodium: 4872mg | Carbohydrates: 35g | Fiber: 0g

Citrus Marinade

This marinade is perfect for both fish and chicken. Pour the marinade over the uncooked food and freeze. You can cook the meat by broiling, grilling, or cooking in a skillet.

INGREDIENTS | YIELDS ½ CUP

½ cup orange juice
1 tablespoon orange juice concentrate
1 clove garlic, minced
1 tablespoon fresh basil, chopped
1 teaspoon minced onion

Freezing Day

Combine all ingredients and freeze in a freezer bag or Tupperware.

Reheating Instructions

Defrost marinade in the refrigerator overnight and use as desired.

PER SERVING
Calories: 67 | Fat: 0g | Protein: 1.5g | Sodium: 2mg | Carbohydrates: 15g | Fiber: 0g

Ginger Marinade

Add this Ginger Marinade to beef and make a delicious beef and vegetable stir-fry that tastes fantastic served over rice. The marinade also works well with pork.

INGREDIENTS | YIELDS ABOUT ¾ CUP

½ cup balsamic vinegar
4 tablespoons cooking sherry
4 tablespoons fresh ginger, grated
2 cloves garlic, minced

Building on the Marinade

This ginger marinade recipe stands well on its own, but ginger goes well with a variety of other flavors you may want to include in your marinade. You can include: curry, honey, lime juice, scallions, basil, chili peppers, cilantro, cumin, lemon, mint, sesame oil, or turmeric.

Freezing Day

Combine all ingredients and freeze in a freezer bag or Tupperware.

Reheating Instructions

Defrost marinade in the refrigerator overnight and use as desired.

PER SERVING
Calories: 172 | Fat: 0g | Protein: 0.5g | Sodium: 6mg | Carbohydrates: 41g | Fiber: 0.5g

Marsala Mushroom Sauce

Keep a supply of this sauce in your freezer for a quick and easy meal.
It tastes delicious served over fettuccine.

INGREDIENTS | YIELDS 2–2½ CUPS

½ onion, chopped

1 bell pepper, chopped

2 cloves garlic, minced

1½ cups shitake mushrooms

3 tablespoons olive oil

¼ cup Marsala wine

1 (10.5-ounce) can cream of mushroom soup

⅓ cup milk

Upgrading Marsala Sauce

Want to take this, or any, Marsala sauce to the next level? To begin, be sure to use an authentic imported Italian Marsala wine. Use the wine to deglaze the pan from whatever meat you cook and add a couple tablespoons of real unsalted butter (and optionally sliced mushrooms). Cook on medium heat until the mixture thickens into a sauce-like consistency.

Freezing Day

In skillet over medium-high heat, sauté the onion, pepper, and mushrooms in olive oil for 5–10 minutes. Add garlic and sauté an additional 1–2 minutes. Cook until vegetables are tender. Add Marsala wine, reduce heat, and simmer for 5 minutes. In separate bowl, combine the soup and milk. Whisk until smooth. Add to skillet and stir to mix. Immediately remove from heat to cool. Freeze in a freezer bag.

Reheating Instructions

Defrost sauce in the refrigerator overnight and use as desired.

PER SERVING
Calories: 719 | Fat: 59g | Protein: 12g | Sodium: 1664mg | Carbohydrates: 39g | Fiber: 3g

Pork Marinade

This is a great marinade to have on hand to marinate a pork roast.
You can also inject this marinade into your pork.

INGREDIENTS | YIELDS 1½ CUPS

1 cup apple juice
2 tablespoons Worcestershire sauce
2 tablespoons apple cider vinegar
1 tablespoon oil
1 tablespoon lemon juice
1½ teaspoons hot sauce
2 tablespoons dark brown sugar
½ teaspoon cumin
¾ teaspoons salt

Freezing Day

In a saucepan combine apple juice, Worcestershire sauce, apple cider vinegar, oil, lemon juice, and hot sauce. Simmer for 10 minutes. Add dark brown sugar, cumin, and salt. Whisk until dry ingredients are completely dissolved. Remove from heat, cool, and freeze.

Reheating Instructions

Defrost in the refrigerator overnight and use as desired.

PER SERVING
Calories: 369 | Fat: 14g | Protein: 0g | Sodium: 2104mg | Carbohydrates: 63g | Fiber: 0g

Chicken Marinade

Marinating your chicken lets it soak up delicious flavors until you are ready to cook. Slice up the chicken and wrap it in a burrito with enchilada sauce, or put it on top of a green salad.

INGREDIENTS | YIELDS 1 CUP

2 teaspoons soy sauce
¼ cup chicken broth
½ cup lime juice
¼ cup olive oil
1 teaspoon salt
2 teaspoons brown sugar
1 teaspoon onion powder
½ teaspoon liquid smoke
1 teaspoon chili powder
½ teaspoon black pepper

Freezing Day

Combine all ingredients in a food processor. Freeze in a freezer bag.

Reheating Instructions

Defrost marinade in the refrigerator overnight and use as desired.

PER SERVING
Calories: 523 | Fat: 54g | Protein: 2g | Sodium: 3082mg | Carbohydrates: 9g | Fiber: 0g

Swedish Meatball Sauce

To make Swedish Meatballs, defrost the desired number of Basic Meatballs (Chapter 15) and heat in sauce. Serve over egg noodles.

INGREDIENTS | YIELDS 3½ CUPS

6 tablespoons butter

⅓ cup flour

3 cups beef broth

⅓ cup heavy cream

Transforming Swedish Meatball Sauce

Swedish Meatball Sauce is a variation of a standard white sauce that can be used in many dishes. You can easily adapt this sauce to a variety of recipes; for instance, add some sautéed mushrooms and serve over chicken, add some red wine and serve with beef, or add lemon or lime and serve over fish.

Freezing Day

Melt butter in a saucepan over low heat. Add flour to butter, a tablespoon at a time. Whisk each tablespoon in with the butter before adding the next. Whisk for 1 minute more until the flour and butter are mixed and it turns a golden color. Add the broth, slowly whisking as you pour. Continue whisking 8–15 minutes until the sauce thickens. Stir in the cream. Remove from heat and cool. Freeze in a freezer bag or plastic container.

Reheating Instructions

Defrost in the refrigerator overnight and use as desired.

PER RECIPE
Calories: 1076 | Fat: 98g | Protein: 13g | Sodium: 3421mg | Carbohydrates: 37g | Fiber: 1g

Pineapple Marinade

Want a spicier alternative? Add 2 teaspoons of red pepper flakes or 4 shakes of Tabasco to give this marinade some extra zest.

INGREDIENTS | YIELDS 2½ CUPS

¼ cup apple cider vinegar

4 tablespoons lemon juice

⅓ cup soy sauce

2 tablespoons dark brown sugar, packed

1 (16-ounce) can crushed pineapple with juice

¼ cup honey

2 cloves garlic, minced

1 teaspoon ginger powder

Understanding Citrus Marinades

Citrus-based marinades provide flavor as they tenderize. The citric acid breaks down protein fibers, making the meat more tender. Be careful not to leave the meat in the marinade too long as it can make the meat mushy. When thawing meat frozen in a citrus marinade, remove the meat as soon as it is thawed.

Freezing Day

In a saucepan, mix apple cider vinegar, lemon juice, soy sauce, and dark brown sugar. Bring to a boil, reduce heat, and simmer 1 minute. Remove from heat and add pineapple, honey, garlic, and ginger powder. Mix well, let cool, and freeze in ½-cup portions in freezer bags or Tupperware containers.

Reheating Instructions

Defrost in the refrigerator overnight and use as desired.

PER SERVING
Calories: 586 | Fat: 0.5g | Protein: 11g | Sodium: 4880mg | Carbohydrates: 137g | Fiber: 5g

Tzatziki Sauce

Tzatziki is a Greek sauce also known as cucumber sauce. It is made from yogurt, cucumbers, and fresh dill. Greek yogurt is used in this recipe because it is a thicker yogurt and doesn't need to be strained of water like regular yogurt.

INGREDIENTS | YIELDS 1⅔ CUP

1 cup finely chopped seedless cucumber

8 ounces Greek yogurt

1 tablespoon lemon juice

½ teaspoon salt

¼ teaspoon pepper

1 tablespoon fresh dill

1 clove garlic, minced

Freezing Day

Press the extra liquid out of the cucumbers. Mix cucumber with Greek yogurt, lemon juice, salt, pepper, dill, and garlic. Freeze in a freezer bag or plastic freezer container.

Reheating Instructions

Defrost in the refrigerator overnight and served chilled.

PER SERVING
Calories: 165 | Fat: 8g | Protein: 16g | Sodium: 1278mg | Carbohydrates: 14g | Fiber: 1g

Strawberry Fruit Topping

Add a fruity flavor to your pancakes and waffles with this simple topping. You can also use it as a topper on ice cream, cheese cake, or mixed with yogurt. Try adding almonds to the topping for a nutty treat.

INGREDIENTS | YIELDS 1 CUP

1 cup fresh strawberries

1 tablespoon brown sugar

1 teaspoon lemon juice

Freezing Day

In a food processor, mix all ingredients. Freeze in a freezer bag or Tupperware. For single servings, flash freeze in a plastic ice cube tray, then transfer cubes to a freezer bag.

Reheating Instructions

Defrost in the refrigerator overnight and serve.

PER SERVING
Calories: 127 | Fat: 0.5g | Protein: 2g | Sodium: 7mg | Carbohydrates: 32g | Fiber: 5g

Mix and Match

Spicy Refried Beans

Divide the beans into portions to make vegetarian bean burritos, or put them on your tacos with meat. Use them as a layer in South of the Border Lasagna (Chapter 8), a topping for nachos, or a dip for chips.

INGREDIENTS | SERVES 8–10

6 (15.5-ounce) cans refried beans

2 (10-ounce) cans enchilada sauce

1 (4.5-ounce) can green chilies

Freezing Day

Mix all ingredients together, separate into desired portions, and freeze in a freezer bag or plastic container.

Reheating Instructions

Defrost in the refrigerator overnight, heat, and use as desired.

PER SERVING
Calories: 314 | Fat: 5g | Protein: 15g | Sodium: 1539mg | Carbohydrates: 53g | Fiber: 16g

Basic Ground Beef Mixture

Keep this on hand, in 1 pound portions, for easy meals. Mix with Gravy for Any Occasion (Chapter 15) and serve over open-faced biscuits. Make a meaty dip by combining with Queso Dip (Chapter 13), or add Basic Marinara Sauce (Chapter 15) and make a quick spaghetti dinner.

INGREDIENTS | SERVES 30–32

8 pounds ground beef

½ cup onion, chopped

4 batches Ground Beef Seasoning Mix (Chapter 13)

Freezer Burgers

Instead of browning the ground beef, mix the raw beef with the seasoning mix and form into hamburger patties. Flash freeze the patties on a baking sheet, and then transfer them to freezer bags. Separate layers of burgers with wax paper to keep them from sticking together.

Freezing Day

Brown ground beef with onion. Drain pan if necessary. Add 4 batches of Ground Beef Seasoning Mix and simmer for 5–10 minutes. Divide mixture into 8 equal portions and freeze in freezer bags.

Reheating Instructions

Defrost meat in the refrigerator overnight and use as desired.

PER SERVING
Calories: 309 | Fat: 19g | Protein: 31g | Sodium: 103mg | Carbohydrates: 0g | Fiber: 0g

Basic Seasoned Chicken

Keep a batch on hand to use in a salad or to wrap in a burrito with refried beans and salsa. It also tastes great on the Easy Stuffed Crust Pizza (this chapter), with Alfredo Sauce (Chapter 14), Roasted Garlic (this chapter), and mozzarella cheese.

INGREDIENTS | SERVES 12

3 tablespoons sage, crumbled

1 tablespoon leaf thyme, crumbled

1 teaspoon white pepper

1 teaspoon paprika

1 tablespoon onion powder

1 teaspoon garlic powder

6 pounds boneless, skinless chicken

3–5 tablespoons olive oil

Freezing Day

Mix all spices together. Cut chicken into cubes and season the cubes with the desired amount of seasoning. Heat olive oil in a skillet over medium-high heat. Add chicken. Brown chicken on all sides about 3–6 minutes until it is fully cooked and no longer pink in the middle. You can either flash freeze the chicken pieces and put into a freezer bag, or divide the chicken into portions and freeze.

Reheating Instructions

Defrost chicken in the refrigerator overnight and use as desired.

PER SERVING
Calories: 315 | Fat: 9g | Protein: 54g | Sodium: 127mg | Carbohydrates: 1g | Fiber: 0g

Easy Stuffed Crust Pizza Crust

NO DEFROSTING NEEDED!

INGREDIENTS | YIELDS 1 PIZZA

1 package refrigerator pizza dough

6–7 pieces mozzarella string cheese

Frozen Pizzas

You can also load your pizza crust with toppings before you put it in the freezer. Simply add desired toppings after browning your pizza crust and then put the pizza in the freezer to flash freeze. This pizza can go directly from the freezer to the oven. Cook at 375°F for 15–25 minutes, depending on the thickness of your crust.

Freezing Day

Take out your pizza pan. (You will be forming the crust in the shape of your pizza pan so on reheating day it will be a perfect fit. Make sure your pan will fit in the freezer because you will be using it to flash freeze the crust.) Lightly grease pan. Open pizza dough and, with your fingers, press it outward to fit pan. Continue to press it so it overhangs pan by 2 inches. Lay string cheese along inside edge of pan. Bring overhanging dough over string cheese and use your fingers to seal the edges into the dough. Wet fingers if needed to create seal. Partially bake crust at 400°F for 6 minutes or until it is very lightly browned. Remove from oven and cool. Put in freezer to flash freeze. Once frozen, wrap well with plastic wrap and return to freezer.

Reheating Instructions

Add desired toppings and cook at 400°F for 15–30 minutes, or until crust is golden brown. Cooking time depends on the thickness of dough and size of pizza.

PER PIZZA
Calories: 1441 | Fat: 38g | Protein: 80g | Sodium: 1957mg | Carbohydrates: 198g | Fiber: 10g

Gravy for Any Occasion

This basic gravy recipe can be used with any type of broth, and as a complement to a variety of dishes. To make this gravy, you can use broth (or meat juices) from the dish you are cooking, canned broth, or even make broth from bouillon cubes.

INGREDIENTS | YIELDS 1½ CUPS

3 tablespoons cornstarch
½ cup cold water
2 cups broth
¼ cup milk
3 tablespoons butter or margarine
Salt and pepper to taste

Freezing Day

In a small dish, combine cornstarch with cold water. Mix well. Add broth to a saucepan. Slowly stir in the cornstarch and water mixture. Cook over medium heat, stirring constantly until gravy begins to boil. Add milk, margarine, and salt and pepper to taste then remove from heat. Let gravy cool, and freeze in a freezer bag.

Reheating Instructions

Defrost in the refrigerator overnight and heat gravy.

PER SERVING
Calories: 466 | Fat: 37g | Protein: 6g | Sodium: 2175mg | Carbohydrates: 27g | Fiber: 0g

Shredded Chicken

This versatile chicken should always be kept on hand. It can be used in Mini Chicken Turnovers (Chapter 2), Curried Chicken (Chapter 4), Chicken Verde Wraps (Chapter 4), and many more recipes. Try mixing it with barbecue sauce and serving it on a toasted garlic roll for an easy dinner.

INGREDIENTS | YIELDS 8 CUPS

4 large bone-in, skin-on chicken breasts
Salt and pepper to taste
Garlic powder to taste
½ cup chicken broth

Freezing Day

Season the chicken with salt, pepper, and garlic powder. Put in slow cooker with chicken broth. Cook for 6–8 hours. Remove chicken from slow cooker and let cool. Separate the chicken from the skin and bones, and shred. Freeze chicken in 2-cup portions. Strain the broth in the slow cooker and freeze in small portions.

Reheating Instructions

Defrost in the refrigerator overnight and use as desired.

PER SERVING
Calories: 435 | Fat: 9g | Protein: 83g | Sodium: 469mg | Carbohydrates: 0.5g | Fiber: 0g

Easy Pie Crust

NO DEFROSTING NEEDED!

INGREDIENTS | YIELDS 1 (10″) PIE CRUST

1 cup flour
Pinch salt
⅓ cup shortening
3–8 tablespoons water
10″ aluminum pie tin

How to Transfer the Dough to the Pie Tin

To check the size, lay your pie tin upside down over the crust. You should have an extra 2″ all around. Gently fold your crust in half, then fold in half again. Lay the crust in the pie tin, with the pointed end of the crust in the center. Unfold and use your fingers to push the bottom into place.

Freezing Day

In a food processor, combine flour and salt. Add shortening and pulse until mixture has a mealy texture. Add 3 tablespoons water to mixture and pulse about 5 times. Check consistency by pinching together the mixture with your fingers. If it holds together, you have the right amount of water. If it doesn't hold together, continue to add water until it does. Roll dough into a ball. On a floured surface, roll dough into a 12″ circle. Place rolled out dough into the aluminum pie tin. Crimp outside edge of crust by pinching crust all the way around so it forms a wavy line. As an alternative to crimping, use a fork and press down outside edge of pie into side of pan, leaving tine marks along the edge. Wrap well with plastic wrap and freeze.

Reheating Instructions

Use frozen pie crust according to pie recipe.

PER CRUST
Calories: 1053 | Fat: 69g | Protein: 13g | Sodium: 584mg | Carbohydrates: 95g | Fiber: 3.5g

Homemade Pizza Sauce

This recipe contains enough sauce to make 4 pizzas, so freeze the sauce accordingly and you'll always have just the right amount for pizza night!

INGREDIENTS | YIELDS SCANT 3 CUPS

1 (15-ounce) can tomato sauce

1 (6-ounce) can tomato paste

2 teaspoons basil

2 teaspoons oregano

1½ teaspoons garlic powder

1 teaspoon paprika

½ teaspoon onion powder

½ teaspoon sugar

Freezing Day

Add all ingredients to a food processor and mix well. Divide into 1-cup portions and freeze in a freezer bag.

Reheating Instructions

Defrost overnight in the refrigerator and use as desired.

PER SERVING
Calories: 326 | Fat: 2g | Protein: 14g | Sodium: 286mg | Carbohydrates: 72g | Fiber: 19g

Sweet Berry Filling

Pair this fruit filling with the Easy Pie Crust (this chapter) for a delicious homemade pie or use the fruit as a topping on ice cream and other desserts. You can even put it in the blender and make a fruit syrup to pour over the Chocolate Chip Pancakes (Chapter 7).

INGREDIENTS | YIELDS 1 QUART

1 quart fruit of your choice

½ cup sugar

Freezing Day

Wash and dry fruit and remove any that are bruised or have bad spots. In large bowl, mix fruit and sugar together, coating thoroughly. Freeze in freezer bags.

Reheating Instructions

Defrost in the refrigerator overnight, and use as desired.

PER SERVING
Calories: 717 | Fat: 2g | Protein: 6g | Sodium: 6mg | Carbohydrates: 181g | Fiber: 12g

Crepes

Crepes can be used for either sweet or savory dishes. To make a delicious and easy dinner, stuff crepes with spinach and feta cheese, or mozzarella cheese and tomatoes.

INGREDIENTS | SERVES 2–4

4 eggs

4 tablespoons vegetable oil

1 tablespoon vanilla, or to taste

1 cup water

1 cup milk

2 cups flour

Cooking spray

Banana Crepes Dessert

Spread cream cheese over the surface of crepe. Add cinnamon and sugar and drizzle melted butter over it. Put banana in and wrap it up. Roll in melted butter and a cinnamon sugar mixture and place seam side down on a cookie sheet. Bake at 350°F until golden brown, 5–10 minutes. Top with caramel sauce.

Freezing Day

In a mixing bowl, whip the eggs and oil until foamy. Add remaining ingredients and blend until smooth. Spray a small skillet with cooking spray. Heat skillet to medium high, and add enough batter to coat bottom of preheated pan. Tilt skillet so that batter spreads evenly on the bottom of the pan. Flip after 1–2 minutes when edges separate from pan sides and bubbles appear on surface of crepe. It only needs about 30 seconds on the second side. Cool on a plate and keep adding new crepes on top. Freeze in a freezer bag and use wax paper between the crepes.

Reheating Instructions

Defrost by carefully separating the crepes, then defrosting at room temperature. Use according to recipe.

PER SERVING
Calories: 466 | Fat: 22g | Protein: 14g | Sodium: 94mg | Carbohydrates: 52g | Fiber: 2g

Chicken Broth

Because this chicken broth is made from chicken breasts, you get multiple meals from the recipe in addition to the broth. The chicken is used to make the broth, and is then frozen and can be used in any recipes calling for cooked chicken.

INGREDIENTS | YIELDS 6–7 CUPS

2½ pounds bone-in chicken breasts

5 sprigs thyme

5 sprigs parsley

1 bay leaf

8 whole peppercorns

2 quarts cold water

2 ribs celery

2 onions

2 carrots

1 clove garlic, peeled

Freezing Day

Put chicken breasts, thyme, parsley, bay leaf, and peppercorns in stockpot with 2 quarts cold water. Cut up celery, onions, carrots, and garlic into chunks and add to water. Bring to a boil, turn down heat, and simmer 4 hours uncovered. Skim foam off the top of the water throughout the cooking time. Remove chicken from water and set aside to cool. Remove chicken from bones and freeze for another use. Strain broth and put it in refrigerator overnight. In the morning, remove and discard fat from the surface of the broth. Divide broth into 1 cup servings and freeze in a freezer bag or plastic container.

Reheating Instructions

Defrost chicken broth in the refrigerator overnight. Boil for 2 minutes and use according to recipe.

PER SERVING
Calories: 102 | Fat: 1g | Protein: 18g | Sodium: 633mg | Carbohydrates: 6g | Fiber: 0g

Caramelized Onions

Caramelized onions make a great topping for burgers like the Blue Cheese Burger found in Chapter 10. You can use them for soups, sandwiches, or as an addition to a vegetable dish.

INGREDIENTS | YIELDS 1 ONION

1 yellow onion
3 tablespoons olive oil
Pinch of salt

Freezing Day

Peel onion and slice into rings. Separate rings. Put 3 tablespoons olive oil in skillet and heat over medium-high heat. When oil is hot, add onions and a pinch of salt. Stir onions to coat in oil. Continue to let onions cook. Stir to keep them from sticking. The onions will get darker in color as they caramelize. Remove onions from heat when they've reached the desired color. Allow onions to cool, then flash freeze in an ice cube tray, muffin tin, or on a baking sheet lined with waxed paper. Once frozen, transfer to a freezer bag.

Reheating Instructions

Defrost onions in the refrigerator overnight, or put frozen onions directly into a skillet and heat over medium heat 5–10 minutes until defrosted. Use as desired.

PER SERVING
Calories: 425 | Fat: 41g | Protein: 1.5g | Sodium: 587mg | Carbohydrates: 16g | Fiber: 2g

Basic Meatballs

NO DEFROSTING NEEDED!

INGREDIENTS | SERVES 6

2 pounds ground beef

1 cup bread or cracker crumbs

½ cup grated Parmesan

1 sprig chopped parsley

1 teaspoon garlic salt

2 beaten eggs

Red wine, as needed for meatballs to
 hold together

Diced mushrooms (optional)

Meatball Mania

Who doesn't love a good meatball? These
can be paired with Basic Marinara Sauce
(Chapter 14) for spaghetti and meatballs,
or Alfredo Sauce (Chapter 14), or made
into meatball sandwiches topped with
mozzarella cheese.

Freezing Day

Combine all ingredients. Form into balls and bake at
350°F for 30 minutes–1 hour depending upon the size of
the meatball, until it is no longer pink in the middle.
Flash freeze on a baking sheet and transfer into freezer
bag.

Reheating Instructions

Add frozen meatballs to desired sauce and cook over
medium temperature 20–25 minutes or until heated to
desired temperature. Meatballs can also be defrosted in
the refrigerator overnight and used as desired.

PER SERVING
Calories: 543 | Fat: 31g | Protein: 48g | Sodium: 564mg |
Carbohydrates: 14g | Fiber: 1g

Roasted Garlic

NO DEFROSTING NEEDED!

INGREDIENTS | YIELDS APPROXIMATELY 10 TABLESPOONS

5 whole garlic bulbs

5 teaspoons olive oil, divided

Salt and pepper to taste

Freeze Roasted Garlic in Single-Use Sizes

If you do not have ice cube trays to freeze the garlic in, try this alternative. Line a baking sheet with wax paper. Put mounded tablespoons (or teaspoons) of garlic on tray and flash freeze. Once the garlic freezes, transfer to a freezer bag. Now, when a recipe calls for a measured amount of roasted garlic, it will be ready to go.

Freezing Day

Cut the top (the pointed part) off each garlic bulb and pour 1 teaspoon of olive oil on each. Sprinkle with salt and pepper. Wrap each bulb in aluminum foil and bake at 350°F for 45 minutes–1 hour until garlic is soft and turning golden brown. Carefully unwrap the foil and squeeze the garlic cloves from the skin. Mash the garlic cloves with a fork. Divide and freeze in ice cube trays sprayed with cooking spray. Once frozen, transfer garlic to a freezer bag.

Reheating Instructions

Frozen roasted garlic can be added to a dish frozen, or defrosted first in the refrigerator.

PER SERVING
Calories: 262 | Fat: 23g | Protein: 2.5g | Sodium: 8mg | Carbohydrates: 14g | Fiber: 1g

Spiced Pecans

The chili powder in these pecans give them a spicy little kick! Wrap them up in cellophane, or put into a small mason jar, tie with a ribbon, and give as a gift.

INGREDIENTS | YIELDS 1 POUND

1 egg white

1 teaspoon cold water

1 pound pecan halves

1 cup sugar

½ teaspoon salt

½ teaspoon chili powder

1 teaspoon cinnamon

¼ teaspoon nutmeg

Spiced Pecan Salad

The spiced pecans are a great snack by themselves, but they are also a flavorful addition to most salads. For a real taste treat, sprinkle the pecans over a salad of fresh spring greens, dried cranberries, baby spinach, crumbled goat cheese or blue cheese, pine nuts, and balsamic or raspberry vinaigrette.

Freezing Day

Beat egg white and water until frothy. Add pecans and stir to coat. In a separate bowl, mix sugar, salt, chili powder, cinnamon, and nutmeg. Add pecans and mix well. Line a baking sheet with foil and put the pecans on the foil. Bake at 300°F for 20–30 minutes. Stir pecans every 8–10 minutes. Cool pecans and freeze in freezer bag or plastic container.

Reheating Instructions

Defrost at room temperature for 1–2 hours and use as desired.

PER ⅛ POUND
Calories: 491 | Fat: 41g | Protein: 6g | Sodium: 153mg | Carbohydrates: 33g | Fiber: 6g

CHAPTER 16

Desserts

Chocolate Banana Pops

These pops are a fun and messy dessert the kids will love making! They are the perfect snack on those hot summer days when the kids want something cool to eat.

INGREDIENTS | SERVES 6–8

1 package chocolate chips

6 ripe bananas

1–2 cups crushed peanuts

12 Popsicle sticks

Let Your Imagination Run Wild!

Try dipping half the banana into chocolate and the other half in melted peanut butter chips. Instead of crushed peanuts, try different toppings such as crushed M&Ms, crushed Oreo cookies, or even crushed pineapple. Or a mixture of all of them! You are only limited by your imagination.

Freezing Day

Melt chocolate chips in the microwave on 50% power for 30 seconds. Stir chips and return to microwave another 30 seconds at 50%. Continue until chips are melted. Cut bananas in half. Push a Popsicle stick into the cut side of the banana. Spread peanuts out in a shallow dish. Dip the banana into the chocolate, then into the peanuts. Lay the pops on a baking sheet lined with wax paper and flash freeze. Transfer to a freezer bag.

Reheating Instructions

No defrosting necessary. Eat the frozen treats straight from the freezer.

PER SERVING
Calories: 465 | Fat: 22g | Protein: 6.5g | Sodium: 5mg | Carbohydrates: 69g | Fiber: 7g

Hot Fudge Sundae Pie

This dessert takes minutes to make, so with very little preparation you can serve a treat everyone loves.

INGREDIENTS | YIELDS 1 PIE

1 quart vanilla ice cream

1 ready-made graham cracker pie crust

Hot fudge to taste (used on reheating day)

Coconut flakes to taste (used on reheating day)

Chopped nuts to taste (used on reheating day)

Maraschino cherries to taste (used on reheating day)

Whipped cream to taste (used on reheating day)

Freezing Day

Allow the ice cream to soften just a bit. Spread the ice cream into the pie shell to make an ice cream pie. Wrap well with plastic wrap and freeze.

Reheating Instructions

Serve the ice cream pie frozen. Set out toppings, cut the pie into wedges, and let everyone customize their own piece of pie.

PER PIE
Calories: 4591 | Fat: 253g | Protein: 59g | Sodium: 3072mg | Carbohydrates: 603g | Fiber: 12g

Ann van Huizen's Spice Cake

This spice cake has a unique flavor that will have your friends talking about it long after they've enjoyed it. It tastes especially good paired with a cup of coffee.

INGREDIENTS | YIELDS 1 CAKE

4 cups flour

2 teaspoons baking powder

2 teaspoons baking soda

3 teaspoons cinnamon

1 teaspoon nutmeg

1 teaspoon allspice

¼ teaspoon ground cloves

1 teaspoon ginger

1½ tablespoons molasses

1 cup hot coffee

1 cup cold water

1 cup brown sugar

1 cup white sugar

1 cup honey

Freezing Day

Mix ingredients, starting with the dry ones and then adding the wet ones. Pour into a long loaf pan. Bake at 350°F for 30 minutes, then 300°F for 30 minutes. Cool, wrap with plastic wrap, and freeze.

Reheating Instructions

Defrost at room temperature for 2–3 hours, or in the refrigerator overnight, and serve.

PER CAKE
Calories: 4557 | Fat: 5g | Protein: 50g | Sodium: 3571mg | Carbohydrates: 1100g | Fiber: 15g

Fruity Frozen Pie

This is another great summer treat for your friends and family. Let this dessert defrost 15–20 minutes at room temperature before serving—it makes cutting it easier.

INGREDIENTS | SERVES 6–8

¾ cups sugar

1 (10-ounce) package cream cheese, softened

1 (16-ounce) bag frozen strawberries with juice, thawed

1 (15-ounce) can crushed pineapple, drained

1 (12-ounce) container Cool Whip

2 large bananas, peeled and sliced

Freezing Day

In large mixing bowl, mix sugar and cream cheese. Cut strawberries into pieces and add them and all the extra strawberry juice into the mixing bowl. Add pineapple and Cool Whip. Fold in bananas. Spread mixture into a 9" x 13" pan and freeze.

Reheating Instructions

Remove dessert from freezer and serve.

PER SERVING
Calories: 313 | Fat: 15g | Protein: 4g | Sodium: 122mg | Carbohydrates: 44g | Fiber: 3.5g

Ice Cream Sandwiches

NO DEFROSTING NEEDED!

INGREDIENTS | YIELDS 12 SANDWICHES

24 Chocolate Chip Cookies (this chapter)

1 quart vanilla ice cream

1 (12-ounce) package chocolate chip morsels

Freezing Day

Line a baking sheet with wax paper. Lay 1 cookie, flat side up, on the baking sheet. Put a small scoop of ice cream on the cookie and put another cookie on top of the ice cream. Press it down until the ice cream reaches the edge of the cookies. Roll the edge of the ice cream sandwich in the chocolate chip morsels. Flash freeze on the baking sheet, then transfer to a freezer bag.

Reheating Instructions

Eat straight from the freezer.

PER SERVING
Calories: 572 | Fat: 31g | Protein: 5g | Sodium: 219mg | Carbohydrates: 70g | Fiber: 1.5g

Mom's Sugar Cookies

This wonderful sugar cookie recipe has been passed down through three generations. The cookies taste delicious plain, or you can decorate them with frosting and sprinkles. Also try the Sugar Cookie Filling.

INGREDIENTS | SERVES 30

1 cup butter

2 cups sugar

4 eggs

2 teaspoons vanilla

5 cups flour

4 teaspoons baking powder

¼ teaspoon salt

Freezing Day

In a mixing bowl, cream butter and sugar. Beat in eggs and vanilla. In separate bowl, combine dry ingredients. Add to the butter mixture. Roll out dough ¼-inch thick and cut out cookie shapes using a cookie cutter. Bake at 400°F for 6 minutes. The cookies should be almost white when done. Flash freeze cookies and transfer to freezer bag.

Reheating Instructions

Defrost cookies at room temperature for 1–2 hours and serve.

PER SERVING
Calories: 192 | Fat: 7g | Protein: 3g | Sodium: 123mg | Carbohydrates: 29g | Fiber: 0.5g

Sugar Cookie Filling

Use this recipe with Mom's Sugar Cookies (above).
It is a good idea to use a plastic container when you freeze cookies to protect them from breaking. Layer the cookies in the container, and separate each layer with wax paper.

INGREDIENTS | SERVES 30

½ cup raisins

½ cup chopped dates

½ cup chopped walnuts

½ cup sugar

Pinch salt

1 tablespoon flour

½ cup water

½ teaspoon vanilla

Mom's Sugar Cookies (see above)

Freezing Day

Combine all ingredients except the vanilla in a sauce pan. Stir and boil until smooth and thick. Remove from stove and add vanilla. Put 1 tablespoon of filling on one (unbaked) Mom's Sugar Cookie. Top with a second cookie and seal edges. Bake at 400°F for 6–8 minutes. Cool and flash freeze, then transfer to plastic container.

Reheating Instructions

Defrost cookies at room temperature for 1–2 hours and serve.

PER SERVING
Calories: 50 | Fat: 1g | Protein: 0.5g | Sodium: 0.5mg | Carbohydrates: 10g | Fiber: 0.5g

Dark Chocolate Cake

Top off this delicious and rich cake with a simple frosting, a glaze, or even a scoop of vanilla ice cream.

INGREDIENTS | SERVES 8–10

1 cup vegetable oil

2 cups sugar

4 eggs

1 cup sour milk

2½ cups flour

¼ teaspoon salt

3 teaspoons baking soda

¾ cup cocoa

¾ cup boiling water

1 teaspoon vanilla

Freezing Day

In a mixing bowl, beat together oil, sugar, and eggs. Add remaining ingredients and beat well. Grease cake pan, pour in batter, and bake at 350°F for 45–50 minutes for a 9" x 13" pan, or 1 hour and 10 minutes for a tube pan. Remove from oven, cool, wrap cake in plastic wrap, and freeze.

Reheating Instructions

Defrost cake at room temperature for 1–2 hours and serve at room temperature.

PER SERVING
Calories: 533 | Fat: 27g | Protein: 7g | Sodium: 470mg | Carbohydrates: 68g | Fiber: 3g

Freezer Derby Pie

NO DEFROSTING NEEDED!

INGREDIENTS | YIELDS 2 PIES

1 cup butter

4 eggs

½ cup brown sugar

1⅛ cups white Karo

1 tablespoon flour

1 teaspoon vanilla

⅓ cup bourbon

1½ cups chopped pecans

2 frozen Easy Pie Crusts (Chapter 15)

1½ cups chocolate chips

Freezing Day

In a small saucepan, melt butter. In a mixing bowl, beat eggs slightly. Add melted butter, brown sugar, Karo, flour, vanilla, bourbon, and pecans. Mix well. Line the bottoms of the pie crusts with chocolate chips. Pour the mixture over the chocolate chips. Bake at 350°F for 45 minutes. Cool pie, wrap well with freezer wrap, and freeze.

Reheating Instructions

Heat frozen pie at 375°F for 20–30 minutes.

PER PIE
Calories: 3072 | Fat: 210g | Protein: 21g | Sodium: 1283mg | Carbohydrates: 308g | Fiber: 8.5g

Apple Crisp with Almond Topping

Serve this warm out of the oven with a scoop of vanilla ice cream.
If you want to vary it, try adding blueberries or peaches instead of apples!

INGREDIENTS | SERVES 8–10

1½ cups flour

2 cups oats

1½ cups brown sugar

1 teaspoon cinnamon

½ teaspoon nutmeg

1½ cups butter, softened

11–12 medium-sized Golden Delicious apples, or Granny Smith (if you prefer more tartness) apples, peeled and sliced

1 cup skinless, toasted almonds

Freezing Day

In mixing bowl, combine flour, oats, brown sugar, cinnamon, and nutmeg. Cut in butter until mixture is crumbly. Press ½ of the crumb topping mixture on the bottom of a baking dish, and top with cut apples. In a food processor, finely grind almonds. Mix with remaining crumb topping and sprinkle over the apples. Bake at 350°F for 45 minutes–1 hour or until apples are tender. Cool, wrap tightly with plastic wrap, and freeze.

Reheating Instructions

Defrost apple crisp at room temperature for 2–3 hours and heat approximately 10–15 minutes in 350°F oven until heated through.

PER SERVING
Calories: 648 | Fat: 35g | Protein: 9g | Sodium: 296mg | Carbohydrates: 79g | Fiber: 7g

No Bake Chocolate Cookies

This classic family recipe, also known as boiled cookies, uses only the stovetop to make the cookies! Best of all, they are a cinch to prepare, taste delicious, and freeze wonderfully.

INGREDIENTS | SERVES 24

2 cups sugar

½ cup butter

¼ cup cocoa

½ cup milk

¼ cup peanut butter

1 teaspoon vanilla

3 cups oatmeal

Freezing Day

In a large saucepan, boil the sugar, butter, cocoa, and milk for 1 minute. Remove from the heat and add the peanut butter, vanilla, and oatmeal. Mix well. Drop by full teaspoons on wax paper and let cool. Flash freeze and transfer to freezer bags.

Reheating Instructions

Defrost cookies 1–2 hours at room temperature.

PER SERVING
Calories: 146 | Fat: 6g | Protein: 2g | Sodium: 74mg | Carbohydrates: 23g | Fiber: 1g

Pumpkin Pie

No need to buy a frozen pie for your next Thanksgiving holiday. You'll see how easy it is to make one from scratch with this delicious recipe.

INGREDIENTS | YIELDS 1 PIE

1 (15-ounce) can pumpkin

¾ cup sugar

1 teaspoon salt

1 teaspoon ginger

1¼ teaspoons cinnamon

½ teaspoon nutmeg

½ teaspoon cloves

3 eggs

1 (12-ounce) can evaporated milk, with enough milk added to make 2 cups

1 unbaked Easy Pie Crust (Chapter 15)

Freezing Day

Combine pumpkin, sugar, salt, ginger, cinnamon, nutmeg, cloves, and eggs. Blend in milk. Pour mixture into pie crust. Bake at 400°F for 50 minutes or until knife inserted into center comes out clean. Wrap well with freezer wrap and freeze.

Reheating Instructions

Defrost pie at room temperature for 1–2 hours and serve at room temperature.

PER PIE
Calories: 1470 | Fat: 45g | Protein: 49g | Sodium: 2937mg | Carbohydrates: 228g | Fiber: 13g

Mincemeat

Traditionally, mincemeat was served with the main dish at Christmas. Over time and with the addition of several kinds of fruit, it has become known as a dessert. Make individual pies with frozen puff pastry, or a large pie using an Easy Pie Crust (Chapter 15) covered with latticed dough or puff pastry.

INGREDIENTS | YIELDS 5 QUARTS

2½ pounds ground beef

4 pounds apples, finely chopped

2½ pounds raisins

1½ pounds currants, blanched and drained

1 pound walnuts, coarsely chopped

1 teaspoon cloves

1 teaspoon nutmeg

1½ teaspoons cinnamon

½ teaspoon mace

2 teaspoons salt

4 cups brown sugar

½ cup molasses or honey

Apple juice as needed

Freezing Day

In large skillet, fully brown the ground beef and drain. Add remaining ingredients, except juice, to ground beef. Add enough apple juice to moisten and hold mixture together. Cook over medium-low heat until all fruit is soft, about 30 minutes. Cool. Freeze mincemeat in freezer bags in 2-cup portions.

Reheating Instructions

Defrost mincemeat in the refrigerator overnight and use as desired. A 2-cup portion is the right amount for making a pie.

PER QUART
Calories: 3,005 | Fat: 100g | Protein: 84g | Sodium: 1253mg | Carbohydrates: 480g | Fiber: 24g

The Spice Mace

Mace, made from the hull of the seed used to make nutmeg, is a spice that many are unfamiliar with. Mace has an aroma reminiscent of a combination of cinnamon and pepper. Milder in flavor than nutmeg, it can be used as a nutmeg substitute. Mace is used in both sweet and savory recipes.

Chocolate Meringue Pie

Because meringue tends to get tough when it is frozen, this pie is baked in two steps. The first step, the chocolate base of the pie, is completed on Freezing Day. On the day you plan to serve the pie, you will complete the second step, the meringue topping.

INGREDIENTS | YIELDS 1 PIE

1½ cups sugar

4 tablespoons flour

4 tablespoons cocoa powder

3 egg yolks

1½ cups milk

½ stick butter

1 teaspoon vanilla

1 baked pie crust

3 egg whites, at room temperature (for use on reheating day)

1 teaspoon vanilla (for use on reheating day)

¼ teaspoon cream of tartar (for use on reheating day)

6 tablespoons sugar (for use on reheating day)

Freezing Day

In saucepan, combine sugar, flour, and cocoa. Add egg yolks, then slowly stir in milk. Place over medium heat, and add butter. Continue to heat and stir 3–5 minutes until mixture thickens. Remove from heat and add vanilla. Allow to cool. Pour into pie crust and freeze.

Reheating Instructions

Defrost pie in the refrigerator overnight, or at room temperature for 1–2 hours. In mixing bowl, beat egg whites, vanilla, and cream of tartar to soft peaks. Add sugar one tablespoon at a time and beat until stiff. Spread meringue on pie and bake at 350°F about 10 minutes until browned.

PER PIE
Calories: 2413 | Fat: 126g | Protein: 47g | Sodium: 1688mg | Carbohydrates: 291g | Fiber: 8.5g

Chocolate Chip Cookies

Add variety to your chocolate chip cookies by throwing some chopped macadamia nuts or walnuts in the batter at the same time you put in the chocolate chips. You can also vary this recipe by using white chocolate chips, or half peanut butter chips and half chocolate chips.

INGREDIENTS | YIELDS ABOUT 40 COOKIES

2¼ cups flour

1 teaspoon baking soda

½ teaspoons salt

1 teaspoon cinnamon

1 cup butter, softened

¾ cup packed light brown sugar

½ cup sugar

2 eggs

2 teaspoons pure vanilla extract

2 cups chocolate chips

Chocolate Chip Substitutions

There is a wonderful assortment of other chips available to today's baker that can be substituted for traditional chocolate chips. Besides several varieties of chocolate chips, like white, semi-sweet, special dark, and milk chocolate, other flavors include butterscotch, peanut butter, carob, and even cherry.

Freezing Day

In a small bowl, mix flour, baking soda, salt, and cinnamon. In a large mixing bowl, cream butter, brown sugar, and sugar until it becomes light and airy. Add eggs and vanilla to the butter mixture, and beat well. Add flour to butter mixture and beat only until blended. Fold in the chocolate chips. Drop by the heaping teaspoonful onto an ungreased cookie sheet. Bake at 375°F for 8–10 minutes. Cool completely on a wire rack, wrap well in plastic wrap, or put in plastic container, and freeze.

Reheating Instructions

Defrost cookies at room temperature for 1–2 hours and serve at room temperature.

PER SERVING

Calories: 151 | Fat: 8g | Protein: 1g | Sodium: 112mg | Carbohydrates: 19g | Fiber: 0g

Macadamia Chocolate Squares

Vary this recipe by using pecans or almonds instead of macadamia nuts. You can also stir in ½ cup of peanut butter chips or top the squares with toasted coconut.

INGREDIENTS | SERVES 12

½ cup butter

2 squares unsweetened chocolate

1 cup sugar

2 eggs

½ cup flour

¼ teaspoon salt

½ teaspoon pure vanilla extract

½ cup chopped macadamia nuts

Marble It!

Before you put the squares in the oven, try marbling them. In a separate bowl, use an electric beater to beat 8 ounces cream cheese with ⅓ cup sugar. Put small spoonfuls of the cream cheese over the top of the chocolate squares batter. Use a knife to pull the cream cheese through the batter, making a marbled effect. Bake as directed.

Freezing Day

In a saucepan, melt the butter and chocolate over medium-low heat. Stir in sugar and mix well. Add eggs one at a time, mixing well in between each egg. Add flour, salt, vanilla, and nuts. Mix well. Grease and flour a 10" x 15" jellyroll pan and pour in batter. Bake at 400°F for 10–15 minutes. Cool completely and cut into squares. Wrap chocolate squares well with plastic wrap and freeze.

Reheating Instructions

Defrost at room temperature 1–2 hours and serve at room temperature.

PER SERVING
Calories: 274 | Fat: 16g | Protein: 3g | Sodium: 195mg | Carbohydrates: 31g | Fiber: 1g

Peanut Butter Cookies

To make Peanut Butter Chocolate Kiss Cookies,
form the dough into a ball but don't flatten. Bake at 350°F for 9–10 minutes.
When cookies come out of the oven, press a chocolate kiss into the middle. Let cool.

INGREDIENTS | YIELDS 3 DOZEN COOKIES

1 cup shortening
1½ cups crunchy peanut butter
1 cup brown sugar
1 cup white sugar
2 eggs
1 teaspoon vanilla
3 cups flour
1 teaspoon baking soda
½ teaspoon salt

Peanut Butter Basics

Peanut butter is nearly 100 percent peanuts; there are very few additional ingredients or additives. The biggest difference between most commercial peanut butters and natural peanut butters is that natural peanut butter does not have hydrogenated oils added to keep the peanut oil from separating from the peanut paste. Natural peanut butter usually needs some mixing prior to use.

Freezing Day

Cream together shortening, peanut butter, white sugar, and brown sugar. Add eggs one at a time, followed by vanilla. Mix well. In a separate bowl, sift together flour, baking soda, and salt. Add to peanut butter mixture. Mix dough (it will be very thick). Form into small balls and put on baking sheet. Press the balls down with a fork. Bake at 350°F for 9–10 minutes until cookies are lightly browned. Cool and freeze in a plastic container.

Reheating Instructions

Defrost cookies at room temperature for 1–2 hours and serve at room temperature.

PER SERVING
Calories: 200 | Fat: 11g | Protein: 4g | Sodium: 125mg | Carbohydrates: 22g | Fiber: 1g

Light Fruit Cake

Homemade fruit cakes taste far better than store-bought fruit cakes.
They are a traditional holiday treat, and make great gifts for your family and friends.

INGREDIENTS | YIELDS 2 LOAVES

1 cup butter

1 cup sugar

4 eggs

3 cups flour

1 teaspoon baking powder

½ cup orange juice

¼ cup light corn syrup

1 teaspoon lemon juice

2 (10-ounce) jars maraschino cherries, drained, chopped

1 cup light raisins

2¼ cups mixed candied fruit

1 cup walnuts, chopped

Freezing Day

In a large mixing bowl, beat butter and sugar until fluffy. Mix in eggs, followed by the rest of the ingredients. Pour into 2 greased and floured loaf pans. Bake at 300°F for 1 hour 10 minutes. Cool. Wrap well in plastic wrap and freeze.

Reheating Instructions

Defrost fruit cake 2–3 hours at room temperature and serve.

PER CAKE
Calories: 3402 | Fat: 144g | Protein: 42g | Sodium: 1457mg | Carbohydrates: 504g | Fiber: 21g

Fruit Salad Cupcakes

This makes a cool summertime treat that kids love and is also a
delicious addition to a breakfast or brunch.

INGREDIENTS | SERVES 8

1 (20-ounce) can crushed pineapples, drained

3 bananas, mashed

1 cup frozen blueberries

8 ounces sour cream

½ cup sugar

½ cup nuts, chopped

1 (16-ounce) container Cool Whip

Freezing Day

Combine pineapples, bananas, blueberries, sour cream, sugar, and nuts in a large mixing bowl. Fold in Cool Whip. Fill muffin tins with mixture and freeze. Once frozen, remove from muffin tins and put in a freezer bag.

Reheating Instructions

Remove from freezer and allow to soften for 15–30 minutes before serving.

PER SERVING
Calories: 349 | Fat: 17g | Protein: 5g | Sodium: 109mg | Carbohydrates: 51g | Fiber: 4g

Peanut Butter Balls

This is a great recipe to let the kids make since it's a fun hands-on cooking project that is simple to make and yummy to eat.

INGREDIENTS | YIELDS 30

⅔ cup creamy peanut butter
2½ cups Cool Whip
⅓ cup mini chocolate chips
½ cup coconut flakes

Delicious Toppings

For recipes that call for shredded coconut as a topping, consider using one or more of these alternatives: crushed graham crackers, crispy rice cereal, cocoa rice cereal, crushed nuts (such as peanut, cashew, pecan, pistachio, or macadamia nuts), crushed candy bars, crushed Oreo cookies, or crushed chocolate chip cookies.

Freezing Day

Mix together peanut butter, Cool Whip, and chocolate chips in a medium mixing bowl. Put in freezer for 15 minutes. Remove from freezer and roll into balls. Put coconut on a plate. Roll the balls in coconut. Flash freeze on a baking sheet lined with wax paper. Transfer to freezer bag.

Reheating Instructions

No need to defrost—eat straight from the freezer.

PER SERVING
Calories: 76 | Fat: 6.5g | Protein: 2g | Sodium: 30mg | Carbohydrates: 4g | Fiber: 1g

Applesauce Raisin Spice Cake

Make muffins out of this recipe by baking in paper-lined muffin or cupcake tins at 350°F for 35 minutes. You can thaw them as you need them if you freeze the muffins individually.

INGREDIENTS | SERVES 6

1¾ cups flour
1 teaspoon baking soda
½ teaspoon salt
1½ teaspoons cinnamon
½ teaspoon nutmeg
½ cup shortening
1 cup sugar
1 egg, beaten
1 cup unsweetened applesauce
1 cup raisins

Freezing Day

In a bowl, sift together flour, baking soda, salt, cinnamon, and nutmeg. In separate bowl, cream shortening with sugar. Beat in the egg. Alternate adding sifted ingredients and applesauce to butter and sugar mixture. Stir in raisins. Pour into greased square pan and bake at 350°F for 45–50 minutes. Cool, wrap with plastic wrap, and freeze.

Reheating Instructions

Defrost cake at room temperature for 2–3 hours. Top with a cream cheese icing.

PER SERVING
Calories: 524 | Fat: 18g | Protein: 5.5g | Sodium: 416mg | Carbohydrates: 87g | Fiber: 2.5g

Peanut Butter and Chocolate Bars

*Serve on a small plate topped with whipped cream and
dusted with cocoa powder or drizzled with chocolate syrup.*

INGREDIENTS | SERVES 6

½ cup butter

1 cup graham crackers, crushed

1 cup peanut butter chips

1 cup chocolate chips

1 (15-ounce) can sweetened condensed
  milk

Freezing Day

In saucepan, melt butter. Add graham cracker crumbs
and mix. Press into the bottom of an 8" x 8" pan. Add
peanut butter chips and chocolate chips on top of the
crust. Pour condensed milk over top. Bake at 350°F for
30 minutes. Let cool, cut into squares, wrap well with
plastic wrap, and freeze.

Reheating Instructions

Defrost at room temperature for 1–2 hours and serve.

PER SERVING
Calories: 815 | Fat: 47g | Protein: 14g | Sodium: 461mg |
Carbohydrates: 122g | Fiber: 2g

Pecan Cookies

*These cookies are perfect for the holidays. Make them ahead of time so you'll
have one less thing on your to-do list when the holidays roll around.*

**INGREDIENTS | YIELDS ABOUT 4 DOZEN,
DEPENDING UPON SIZE**

1 cup butter

¼ cup sugar

2 cups flour

2 teaspoons vanilla

2 cups pecans, finely chopped

Powdered sugar, for dipping

Freezing Day

In a mixing bowl, cream butter and sugar. Add flour and
vanilla. Mix well, then stir in pecans. Form dough into
small balls, then press down to make a cookie. Bake at
325°F for 25 minutes. Once out of oven, dip the top of the
cookie in the powdered sugar. Flash freeze on a baking
sheet, then transfer to a freezer bag.

Reheating Instructions

Defrost at room temperature for 1–2 hours and serve.

PER SERVING
Calories: 89 | Fat: 7g | Protein: 1g | Sodium: 39mg |
Carbohydrates: 6g | Fiber: 0.5g

APPENDIX A

Glossary of Terms

Al dente

An Italian phrase meaning "to the tooth." It refers to pasta that is cooked to the point where it offers resistance to the tooth.

Baste

To brush or pour a sauce over food as it cooks to keep it from drying out. Basting also adds flavor to the food.

Blanch

A process of putting food in boiling water for a short period of time, then immediately submerging it in ice-cold water to stop the cooking process. It is used for many fruits and vegetables to prepare them for freezing.

Boil

To bring a liquid to a point of heat where it bubbles vigorously. Water boils when it reaches 212°F.

Bouillon

A broth that is made by cooking meat, poultry, or vegetables in water. Bouillon cubes are a dry, concentrated form that must be mixed with hot water to form broth.

Braise

A process in which food is first browned, then a small amount of liquid such as broth, water, wine, or juice is added to the pan. The food cooks in the liquid at a low temperature, over a long period of time, covered tightly. The liquid has concentrated flavor and can be used to make sauce or gravy.

Broil

Most often associated with cooking in an oven, food is broiled when it is cooked directly under the heat source.

Broth

The liquid that results from cooking meat, poultry, or vegetables in water.

Caramelize

To cook sugar, or food containing a natural sugar, until the sugar turns into a golden brown syrup.

Casserole

Can refer to a type of meal that is cooked together in one dish, or can refer to the dish itself.

Chorizo sausage

Spanish chorizo is made with smoked pork, while Mexican chorizo is made with fresh pork. They both are very flavorful due to the high amount of seasoning they contain. Chorizo is wrapped in a casing which should be removed before cooking.

Consommé

A broth that has been clarified. A broth is clarified when egg whites are used to remove all the fat from the broth making it clear in appearance.

Deglaze

When a meat has been browned in fat, a liquid such as wine or broth is poured into the skillet to loosen and mix with the brown pieces of cooked food on the bottom. The liquid is then used in making a sauce.

Dice

To cut food into cubes.

Dredge

To dip something in flour or other coating to cover it.

Froth

To become foamy.

Fry

To cook food in a type of fat over medium-high heat.

Mince

To chop into very small and fine pieces.

Mix

To combine ingredients, by hand or with an electric mixer.

Prosciutto

An Italian ham that has been salt-cured and air dried. It has a strong flavor because it has been pressed.

Purée

To combine ingredients until they become completely smooth.

Quick bread

A bread that uses ingredients such as baking powder and baking soda to cause the bread to rise quickly. Quick bread is much faster to prepare than yeast bread because it does not need to be kneaded and you don't have to wait for it to rise.

Roux

Roux is formed when a fat such as butter is melted and mixed with flour over low heat. Liquid is then mixed with the roux, thereby thickening the liquid into gravies and sauces.

Sauté

To cook food over a high heat in butter or other fat.

Scald

To heat milk to just below the boiling point.

Sear

To brown meat over high heat in order to seal in the juices.

Steam

To cook vegetables or other foods in a basket over boiling water. This method is best for retaining vitamins and minerals in food.

Zest

The colored outside skin of the fruit, not including the white pith underneath it.

Additional Resources for Freezer Cooking

Websites

Frugal Mom.net
www.frugalmom.net

Menus4Moms
www.menus4moms.com

Cook of the Month
www.cookofthemonth.com

30 Day Gourmet
www.30daygourmet.com

Dinner's in the Freezer
www.dinnersinthefreezer.com

Freezer Meals and Freezer Recipes from Scratch
www.favoritefreezerfoods.com

Books

Fix, Freeze, Feast: Prepare in Bulk and Enjoy by the Serving by Kati Neville and Lindsay Tkacsik

Don't Panic–Dinner's in the Freezer by Susie Martinez, Vanda Howell, and Bonnie Garcia

Holly Clegg's Trim & Terrific Freezer Friendly Meals by Holly Berkowitz Clegg

Fix, Freeze, Take & Bake by G & R Publishing.

Prevention's Low-Fat, Low-Cost Freezer Cookbook: Quick Dishes for and from the Freezer by Sharon Sanders

Taste of Home: Freezer Pleasers by Taste of Home

APPENDIX C

Charts and Extras

FREEZING CHART: MAXIMUM FOOD-STORAGE TIMES

According to the USDA, food frozen at 0°F will remain safe to eat indefinitely. This chart represents how long a food can stay in your freezer until its quality is affected.

Food	Freezer Storage Time
Bread	2–3 months
Butter	6–9 months
Cake	2–4 months
Casseroles	2–3 months
Cheese	6 months
Cookies	6–12 months
Crab and Lobster	2–3 months
Fish (cooked)	4–6 months
Fish (fatty)	2–3 months
Fish (lean)	6 months
Fruit	12 months
Gravy	2–3 months
Ice Cream	2–3 weeks
Meat, cooked	2–3 months
Meat, ground	3–4 months
Meat, uncooked (excluding ground)	Up to 12 months
Milk	3 months
Muffins	6–7 months
Pie, baked fruit	6–8 months
Pie, pumpkin or chiffon	1–2 months
Pie crust	12 months
Pizza	1–2 months
Poultry, cooked	4 months
Poultry pieces, uncooked	9 months
Shellfish, cooked	3 months
Shrimp and Scallops	3–6 months
Soups and Stews	2–3 months
Vegetables	8 months

Tips, Tips, and More Tips

1. **Easy slow cooker cleanup:** Spray the inside of your slow cooker with cooking spray before putting food in. You can also line the slow cooker with a disposable cooking bag.

2. **Cool food in a hurry:** Fill your sink with enough ice and water to come up the sides of your pot. Set your pot filled with hot food in the sink, and the ice bath will help food cool down quickly.

3. **Easily remove air from a freezer bag:** Ever have a hard time getting that last bit of air out of the freezer bag? Leave a small opening at the seal, and stick a small straw inside the bag. Suck out as much air as possible through the straw and quickly seal the bag.

4. **Vacuum sealers:** These are a great solution for packaging your frozen foods. If you use one, make sure before vacuum sealing any soft food that you flash freeze the food first. Otherwise your food will become mushy as the air is vacuumed out of the bag.

5. **A mug of soup:** Try this tip for making a mug-sized (and shaped!) portion of soup. Allow your soup to cool. Line your favorite mug with a freezer bag and spoon the soup into the bag. Put the mug with soup in the freezer and leave it there until the soup is frozen. Lift the freezer bag out of the mug and seal. Next time you want a mug of soup, take it out of the bag and it will fit perfectly in your favorite mug.

6. **Warning about defrosting in the microwave:** The microwave is a great way to quickly defrost food, but be careful about defrosting food while in the plastic bag; not all bags withstand defrosting in the microwave. They may melt or split along the sides as the food defrosts. For best results, transfer to a microwavable dish to defrost.

7. **Casseroles from freezer to oven:** One thing to love about freezer cooking is the time it saves in the kitchen. However, defrosting a casserole in the refrigerator usually takes about 24 hours. What about those nights you didn't plan ahead or forgot to defrost it first? If you need to go from the freezer directly to the oven, the general rule is to add 40 minutes–1 hour to the defrosted cooking time.

8. **Labeling freezer bags:** When labeling your freezer bags, use a permanent marker and write the name of the dish, the date, and reheating instructions on the bag before you add the food.

9. **Freezing pasta:** It is a good idea to undercook pasta before freezing. Because pasta absorbs liquids it is frozen with, it can become soggy when defrosted if it is fully cooked. If adding spaghetti to a soup, there is no need to cook it first; add dry spaghetti to the soup and the pasta will be perfect when you defrost and reheat the soup.

10. **Double the sauce:** Different cooks like different amounts of sauce with their food. If you find you enjoy more sauce with your meals, try doubling the sauce before freezing. You also have the option of adding more liquid as the meal is cooking.

11. **How to organize a chest freezer:** Try using plastic milk crates to organize your chest freezer. You can use one crate for beef meals, one for chicken meals, etc. The crates can easily be rearranged in your freezer and will save you from a lot of digging!

12. **Neatly fill your freezer bags:** Line a large coffee can with a gallon-sized freezer bag. Fold the top of the bag over the side of the can and you can easily fill the bag without making a mess.

SUBSTITUTIONS FOR COMMON INGREDIENTS
1 cup tomato sauce–½ cup tomato paste plus ½ cup cold water
1 teaspoon vinegar–2 teaspoons lemon juice
1 cup brown sugar–1 cup granulated sugar plus 2 tablespoons molasses
1 cup half and half–½ cup coffee creamer plus ½ cup milk
1 teaspoon baking powder–¼ teaspoon plus ⅝ teaspoon cream of tartar
2 tablespoons minced onion–teaspoon onion powder
1 tablespoon cornstarch for thickening–2 tablespoons flour
1 cup sugar–1 cup brown sugar
1 cup honey–1¼ cups sugar plus ¼ cup water
1 cup corn syrup–1 cup sugar plus ¼ cup water
1 small onion, chopped–1 teaspoon onion powder or 1 tablespoon dried minced onion
1 teaspoon dry mustard–1 tablespoon prepared mustard

MEASURING EQUIVALENTS
3 teaspoons = 1 tablespoon
4 tablespoons = ¼ cup
5⅓ tablespoons = ⅓ cup
8 tablespoons = ½ cup

12 tablespoons = ¾ cup	
16 tablespoons = 1 cup	
1 cup = 8 ounces	
2 cups = 1 pint	
4 cups = 1 quart	
2 pints = 1 gallon	

Freezer Cooking FAQ

Do I need a separate freezer to store freezer meals?

No, you do not need a separate freezer for your meals but you will need to pack your refrigerator in an efficient manner to maximize your space. Whenever possible, use freezer bags instead of plastic containers because the bags freeze flat and stack nicely on top of each other.

Is there a quick way to defrost my freezer meals?

Meals need up to 24 hours in the refrigerator to defrost. If you forgot to put something in the fridge to defrost ahead of time, you still have a couple of alternatives. The first is the microwave as many microwaves have a defrost setting that works according to weight. It is better to put a lower weight, because the edges will begin to cook if food is in the microwave too long. The second way to quickly defrost is in a sink or bowl filled with ice-cold water.

How can I quickly cool down food?

As you know, food needs to be cooled before it is put in the freezer. Have a large cooler filled with ice on hand to help this process along. Put pots of soup or casserole dishes in the cooler, being careful that the ice only touches the sides of the dish and doesn't get inside it. You never want to put a glass dish directly from the oven into the ice because the quick change in temperature can cause the glass to shatter.

I am so busy—does freezer cooking take up a lot of time?

Freezer cooking works best when you fit it around your lifestyle. If you work full time and are very busy, try filling your freezer with meals by cooking double or triple batches of these recipes at one time. You may not have an entire day to spend cooking meals, but you can certainly cook larger batches of planned meals.

Is a chest or upright freezer better for storing my freezer meals?

Both chest and upright freezers have their advantages and disadvantages. It is much easier to get meals in and out of an upright freezer, but a chest freezer is more energy-efficient. Upright freezers generally cost more than chest freezers, but often have a self defrost feature that most chest freezers do not.

What are the best containers to use?

When using freezer bags, always purchase bags made specifically for the freezer. This is not an area to skimp. Most heavy plastic containers, like Tupperware, freeze well so long as the lid fits on snugly around all sides. Plastic containers tend to warp over time, and this will prevent the lids from getting a good seal to keep out air.

How do I prevent freezer burn?

Very simply, wrap your food well. Do not allow any air from the freezer to touch any part of your food, unless you are flash freezing for a couple of hours only.

I am single—will freezer cooking work for me?

Absolutely! Choose the recipes you'd like to cook and divide the recipe into single-serving portions when you are ready to freeze. This way you do not have to defrost an entire casserole for one meal—you eat it as you want it.

What to Do If Your Freezer Stops Working

- Do not open the door. Every time you open the door, cold air escapes and warm air enters. A well-packed freezer can stay frozen up to two days if the door stays closed.
- Determine the problem. If it is a power failure, attempt to find out how long the outage will last. If there is something wrong with the freezer

and you can't fix it yourself, contact a repair service and see how long before you can be seen.

- On any occasion when your freezer will be out of commission for longer than a day, try relocating your food. If you have another freezer in your house that is still working, try relocating it there. It's also not a bad idea to ask your neighbors if they have extra freezer space.
- If you are unable to relocate your food, pack your freezer with dry ice.

Index

We Have EVERYTHING® on Anything!

With more than 19 million copies sold, the Everything® series has become one of America's favorite resources for solving problems, learning new skills, and organizing lives. Our brand is not only recognizable—it's also welcomed.

The series is a hand-in-hand partner for people who are ready to tackle new subjects—like you!

For more information on the Everything® series, please visit *www.adamsmedia.com*

The Everything® list spans a wide range of subjects, with more than 500 titles covering 25 different categories:

Business	History	Reference
Careers	Home Improvement	Religion
Children's Storybooks	Everything Kids	Self-Help
Computers	Languages	Sports & Fitness
Cooking	Music	Travel
Crafts and Hobbies	New Age	Wedding
Education/Schools	Parenting	Writing
Games and Puzzles	Personal Finance	
Health	Pets	

Made in the USA
San Bernardino, CA
16 February 2014